The Political Economy of Fiscal Decisions

Contributions to Economics

Christoph M. Schneider
Research and Development Management: From the Soviet Union to Russia
1994. ISBN 3-7908-0757-5

Bernhard Böhm/Lionello F. Punzo (Eds.)
Economic Performance
1994. ISBN 3-7908-0811-3

Lars Olof Persson/Ulf Wiberg
Microregional Fragmentation
1995. ISBN 3-7908-0855-5

Ernesto Felli/Furio C. Rosati/ Giovanni Tria (Eds.)
The Service Sector: Productivity and Growth
1995. ISBN 3-7908-0875-X

Giuseppe Munda
Multicriteria Evaluation in Fuzzy Environment
1995. ISBN 3-7908-0892-X

Giovanni Galizzi/ Luciano Venturini (Eds.)
Economics of Innovation: The Case of Food Industry
1996. ISBN 3-7908-0911-X

David T. Johnson
Poverty, Inequality and Social Welfare in Australia
1996. ISBN 3-7908-0942-X

Rongxing Guo
Border-Regional Economics
1996. ISBN 3-7908-0943-8

Oliver Fratzscher
The Political Economy of Trade Integration
1996. ISBN 3-7908-0945-4

Ulrich Landwehr
Industrial Mobility and Public Policy
1996. ISBN 3-7908-0949-7

Arnold Picot/Ekkehard Schlicht (Eds.)
Firms, Markets, and Contracts
1996. Corr. 2nd printing 1997. ISBN 3-7908-0947-0

Thorsten Wichmann
Agricultural Technical Progress and the Development of a Dual Economy
1997. ISBN 3-7908-0960-8

Ulrich Woitek
Business Cycles
1997. ISBN 3-7908-0997-7

Michael Carlberg
International Economic Growth
1997. ISBN 3-7908-0995-0

Massimo Filippini
Elements of the Swiss Market for Electricity
1997. ISBN 3-7908-0996-9

Giuseppe Gaburro (Ed.)
Ethics and Economics
1997. ISBN 3-7908-0986-1

Frank Hoster/Heinz Welsch/ Christoph Böhringer
CO_2 Abatement and Economic Structural Change in the European Internal Market
1997. ISBN 3-7908-1020-7

Christian M. Hafner
Nonlinear Time Series Analysis with Applications to Foreign Exchange Rate Volatility
1997. ISBN 3-7908-1041-X

Sardar M.N. Islam
Mathematical Economics of Multi-Level Optimisation
1998. ISBN 3-7908-1050-9

Sven-Morten Mentzel
Real Exchange Rate Movements
1998. ISBN 3-7908-1081-9

Lei Delsen/Eelke de Jong (Eds.)
The German and Dutch Economies
1998. ISBN 3-7908-1064-9

Mark Weder
Business Cycle Models with Indeterminacy
1998. ISBN 3-7908-1078-9

Tor Rødseth (Ed.)
Models for Multispecies Management
1998. ISBN 3-7908-1001-0

Michael Carlberg
Intertemporal Macroeconomics
1998. ISBN 3-7908-1096-7

Sabine Spangenberg
The Institutionalised Transformation of the East German Economy
1998. ISBN 3-7908-1103-3

continued on page 151

Jessica de Wolff

The Political Economy of Fiscal Decisions

The Strategic Role of Public Debt

With 44 Figures
and 2 Tables

Physica-Verlag
A Springer-Verlag Company

Series Editors
Werner A. Müller
Martina Bihn

Author
Dr. Jessica de Wolff
Economics Department
Sekr. WW4
Technical University of Berlin
Uhlandstr. 4–5
D-10623 Berlin, Germany

ISBN 3-7908-1130-0 Physica-Verlag Heidelberg New York
D83 (1997)

Cataloging-in-Publication Data applied for
Die Deutsche Bibliothek – CIP-Einheitsaufnahme
Wolff, Jessica de: The political economy of fiscal decisions: the strategic role of public debt / Jessica de Wolff. – Heidelberg; New York: Physica-Verl., 1998
(Contributions to economics)
Zugl.: Berlin, Techn. Univ., Diss.
ISBN 3-7908-1130-0

Softcover Design: Erich Kirchner, Heidelberg

SPIN 10684458 88/2202-5 4 3 2 1 0 – Printed on acid-free paper

To Dati

Preface

This Ph.D. was conceived and written while I was working at the Economics Department of the Technical University Berlin. First of all, I want to thank my supervisor Prof. Dr. Jürgen Kromphardt for his encouragement and his decisive comments. I am especially grateful to Prof. Dr. Georg Meran for serving as my second advisor. Avner Shaked accompanied the development of this study over the years with helpful comments on various versions and with moral support. I have also benefitted from very helpful comments by Pio Baake, Diana Barrowclough, Patrick Bolton, Gesa Bruno-Latocha, Sven Feldmann, Gilat Levy, Torsten Persson and Ailsa Roell as well as from participants at the Doktorandenkolloquium at the TU Berlin and seminar participants at ECARE at the Université Libre Brussels, at the 7th summer school in Economic Theory on Political Economy at the Institute for Advanced Studies at the Hebrew University of Jerusalem, at the EEA'96 and ESEM'96 conferences in Istanbul and at the Free University Berlin. A very special thanks goes to Heinz-Dieter Kretzmer who saved me when my work got lost in the depths of my computer. Moreover, I would like to thank Wenzel Matiaske and Thorsten Wichmann for computer assistance and Stephanie Behrendt for guiding me around the bureaucratic hurdles of the *Promotionsverfahren*. Finally, financial support from the Victor Rothschild Foundation, the European Economic Association and the Gesellschaft von Freunden der TU Berlin is gratefully acknowledged.

Of course, I am to blame for all remaining errors and imperfections.

Berlin, March 1998

Table of Contents

List of Figures

List of Tables

1. Introduction

> "This deficit is no despised orphan. It is President Reagan's child and secretly he loves it, as David Stockmann[1] has explained: The deficit rigourously discourages any idea of spending another dime for social welfare." (New York Times, 25 January 1987)

Public debt has been the subject of deep concern to prominent economists already in the 18th century. Almost all of the leading British classical economists were opposed to the maintenance of a national debt. Their negative forebodings were intensified by such gloomy forecasts as Mathus' population doctrine or the existence of diminishing returns in agriculture. Adam Smith helped to establish the mood when he prophesied that "the enormous debts" of his time "will in the long run probably ruin all the great nations of Europe" [1776], p.863.

Two hundred years later, a statement like this would not surprise the readers of any newspaper or even scientific journal. Public debt is still a central subject of the political and economic debate and the views on it are as varied as they were in Smith's times. Then, economists as Smith and Ricardo were in favour of a radical and fast reduction of the debt, since the debt "destroyed the equilibrium of prices, occasioned many persons to emigrate to other countries in order to avoid the burden of taxation which it entailed and hung like a mill-stone round the exertion and industry of the country". (Ricardo cited after Hansard [1819], pp.1022-1024). Ricardo feared the consequences of the debt which has been accumulated in the wars with Napoleon and proposed a once-and-for-all discharge of the existing British debt.) Thomas Malthus and Lord Lauderdale (British economist, 1759-1839), on the other hand, were concerned about the consequences a too rapid retirement of the debt would have on the level of demand in the economy. From America, where the government incurred debt not only to fight wars but also to peacefully increase its territory (for example the Louisiana Purchase in 1803), came arguments such as: If government expenditures are used for projects which yield benefits for future generations then it is appropriate that those generations help meet some of the costs involved, a concept later labelled "pay-as-you-use concept" by Richard Musgrave [1958].

[1] President Reagan's Budget Chief for four and a half years

Other arguments in favour of the expansion of national debts were added to the debate by Keynes and his followers in the 1930s. Especially in periods of economic slow-down government expenditures derived from borrowing would create employment and stimulate growth in the private sector of the economy via multiplier effects. Further, it was argued that whereas an external debt burdens a nation, its domestic debt may entail an internal redistribution of wealth but not necessarily an additional burden on the nation as a whole. This triggered the crowding-out debate: By putting upward pressure on interest rates and by using resources that would otherwise be used by the private sector the government's activity was curtailing private activity. By now, the crowding-out debate is neither empirically nor theoretically resolved[2]. The Keynesian deficit spending which was widely used as a fiscal instrument in the 1960s, has failed if only for reasons of practicability. The idea was that deficits taken on in recessions would be reduced in periods of economic recovery. This "fine tuning" of the demand management proved to be impossible for the political authorities[3].

A third view that a deficit is - under certain conditions - irrelevant for the level of economic activity was added by Barro [1974] and [1979], the so-called Ricardian equivalence theorem. It states that financing government expenditure by taking on a debt instead of increasing taxes will have no effect on the level of economic activity, since rational consumers will foresee the future tax increase necessary for repaying the debt. In order to meet these future costs consumers increase their savings today in order to accumulate resources for the future tax increase.

Realizing that it would be difficult to agree on a final judgement on whether debt is good, bad or irrelevant, economists have in recent years undertaken research on whether there exists such thing as an optimal or sustainable level of debt. Even though indicators have been found (Domar [1944], Blanchard as presented in Galbraith/Darity [1995], p.10) they seem not to have found (yet) entry into actual policy-making. A good example are the fiscal criteria in the Maastricht treaty (3% as an upper limit for the deficit-to-GDP ratio and 60% for the debt-to-GDP ratio). We have not found any evidence for these figures having any economic backing. Robert Eisner has entered the debate arguing that the whole debate about debt is still confused and its arguments misleading, because "we have not measured deficits correctly". Consequently, "we have confused economic analysts, turned economic theory on its head and committed grievous errors in economic policy", [1986], p.2. Deficits can be too small or too large "and you cannot even begin to tell what they are until you measure them right" ([1992], p.295). That this debate is still current show other more recent papers as for example one by Galbraith/Darity [1995] or an article in the Economist of February 10th, 1996.

---

[2] For a short but comprehensive presentation of the crowding-out debate see Kromphardt [1987], pp.164-169, or Gandenberger [1988], pp-176-180.

[3] For a discussion see Kromphardt [1987], pp.171-179.

Both give a nice summary of Eisners main arguments. Galbraith/Darity's paper was a reaction to the unanimous decision of President Clinton and the American Congress to balance the American budget by 2002.

Von Weizsaecker [1992], p.56, comments on the debate about the burden of public debt as follows: "It is surprising and depressing at the same time, how economists cannot agree on a question that all non-economists consider frightening and unsustainable in the long run." An undisputable conclusion that may be drawn from this discussion is that debt is bad for the economy at least when it is too high and apparently the public considers the debt to be too high in most OECD economies at the moment. The question that now arises is, why is the debt not reduced, if apparently the majority of voters and politicians alike are in favour of reducing it? Alesina/Tabellini [1990b], p.37, report on studies in the US that show that the majority of consumers is in favour of a balanced budget. What then keeps the policy-makers from reducing the debt? All the literature described above takes the political environment in which fiscal decisions are taken as a black box. However, fiscal policy is decided by politicians that have been voted into office for a limited period (usually determined by the country's constitution). These politicians are subject to pressures and restrictions and have political interests and ambitions. It makes no sense to ignore these constraints which no doubt influence their decision-making process.

This thesis is part of the literature that takes the political structure as part of the environment influencing the decision-maker. A detailed survey of this literature can be found in section 3, here we only describe the main features of the political process that this thesis considers.

The consumers are also voters, i.e. they can determine who will be in power in the future. The present government, realizing that the public can decide whether it will remain in power, may choose to court the public. They can do that by making themselves more attractive or by taking such actions that restrict and limit the actions of the future government so as to make the opposition less attractive. This scenario becomes more complicated if the government's aim is not only to remain in power but it is concerned about the economy and the welfare of a certain group of voters it chose to represent ("representative voters"). Such a government will attempt to attract a minimal constituency that will guarantee its reelection, so as not to compromise too much on economic issues. However, compromising on economic issues just to stay in power, or in other words deviating from the policy the government would have taken if its staying in power was guaranteed, may result in too large a utility loss for the government's representative voters. In this case the government will prefer to abandon its hopes to be reelected and work towards its economic aims under the assumption that the opposition will gain power. Thus, the government may choose whether to use its fiscal actions strategically in order to manipulate the elections.

A brief detour: The use of the term "Election Manipulation" in the political economy literature. The use of the term "election manipulation" in the political economy literature is somewhat unusual. According to Random House Webster's Dictionary "manipulate" is defined as:

> to manage or influence skillfully and often unfairly: to manipulate peoples' feelings.

Thus, manipulation usually has negative connotations. In the context of elections it usually means that a party deviates from a policy it announced earlier in order to influence voters' preferences and make them vote for the party[4]. In this context the party is assumed to have a preference for being in power that dominates any other aims it may have, (in political economy such a party is called "opportunistic", see page 29). This assumes that the voters can be tricked into believing that the party has a policy which suits them and that they are sufficiently dim-witted not to notice that the party's real aim is to stay in power. With such assumptions about the party and the voters it is easy to explain debt accumulation as an instrument for election manipulation.

However, since we do not want to assume that the party obtains utility just from being in power or that the voters are so short-sighted as to be blinded by the party's short term favours the question of election manipulation becomes more subtle. We assume that a party represents a certain representative voter and maximizes this voter's long run utility. The party in power will then consider various plans of actions, some of which lead to the party staying in power and others to it losing power. For each such plan the party considers the long run consequences for its representative voter. There may be cases where it is best for the voter if the party adopts a plan under which it will lose the elections. It is in this sense that the party may be said to manipulate the elections: Since the election outcome depends on the party's action it can knowingly choose a plan where it stays in power or loses it. This is how in the literature on the political economy of the government budget the term "election manipulation" is used. Another way of putting it is to say that the election outcome is endogeneous.

We so capture another feature of modern democracies: It is well known that governments attempt to influence elections in their favour by choosing seemingly popular policies close to elections time. We identify conditions under which a government will wish to deviate from its desired actions (the fiscal decisions it would take if its staying in power was guaranteed) in order to influence the electorate.

The phenomenon of increased debt in OECD economies is no doubt due to many factors. Our analysis may help to identify one factor: the parties' urge

[4] Chancellor Kohl's announcement, that financing the German reunification would not require any tax increases, can be regarded as such an example. It was quite obvious (or should have been obvious at least for Kohl's advisors) that this policy would prove to be unsustainable later on.

to stay in power even in unfavourable situations. It is usually the case in developed countries that the electoral results cannot be foreseen and that reigning parties are constantly faced with the threat of losing sympathy among voters. It is precisely in these situations that our model predicts that the government will use populist fiscal measures in order to stay in power.

We find that for this analysis the distribution of the voters' political preferences plays a crucial role, for this determines how much a government should deviate from its first best action in order to remain in power. We capture the voters' political preferences by two attributes instead of one as the existing literature does. The latter usually assumes that voters differ in their income *or* their attitudes towards public goods. Our voters are described by both their income *and* their preference for private relative to public goods. We so capture in greater detail the heterogeneity of the voting population. This makes the model more realistic and the analysis more complicated.

Our model shows that the distribution of voters is crucial to the understanding of the fiscal decision-making. The pressures and constraints that a government faces due to the expected elections influence its decisions. Thus, our conclusion is that the distribution of voters' preferences has a large impact on fiscal decisions and in particular, two countries that are otherwise similar but differ in the composition of the voters' preferences may exhibit different fiscal behaviour. Our results may thus help to explain a phenomenon that has among other things triggered the new political approach to fiscal policy, namely the large differences in fiscal behaviour of economies that are otherwise very similar as for example the OECD economies.

The thesis is organized as follows. In section 2 we sketch a rough picture of the debt development in selected OECD economies since the 1960s. Our main intention is to highlight the macroeconomic puzzle that has triggered renewed research interest in the issue of public debt: There has been massive debt accumulation after the oil price shock in 1972 and throughout the succeeding period of economic recovery, i.e. in peacetimes, in most OECD countries and the debt behaviour varies immensely among these nations.

The conclusions economists drew from this was that a) standard economic theory could not explain these observations and b) it might help to integrate the political environment in which fiscal decisions are taken into the analysis. This is what the new literature on the political economy of the government budget does. In section 3 we present a survey of this literature which we organize into four subgroups: (1) models of intergenerational redistribution (section 3.2), (2) models of geographically dispersed interest (section 3.3), (3) models of government weakness (section 3.4) and (4) models of debt as a strategic instrument (section 3.5). We do not intend to give a comprehensive overview of the literature. Rather, we present what we consider the most important papers in greater detail to show how the authors go about modeling and solving the politico-economic set-up which they consider relevant. We so want to convey the reader the flavour of this exciting new literature. We deal with the last of these subgroups in more detail since our model was motivated by the papers presented there.

In the following sections we then present our model; first verbally (section 4) and then formally (section 5). In section 6 we derive the results. To ease the reading we have delegated most of the algebra and the proofs to the appendix. Finally, section 7 concludes.

2. The Evolution of Public Debt

In this section we want to sketch a picture of the fiscal behaviour of the industrialized economies. Of course there are many variables one would have to look at in order to derive a detailed picture. Nevertheless, for our purpose it suffices to provide a rough presentation. Our goal is to bring into focus the empirical puzzle that triggered the literature on the political economy of budget deficits and in particular our approach. Hence, we concentrate on some evidence concerning the trends in budget deficits and public debt in the OECD countries since the mid-1960s.

In figures 2.1 and 2.2 we present the development of the net debt-to-GDP ratio of selected OECD countries[1]. Up until 1973 government deficits were sufficiently low to enable the OECD economies to reduce the debt accumu-

[1] Throughout this section we present data for the net debt of the public sector (liabilities minus financial assets) as calculated by the OECD. The data covers the general government sector, which is a consolidation of central government, state and local government and the social security sector.

We would like to point out that neither the OECD itself nor some of the authors who use the OECD data exhibit a very cautious behaviour dealing with the data. For example, Sachs/ Larrain [1993], p. 207, present data for the net debt to GDP ratios from 1960-90 naming as a source: OECD Economic Outlook, various issues, without stating the year or the page of the issues. If one then takes any OECD Economic Outlook issue one is struck by two observations: (1) It is difficult (or better impossible) to find figures that match those quoted by the authors and (2) even if one takes two OECD Economic Outlook issues the tables for the same year are not identical. This can of course be explained for recent data, since the OECD has to estimate until the exact data materializes. This does not make sense, however, for data from the 1980s. For example, we compared table 35 ("General government net financial liabilities as a ratio of GDP") in the issues of June 1995 and December 1996. The June issue states 22.7% as the 1980 ratio, whereas the December issue states 21.8% for the same year. There is no note about a change in the calculation method explaining these kinds of discrepancies.

Roubini/Sachs [1989a], p. 106, table 3, present data from an OECD Economic Outlook (neither year nor page are mentioned) on total government expenditure as a percentage of GDP. They claim that in the last three decades the government sector has increased continuously in most OECD economies. If one investigates a corresponding table in an OECD Economic Outlook (for example table 28 on p. A31 in the December 1996 issue) one finds that the government expenditure to GDP ratio has remained stable almost everywhere, even in countries as Belgium or Italy.

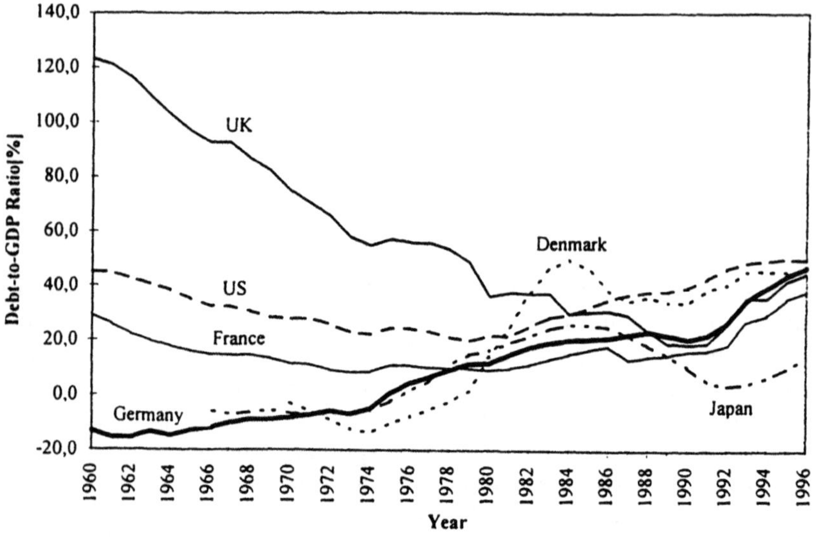

Source: For the years 1960-1979 Roubini/Sachs [1989b], p.914; for 1980-1996 OECD [1996], p.A38; see also comments in footnote 1

Fig. 2.1. Debt-to-GDP Ratios in Selected OECD economies I

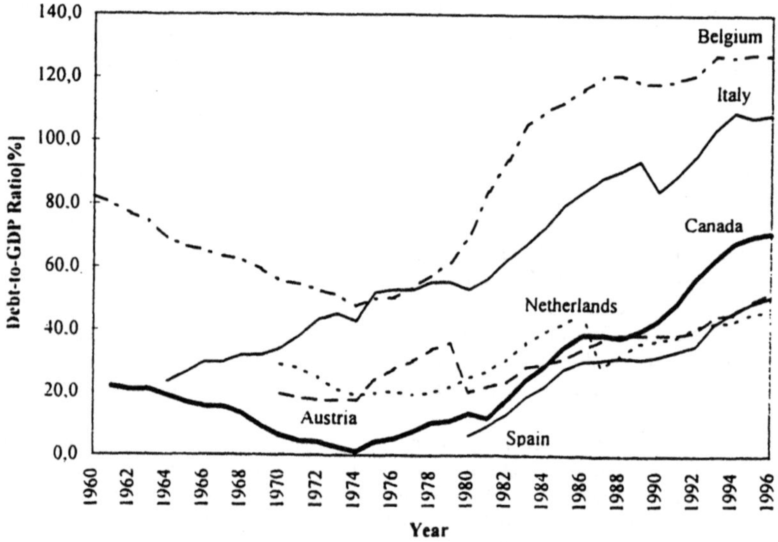

Source: See figure 2.1

Fig. 2.2. Debt-to-GDP Ratios in Selected OECD economies II

lated during and after the second World War, thus achieving falling ratios of net debt-to-GDP. The US for example reduced its net debt-to-GDP ratio from 45% in 1960 to 23% in 1973. France even managed a reduction from 29,1% to 8,3% in the same period, for the exact figures see appendix A.1. But after 1973 this trend was reversed: almost every OECD country experienced a significant rise in the net debt-to-GDP ratio in the years 1973-85. The exceptions are the US, where the debt-to-GDP ratio started to increase only in the 1980s under the reign of Ronald Reagan, the UK and Australia. But also among the countries with rising debt-GDP ratios we can distinguish countries in which the debt-to GDP ratio stabilized around a higher level such as France, Germany and Japan (figure 2.1) and countries that experienced ever increasing debt-to GDP ratios, in some cases reaching levels above 100% as in Belgium and Italy (figure 2.2). Between 1985 and 1992 the ratios more or less remained at their 1985 level in most countries of figure 2.1, whereas they increased further in the countries of figure 2.2. Only in 1992 a new general increase can be observed.

From these observations we can deduce two phenomena:

1. The observed fiscal imbalances occurred in the last 20 years (after 1973), i.e. in peacetimes.
2. We observe significant differences in the fiscal performances of the OECD economies.

Explaining these phenomena by economic arguments alone does not prove appropriate. Of course part of the significant increase in government debt can be attributed to the cyclical downturns in the OECD economies after the first oil price shock in 1973 and in 1992[2]. But the oil price shock and the 1992 recession hit the economies in question (more or less) equally hard, so explaining the observed differences in macroeconomic behaviour entirely by these recessions seems rather dissatisfactory. This becomes even more obvious when taking into account not only the fact that the OECD countries have suffered from the same economic shocks, but also that they bear strong similarities in economic attributes: They are all highly industrialized democracies with high per-capita income, they are members of more or less the same political and economic organizations and are thus highly interconnected. This macoreconomic puzzle, namely why countries as similar as the OECD economies go through such different experience in terms of public debt, has triggered the new literature of the political economy of fiscal policy of which we will now provide a broad survey.

[2] See Roubini/ Sachs [1989a], pp.119, 120, for an econometric study on the extent to which cyclical factors account for the jump in the debt-to-GDP ratios after 1973. Roubini/Sachs, p.120, come to the conclusion that the slowdown in growth and the rise in unemployment after the 1973 oil price shock had added more than two percentage points to the spending-output ratio by 1980 in Belgium, Denmark, France, the Netherlands and the UK and more than one percentage point in Austria, Germany and the US. By 1985, however, in all but the Netherlands and Belgium these cyclical effects had disappeared.

3. Literature Survey: The Political Economy of the Government Budget

The literature on the political economy of fiscal policy is very large and dates back to the 19th century with the Swedish and Italian schools of public finance. Some examples are Wicksell's rejection of the idea of a benevolent dictator, Lindahl's work on the 'fair' distribution of tax shares, Mazzola's and Sax's discussion of the demand side of public goods by identifying collective as distinct from private wants or Puviani's idea that the 'fiscal illusion' of voters governs the evolution of tax structures, see Ekelund/Hébert [1990], pp.631-639 and Buchanan [1960]. The political approach to economics has experienced a strong revival with the public choice school and the work of its founder Buchanan. One crucial assumption of the part of the public choice school that deals with budget deficits is the fiscal illusion of voters: Voters do not understand the government's intertemporal budget constraint. When offered a deficit-financed expenditure program they overestimate the benefits of current expenditures and underestimate the future tax burden. Thus, they vote for "overspending"[1]. Of course it is difficult for the electorate to understand the complexity of the government budget. However, there is a crucial difference between errors and illusion. If voters make uncorrelated errors, on average they do not over- or underestimate the costs and benefits of taxes and spending. An illusion implies a systematic bias in these errors. While it is uncontroversial that voters make mistakes and are imperfectly informed, it is not at all obvious why the mistakes should be biased in a certain direction.

In contrast, a crucial feature of the new political economic approach to fiscal policy we are about to present is that agents are rational. We start our review with a short presentation of the "tax smoothing" theory of the government budget (Barro [1979]). This approach serves as a benchmark for most of the recent political models, in that the latter provide "'positive' explanations of observed deviations from tax smoothing" (Alesina/ Perotti [1995], p.4). We then present the main papers of the political economic approach which we organize into four subgroups: (1) models of intergenerational redistribution, (2) models of geographically dispersed interests, (3) models of government weakness and (4) models of debt as a strategic instrument.

[1] An argument somewhat related can be found in the early political business cycle literature (Nordhaus [1975], Hibbs [1977]). Here expectations are adaptive instead of rational; for a survey of the political business cycle literature see Belke [1993].

3.1 The Tax-Smoothing Theory of the Government Budget

The starting point for Barro's research was his observation that "proponents of the Ricardian view that the choice between debt and taxes does not matter are left with an embarrassing absence of a theory of public debt creation" (Barro [1979], p.940). The underlying Ricardian equivalence theorem is based (among other things) on the crucial assumption that the government raises lump sum taxes. A rational consumer will then be indifferent between tax or deficit financing public expenditure: A deficit-financed increase in the budget will lead to future tax increases. After discounting this tax stream, the present value will be equal to the case of initial tax finance of the government expenditure. Net worth is reduced equally in both cases (see Barro [1974])[2].

This result does not hold when taxes are distortionary instead of lump sum. With distortionary taxes the real effects of deficit or tax financing differ and the policy-maker has to decide on optimal tax paths.

A Brief Detour: Distortionary Taxes and the Dead Weight Loss of Taxation. When a government needs to raise a certain amount of tax revenues it can choose between non-distortionary lump sum taxes and between distortionary taxes. Both reduce a consumer's disposable income but in addition the distortionary tax distorts efficient choice and leads to a loss in consumer's utility without at the same time increasing the government's utility (dead weight loss).

This is demonstrated in figure 3.1. Before the tax a consumer consumes an optimal bundle A given his budget constraint $\overline{RS}$: $p_1x_1 + p_2x_2 = m$, where x_i and p_i denote good and price of good i respectively and m denotes income. A government now needs to raise a certain amount in tax income. We assume that the government imposes a tax τ only on good x_1. The new budget constraint is $\overline{RT}$: $(p_1 + \tau)x_1 + p_2x_2 = m$. The consumer now chooses bundle B and the government has raised τx_1.

If on the other hand the government wants to raise the same amount with a lump sum tax it has to reduce the consumer's income by an amount a such that $a = \tau x_1$, i.e. the lump sum tax has to be such that the bundle B consumed under the distortionary tax scheme is in the new budget set. This new budget constraint is $\overline{R'S'}$. As we see, bundle C will be on a higher utility level than bundle B (except when the two goods are perfect complements).

---

[2] For a detailed presentation of the of the Ricardian equivalence theorem see Myles [1995], pp.499-501, for a critical evaluation see Musgrave/ Musgrave [1989], p.521 or Buchanan [1987], p.1045.

Note that the Ricardian equivalence theorem does not stem from Ricardo himself. He discussed the issue of debt neutrality but then dismissed it. He argued that the individual tax-payer is not fully rational and he feels subjectively richer when a society as a whole rather than he himself is responsible for the debt ("fiscal illusion"), see O'Driscoll [1977], p.208.

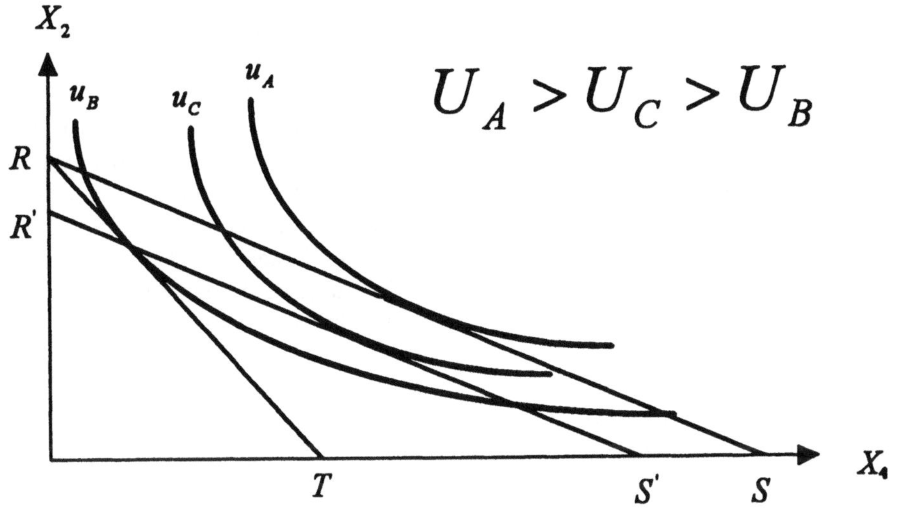

Fig. 3.1. Distortionary Taxes

The dead weight loss of the distortionary tax scheme now becomes obvious. In both cases the government has raised the same revenue, i.e. the government is as well off under both tax schemes. The consumer on the other hand suffers from a loss in utility under the distortionary tax scheme that he is not compensated for by higher government spending. Nevertheless, the taxes most widely used in reality are distortionary. The reason is that even though from an allocative point of view lump sum taxes are the most efficient, they are criticized for reasons of equity[3].

We now return to Barro's tax smoothing theory. Barro [1979] has analyzed the problem of optimal taxation when taxes are distortionary. In an infinite horizon model a government has a given expenditure plan, i.e. an infinite stream of given (and known) expenditure[4]. This expenditure is to be financed by distortionary taxes. However, the government wishes to minimize the loss caused by the tax. So the government's aim is to minimize this loss subject to the tax revenues being sufficient to finance the expenditure stream.

The main result is Barro's famous "tax smoothing hypothesis" which not only states the optimal tax policy but also provides an explanation of the

[3] Note that if leisure can be treated as a good and all goods (inclusive leisure) can be taxed, then a value added tax works like a lump sum tax and is then non-distortionary, see Ramsey [1927].

For a discussion of the optimal balance between equity and efficiency of tax systems see Atkinson/Stiglitz [1980], lecture 12, pp.366-393.

[4] Lucas/ Stokey [1983] present a model where government spending is stochastic. The theory becomes formally more complex but the basic principles of tax smoothing generalize, (for an overview of the theory of dynamic optimal taxation see also Alesina/ Tabellini [1992]).

existence of public debt[5]: An optimal fiscal policy that minimzes tax distortions over time implies a constant tax rate over time. This tax rate is a function of the level of permanent spending[6]. The public debt can then be explained as both "distortion smoother" and "shock absorber" (Grilli et al. [1991], p.342). In periods where government expenditures exceed government revenues, the economy runs a deficit which is erased in periods where revenues exceed expenditures. In particular, temporary expenditure increases or temporary shortfalls in revenue, i.e. temporary shocks, should be financed by issuing debt, whereas tax rates should only be changed in the face of permanent shocks. For example a war should be financed by deficits leaving tax rates unchanged. The accumulated debt will be repaid by the budget surpluses in the following peace-time. (Note that the level of actual spending can be below the level of permanent spending. The latter includes expected expenditures of future wars. Hence, in peace-time actual spending will be less than permanent spending.) This is demonstrated in figure 3.2: From time 0 to time t government spending is constant and is expected to be constant forever. At time t an unexpected "war" occurs, which is known to last until $(t+n)$. If the war increases the level of permanent spending tax rates will have to be adjusted. In addition, the economy runs deficits until $(t+n)$ and surpluses afterwards. For a detailed formal presentation of the tax smoothing

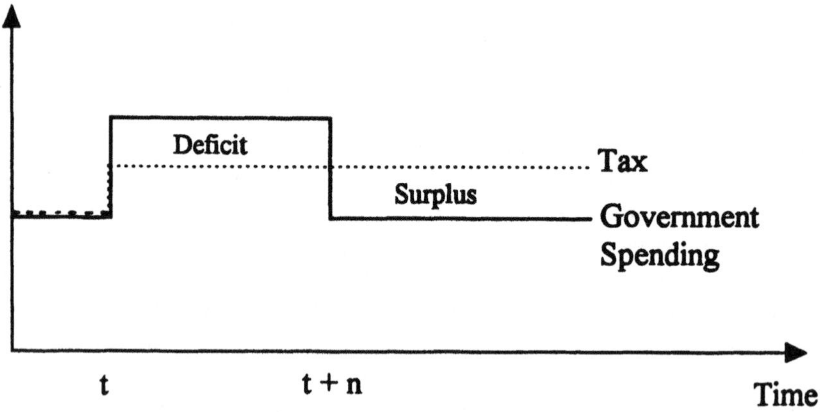

Fig. 3.2. Tax Smoothing Policy

[5] The tax smoothing hypothesis of Barro [1979] can be viewed as an extension of the Ricardian approach of Barro [1974] in that he exchanges the assumption of non-distortionary lump sum taxes by distortionary ones.

[6] Permanent spending is the constant level of government spending such that the discounted value of this constant value is equal to the discounted value of the actual path of government spending, i.e. like Friedman's permanent income, it represents the present discounted value of future spending on a per period basis.

theory see Roubini/ Sachs [1989b] or Aschauer [1988].

The tax smoothing hypothesis can be criticized on many grounds. We here just discuss whether the observed debt behaviour of the OECD economies as presented above can be explained by this approach. The tax smoothing model can certainly explain why debt-to-GDP ratios started to increase after 1973. The sudden and sharp increase in budget deficits after 1973 can be linked directly to the sudden slowdown in OECD growth and the corresponding rise in unemployment after the first oil-price shock. Since it was widely expected during the 1970s that the recession and the rise in unemployment would be transitory, it is consistent with the equilibrium (tax smoothing) view that these shocks would be accommodated initially by budget deficits. By the early 1980s, however, the growth slowdown and the rise in unemployment were widely understood to be highly persistent. Nevertheless, with the exception of the UK and Norway the debt-to-GDP ratios rose further, in some countries they even exploded as for example in Italy, Belgium and Greece. This development is difficult to reconcile with the view that budget deficits were only smoothing the effects of temporary shocks. The tax smoothing theory fails even more when it comes to our second observation, namely the significant differences in debt behaviour in the OECD countries. According to this theory, the various national economies were hit differently by different shocks and/or their expectations of future spending were different. This explanation is quite unconvincing given the fact that the OECD economies are very similar in their economic structure and moreover highly interconnected.

The tax smoothing hypothesis has been tested extensively and rejected at least for the period after 1973, for a detailed overview of the econometric studies see Roubini/ Sachs [1989b].

This leads us to the literature on politico-institutional determinants of the government budget. The political economy approach aims to get a deeper understanding of budgetary processes by integrating the political and institutional environment in which fiscal decisions are taken into the analysis. The political economy models depart from the restricting assumptions of the tax smoothing approach: Instead of a social planer/ benevolent dictator there are different parties with different political preferences who take the fiscal decision. Also, government terms (and thus elections) are explicitly taken into account. The models differ in some important institutional aspects like electoral laws, party structure, budget laws, central bank laws, degree of decentralization, political stability or social polarization and the representative agent assumption is replaced by the assumption of heterogeneous consumers.

We now give a broad overview of the literature on the political economy of budget deficits which we organize into four groups[7]:

1. models of intergenerational redistribution
2. models of geographical redistribution

[7] For other organizations of this literature see the surveys by Grilli et al. [1991] or Alesina/Tabellini [1992].

3. models of coalition governments
4. models of debt as a strategic instrument

and we discuss how well these models explain our two observations from section 2, namely the accumulation of debt in the OECD countries after 1973 and the large differences in debt behaviour in these countries. We do not attempt to present all of the above mentioned subgroups of this literature in greatest depth. The idea is to acquaint the reader with an idea of how these approaches explain debt as a political-economic phenomenon.

3.2 Intergenerational Redistribution

In popular debate, one of the main arguments against government borrowing is that the current generation profits from a wider choice of fiscal instruments and thus consumption, but leaves the burden of repaying the debt to future generations[8][9]. Since only the current generation votes - and given the fact that it votes on issues that affect the future generations who have no say in the vote - a selfish generation could vote for policies that shift the burden of taxation to the future. Then - since people are mortal and thus the voting generation has a finite horizon - Ricardian equivalence does not hold. Barro's [1974] answer was to introduce altruism: Since agents care for the well-being of their offspring, the future generations' assets and liabilities enter the preference functions of the current generation. Hence, the current generation's government borrowing in excess of their own tax revenues (deficit) would be balanced by their need to adjust their bequests to leave their heirs uninjured by the future tax increases necessary to service the debt. Thus, in a way, people do have infinite horizons and Ricardian equivalence is rehabilitated.

Altruism is an intuitive and plausible argument, but nevertheless there are many objections to the strong version of altruism Barro uses (see Eisner [1987], p.295, and also Richter/Wiegard [1993], pp. 375-77): Some current agents have no heirs, others do not care about their heirs and still others are at "corner solutions" so that the amount they give to (or receive from) their

[8] Throughout this section we assume that government borrowing is not entirely used for productive investment in the future. In that case, according to Musgrave's pay-as-you-use concept, taking on a debt would be justified because mainly future generations profit from the revenues of these investment projects and it makes therefore sense to have future generations take part in financing the outlays. In this case, deficit financing can be regarded as an instrument to synchronize revenues and costs, Musgrave [1958], p.72.

[9] A nice example is this extract from Ronald Reagan's Inaugural Address, January 20, 1989: "You and I, as individuals, can, by borrowing, live beyond our means, but only for a limited period of time. Why then do we think that collectively, as a nation, we are not bound by that same limitation? For decades we have piled deficit upon deficit, mortgaging our future and our children's future for the temporary convenience of the present. To continue this long trend is to guarantee tremendous social, cultural, political and economic upheavals."

children will not be affected by expected future tax increases. Moreover, there is uncertainty about the life span of both current agents and their offspring and also with regard to the numbers of their children and of their childrens' children for whom provisions should be made. Hence, Ricardian equivalence of deficit- or tax financing a given amount of government expenditure is quite likely not to hold and debt accumulation can be explained by the behaviour of a "selfish" generation that does not (have to) fully internalize the future cost of servicing the debt, living well at the expense of its offspring.

Nevertheless, some altruism exists. In this section we describe some models that show how debt can be explained by intergenerational redistribution even when people are altruistic. We will discuss first a model in which the main idea is that some agents are more altruistic than others. This leads to a deficit bias in the political equilibrium.

Cukierman/Meltzer [1989] present a model with lump sum taxes in which the current generation decides on the government budget. The paper distinguishes between altruistic "rich" parents and non- altruistic "poor". For rich parents Ricardian equivalence holds: They leave positive bequests to their offspring if they expect their children to be confronted with tax increases in the future and they thus disentangle the redistributive effects across generations. Poor parents, on the other hand, value the redistributive effect of debt since they are bequest-constrained, i.e. they would like to leave negative bequests. However, private negative bequests are not enforceable (a son cannot be forced to pay his father's debt) while public negative bequests are (no-default assumption). Hence, poor individuals favour running government deficits which redistribute in their favour at the expense of their children. So because of the asymmetry that one group of agents is indifferent to any debt policy whereas the other favours debt the social choice will lead to debt, the more so, the larger the fraction of bequest-constrained parents.

A crucial assumption in this model is the no-default assumption. The debt policy redistributes across generations only because future generations decide not to renege on it later on. In any moment in time, the fiscal policy redistributes from the young to the old. However, this model does not address the question why the young should honour these debt obligations inherited from their parents and should not decide to repudiate the debt.

Tabellini [1991] addresses this problem in a model where it is voted on whether or not to repay the debt. He argues that once debt is issued, even some young people, in particular the children of the rich vote for repaying the debt, because through their altruism for their parents they profit from it.

The model is a two-period model. Parents live in both periods, their children only in the second. Parents and children care for each other. Parents have a certain level of wealth according to some given wealth distribution. The children (in the second period) all earn the same income[10]. In the first

[10] Under certain conditions and at the expense of mathematical ease, this assumption can be relaxed, see Tabellini [1991], p.340.

period the parent generation can save i.e. take on a debt, in order to finance a public good. This implies *intra*generational redistribution from the rich to the poor who profit more from the public good than the rich. Goods and wealth are not transferable to the second period. Whether this debt is repaid then depends on a vote of those alive in the second period, i.e. both parents and their children. Of course, the debt-holding parent generation votes for repaying. But the children are faced with the choice between total income equality (reneging on the debt) and wealth inequality: children of parents who saved a lot (usually the rich parents) benefit from repaying via their parent's well-being (altruistic children). Thus, the children of high-saving parents vote for repaying the debt because the tax they will have to pay is negligible compared to the considerable amount their parents get back. Tabellini shows that in the political equilibrium under certain conditions on the parents' wealth distribution debt, once issued, is repaid. So the old generation, knowing that the future vote will be in favour of paying, decides to borrow from the young because issuing debt "creates a constituency in support of repaying it"(p.354). Once debt is issued repudiation has *intra*generational redistributional consequences (from rich to poor, in disfavour of the high-savers and their children).

We have discussed two political models of intergenerational redistribution which explain debt accumulation as a consequence of the behaviour of a selfish generation. The currently alive (and voting) generation has the power to redistribute their childrens' income in their own favour. According to Cukierman/Meltzer [1989] the level of accumulated debt is higher the less altruistic the parent generation is (the more bequest-constrained poor relative to altruistic rich parents there are) whereas Tabellini [1991] shows that it depends on the level of altruism of the children whether (and how much) debt is issued.

How do these approaches score as explanations for the two observations in section 2? According to these models debt has increased so significantly in the last two decades because intergenerational redistribution has increased. Moreover, the differences in debt performance would imply that intergenerational altruism varies across nations. One could for example deduce, that the Italians are less altruistic than the British. Both explanations are not satisfactory. Alesina/ Perotti [1995], p.11, argue that if anything , transferring higher shares of the tax burden to future generations would make sense in economies that exhibit increasing growth rates. However, growth has been decreasing in OECD countries in the last two decades relative to the decades before.

Tabellini's interesting contribution is his focus on *intra*generational redistribution, arguing that purely *inter*generational policies do not exist. A debt policy typically redistributes across generations as well as from rich to poor households. Similarly, reneging on the debt not only harms the old, it also harms the rich (who hold more debt) more than the poor. We will come back to the aspect of *intra*generational redistribution in section 3.3 where it is argued that excessive debts are due to intragenerational geographical conflicts.

One last criticism we would like to mention concerns the approach to altruism in these models. Altruism is crucial in these models but at the same time it is simply assumed to exist. Where does altruism come from? How does it develop? Why do people vary in their levels of altruism? Models that so crucially depend not only on altruism itself but also on its degree should also provide an explanation for it.

In the literature bequest motives are very rarely explained by pure altruism. Hurd [1989] argues that bequests are more or less random due to uncertainty about the time of death. Bernheim et al. [1985] argue that older people use bequests strategically: They use the prospect of a bequest to make the young behave in the desired way towards them. Another approach shows that altruism can be supported as an equilibrium in an overlapping generations model. If deviating from altruism is punished, then nobody will wish to deviate, i.e. if all others follow the custom then each individual has no choice but to follow it too.

3.3 Intragenerational Geographical Redistribution

In this section we want to familiarize the reader with a stream in the political science literature that studies how the organization of legislature leads to inefficient fiscal decisions[11]. Most of the initial papers focus on the US congress, but this literature has lately experienced a revival in the discussion of federalism and of the legislative design of the European Union[12]

Intragenerational redistribution occurs in many ways and it usually favours socio-economic groups. There are programs targeted to the poor (welfare), the retired (social security), the mal-nourished (food stamps) or the unemployed (unemployment benefits). Any citizen may obtain the benefits if he falls in the specific category and benefits cannot be varied without varying them for others in the category. A special case is a beneficiary group that is geographically defined or determined rather than socio-economically. Since geography is also the basis for political organization and representation (there is no party representing exclusively the young, the bus drivers or the unemployed, but US-states or *Bundesländer* have representatives exclusively fighting for their interests) projects can be exclusively targeted and may be

[11] An introductory survey is Inman [1990]. Some of the leading papers are Frerejohn [1974], Fiorina/Noll [1978], Shepsle/Weingast [1981], Weingast/Shepsle/Johnsen [1981], Weingast/Marshall [1988] and Baron/Frerejohn [1989].

[12] See the contributions to the session "Fiscal Federalism" at the 1991 annual congress of the European Economic Association (Casella/Frey [1992], Buiter/Kletzer [1992] and Inman/Rubinfeld [1992]) for an introduction to this literature. Another survey is Hughes/ Smith [1991]. More recent papers that focus on the European Union are Maré/Sarcinelli [1994] or Steunenberg [1994].

independently varied. It is for this reason that part of the literature in the political economy of legislative institutions has as a special feature the focus on geographical issues.

A typical feature of policy projects is that the benefits are concentrated in geographically specified constituencies while the cost of financing them are spread across all constituencies through generalized taxation[13]. A typical example is highway construction. The beneficiaries of such a project have a strong incentive to lobby for it while taxpayers who only bear a small fraction of the cost do not have a similarly strong incentive to oppose it. Weingast/Shepsle/Johnsen [1981] provide a formal presentation of this type of problem. The policy-makers of each district can exclusively decide on projects in their district. The cost of the project will be shared nation-wide. The benefits of each project are unrelated to the benefits of the projects in other districts. Weingast et al. [1981] analyze three different cases: in the extreme case the local policy-makers decide on the basis of the benefits of their constituencies and the fraction of the cost of "their"projects they have to bear. In an intermediate case, Weingast et al. allow members of a constituency to derive some benefits from projects in other constituencies (because they hold shares in the project, say). But in addition, the policy-maker also internalizes the fraction of the costs of projects in other districts that his constituency has to bear. The third case is that of the social planner who internalizes all benefits and all costs of all projects. In the first two cases the political equilibrium is such that each constituency ends up choosing projects that are too large compared to the social optimum (case 3). Efficiency is higher when various (all) costs are taken into account. The principal conclusion of Weingast et al. is that since political institutions fundamentally alter the perceptions and incidence of benefits and costs they systematically bias projects away from the efficient outcomes. Thus, decentralization of expenditures plus taxation according to a cost-sharing rule is a recipe for excessively large government budgets.

At first sight the impression arises that the strict "pork barrel" assumptions, as for example that a local policy-maker can decide independently on projects in his district that then will be financed by the whole economy, can rarely be found in reality. Nevertheless, it is true for most countries that representatives from different districts represent specific geographical interests and for the US congress Weingast et al. [1981], p.651, find evidence for reciprocity (i.e. the exchange of mutual favours) as a common decision rule. This enables district representatives to obtain the support even of those without a stake in the package in exchange for a reciprocal treatment[14]. The relevance of this approach can also be based on the observation that beneficiaries of certain transfer programs as the ones mentioned above (Unemployment ben-

[13] In the American political science literature these projects are called pork barrel projects.

[14] For some empirical evidence see Stockmann [1975] and Fiorina [1978].

efits, welfare, etc.) are often concentrated in certain regions. Then income redistribution and geographical redistribution become highly interconnected. Examples are transfers to the miners in the Ruhr area, Florida with its high concentration of pensioners or the transfer system from northern to southern Italy.

The crucial insight of this literature is that the geographical distribution of costs, benefits and decision power can make an important difference to the aggregate budget. This insight has triggered new research interest in Europe, where recent events have put the working and design of federal constitution on the agenda of public debate. Integration in Western Europe and disintegration in Eastern Europe both involve questions about the form of government institutions; German unification has put fiscal policy under strain and raised questions about budget interactions between the different Bundesländer (*Länderfinanzausgleich*) and also between different individuals (*Solidaritätszuschlag*); in Italy as well as Belgium, public debt problems in conjunction with regional conflict have created demands for a federative structure with more regional autonomy in carrying out government functions; the new federalism in the US involves decentralizing tasks from federal to state hands; perceived problems in Canada with federal schemes for transfers to and income equalization between provinces has generated thorough debate.

This literature makes a valuable contribution in explaining the increase in public debt in the last decades and the differences among economies in debt performance, (see chapter 2). The above evidence suggests that there has been an increase in the fiscal responsibilities of local authorities which can help to explain the increase in government budgets and debt. Hughes/Smith [1991], p.430 argue that this increase in local decentralization of decision power has occurred after 1975. They also find evidence for a "striking diversity of existing fiscal arrangements in different countries", p.426, which could help to explain the differences in fiscal performance among the OECD countries. However, the theory does not explain why for example two centralized economies as France and Italy exhibit such differences in fiscal behaviour. Hence, to thoroughly understand the relationship between fiscal institutions and fiscal performance more research is required.

3.4 Government Fragmentation and Duration and the Electoral System

In this section we discuss the relationship between government stability and budget deficits. In the literature the common indicators for government instability are the degree of government fragmentation (the numbers of participants in the political decision-making process) and the duration of government. The empirical literature (Roubini/Sachs [1989a], [1989b],

Grilli/Masciandaro/Tabellini [1991]) connects these indicators to a third, namely the electoral system, arguing that there is a strong correlation between the type of electoral system and the duration and degree of fragmentation of government as well as with the level of government debt.

Whereas the major part of the literature consists of empirical studies there are a number of theoretical papers on the correlation between government fragmentation and fiscal performance. We start by presenting a paper representative of this literature and then give a brief overview of the main empirical findings.

3.4.1 A War of Attrition Model

The main feature of models on the impact of government fragmentation is that there is a number of decision-makers with conflicting interests involved in the decision-making process at any point in time. One can think of different ministers in a cabinet, a coalition government or different levels of government. As a result, the fragmentation of power and lack of unified control leads to myopic policies, such as borrowing or delaying tax reform[15].

Alesina/Drazen [1991] show in a war of attrition (*Zermürbungskrieg*) model how the distributional struggle among different interest groups delays the adoption of the efficient policy of balancing the budget. A war of attrition can be characterized as follows[16]: A number of players are locked in a battle to win a prize in which all make losses which accumulate as long as the battle lasts. The one who stays longest wins the prize.

The set-up in the model by Alesina/Drazen [1991] can be summarized as follows. Some exogenous permanent shock perturbs the government budget, so that at the existing tax rates a deficit occurs and the debt begins to accumulate. A social planner would react immediately and adjust tax rates according to the optimal tax smoothing policy. However, for the installation of the stabilization program the approval of two interest groups is necessary. As long as they do not agree to stabilize the two groups share the fiscal burden, which arises from distortionary financing of the debt: Instead of implementing the optimal tax the deficit is mainly financed by monetization (inflation tax). In addition, part of the debt can be financed externally. The associated distortions due to high and variable inflation persist over time and the debt increases. Thus, both the welfare loss due to distortionary taxation

15 This idea has been applied to the coordination of fiscal and monetary policies by Sargent/ Wallace [1981] and Tabellini [1986] and to transfer policies in federations by Sanguinetti [1993].

16 The war of attrition model was first formalized in a biological context by Riley [1980], where two animals are fighting over a prize, and further developed by Bliss/Nalebuff [1984]. Kennan/Wilson [1988] apply this model to labour strikes. Backus/Driffill [1985a] and [1985b] and Tabellini [1988] discuss a war of attrition between trade unions and a central bank.

and the taxes needed to service the debt once stabilization is started increase, the longer the implementation of the stabilization program is delayed.

Moreover, each group incurs (individual) political costs (lobbying, political action) of preventing the other group from imposing an undesirable fiscal plan. The welfare losses as well as the political costs may differ across the two groups. Inflation has redistributive effects and thus different socioeconomic groups suffer differently from it. Political costs may differ because groups may vary in their political influence and therefore in the level of effort needed to continue fighting. Moreover, it is private information: each party is not fully informed about the cost borne by its opponent. (Knowing the other's costs is equivalent to knowing how strong your opponent is and is therefore crucial for determining one's own behaviour.)

The two interest groups, knowing that implementation of the stabilization program is inevitable, fight how to share the fiscal burden. The fractions of the burden that the winner and the loser will have to bear is given by an exogenous distribution and known to both groups. The first party to concede bears the larger share of the burden, whereas benefits from starting stabilization benefit everybody. Thus, each player has an incentive to postpone concession hoping that the other will give in first.

Alesina/Drazen now identify some parameters on which the equilibrium outcome depends:

- Delay is longer the more unequal the distribution of stabilization costs. Alesina/ Drazen suggest that the distribution of stabilization costs represents the degree of political cohesion in the economy. In countries with high political cohesion, the fiscal burden of stabilization is shared relatively equally, whereas in more polarized economies the group that concedes first bears a relatively larger share of the burden than the other. In the latter case, the gains from waiting are larger, so that each group holds out longer. The idea, that the degree of a society's political homogeneity plays an important role for macroeconomic performance also plays a central role in our model (see section 5) or in Alesina/ Tabellini [1990a] or [1990b] (see section 3.5.2) and is confirmed by the empirical evidence we will present later in this section.
- If the costs of of waiting are low, i.e. it is for example easy to live with inflation, then there will be longer delays before the correcting policy is implemented. This suggests that in countries with institutions that lower the loss from distortionary financing of government expenditure stabilization will be postponed longer. This could help throw light on the case of Italy whose *scala mobile* (wage and pension indexation) can be regarded as such an institution: by linking all wages and pensions to the inflation rate the population was not affected by inflation. (Note that the scala mobile was abandoned in 1989.)
- Moreover, financing a greater fraction of the deficit via distortionary taxation (which Alesina/ Drazen interpret as an attempt to control the growth

of government indebtedness) implies an earlier date of stabilization. By worsening the economic crisis the necessity of fighting it becomes more pressing. This idea can also be found in Drazen/ Grilli [1993]. They show, in a war of attrition model, how an economic crisis, defined as a period of high (and thus costly) inflation, actually increases total welfare by inducing an agreement over a policy change.

It is not difficult to find empirical examples for the predictions of the model by Alesina/ Drazen. For example, the model can explain why reforms that were repeatedly rejected in the past are suddenly implemented. Alesina/ Drazen themselves mention in their very interesting introductory section the examples of France 1926 and Germany 1923 (p.1174). The components of the successful Poincaré stabilization program are quite similar to his 1924 program[17]; also the German stabilization program implemented by the Stresemann government in November 1923 bears strong similarities to previous proposals[18]. A more recent example is Israel's 1985 stabilization program whose components were discussed by researchers and politicians well before but rejected by the government[19]. Other examples are peace agreements which are finally reached after years of apparently useless fighting as in Korea, Vietnam, Israel or Algiers.

Moreover, Alesina/ Drazen's model agrees with the intuition that reforms are often blocked by conflict over how to distribute the losses. Alesina/ Drazen elaborate on the examples of France and Germany after the first world war (see also Maier [1975]). But one need not go that far back for an example. The current struggle for implementing the tax reform in Germany bears all the ingredients of Alesina/ Drazen's model.

Even though Alesina/ Drazen do not explicitly call the two socioeconomic groups in their model a coalition they can easily be understood as such. Spolaore [1993] presents a very similar model, in which members of a coalition who represent the interests of different constituencies decide on fiscal ad-

---

[17] In the early 1920s France realized that the German war reparations would not solve the French fiscal problems. A period of various policy proposals followed, a stabilization program (higher indirect taxes) was implemented in 1924, which was only temporary due to the election of an internally divided "cartel des gauches" government. In 1926 Poincaré increased both indirect taxes and the income tax on the lower middle class (see Alesina/ Drazen [1991], p.1172, or Maier [1975]

[18] The new government that took power in August 1923 was a "Grand Coalition" of the right and the left. Nevertheless, Stresemann was not able to implement his policy program, because he needed to appease the conservatives who had become "more dangerous and powerful than the socialist left" (Maier [1975], p.384). Only after the new Enabling Act in November 1923, giving the government power to cut through legislative deadlocks and quickly adopt fiscal measures by decree, was Stresemann able to start his stabilization program (Alesina/Drazen [1991], p.1173, 74).

[19] See Bruno [1990], pp. 290-295, for a detailed discussion of "early failures to sell the right programs". The anti-inflation program was originally laid out in 1981 and rejected twice in 1984.

justment. He investigates how fiscal inefficiencies depend on the number of coalition members. Not surprisingly, the accumulation of debt (due to the ongoing war of attrition) is a positive function of the degree of government fragmentation.

3.4.2 Empirical Findings

The significance of the degree of government fragmentation is also emphasized in the empirical papers we review now.

Roubini/ Sachs [1989a] and [1989b] construct a political indicator that is increasing in the degree of government fragmentation. This indicator can take values from 0 to 3; value 0 indicates a one-party majority, values 1 and 2 a coalition government of two and three or more parties respectively and value 3 a minority government; see Roubini/ Sachs [1989b], p. 293, for details. They then estimate a regression where deficits depend on the change in unemployment, income and the real interest rate as well as the political variable interacting with a dummy variable. The dummy is equal to 0 during the rapid growth period 1960-74 and equal to 1 during 1975-85 (period of macroeconomic stress due to the oil price shock). They so aim to test the proposition that "multi-party governments have a bias towards larger budget deficits, but perhaps only during periods of macroeconomic stress" (Roubini/Sachs [1989b], p.923). They find that the political dummy enters significantly. (That the economic variables have a significant coefficient comes as no surprise.) Moreover, they find that coalition governments manage the budget better when overall macroeconomic circumstances are favourable.

Roubini/ Sachs give the following intuition for their results: That coalition governments in general have difficulties in balancing the budget is quite obvious. The coalition members represent distinctive constituencies and thus have distinctive interests. This leads to clashes in the political consensus-finding process and thus to suboptimal or delayed decisions. The coalition members find themselves in a prisoners' dilemma: all members may prefer comprehensive budget cuts, but each of them may have the incentive to protect its particular part of the budget against the consolidation measures. The ideal situation would be if all members cut their respective parts of the budget. However, for each member it is better when the others cut their budget, while he does not cut his own.

Also, coalition members often have considerable power to veto a change in the status quo. This explains the enormous power of even very small coalition partners, as for example the religious parties in Israel. Finally, the mechanism to enforce cooperation of the coalition partners may be very weak[20].

---

[20] Weingast/ Marshall [1988] analyze vote trading as a mechanism for enforcability of cooperation. They argue that trading votes in order to arrive at an efficient overall budget involves exchanges of benefits that are hard to monitor and hard

For their finding that coalition governments manage the budget better when overall macroeconomic circumstances are favourable they give the following explanation ([1989b], p. 925): Whereas coalition members have the power to veto spending cuts they may have less power to push through spending increases without the support of other coalition partners. Since the other coalition partners will not necessarily have an incentive to support excessive spending, the decision for the spending increases is not likely to be made and the budget will be kept at an appropriate level. The spending cuts needed in response to an adverse shock, on the other hand, are unlikely to draw a majority due to the coalition members' veto power.

Another suggestion Roubini/ Sachs make is that the tenure of government matters. This was tested by Grilli et al. [1991] and we come back to that point later in this section.

The work of Roubini/ Sachs [1989a] and [1989b] is one of the first empirical studies investigating the role of institutions for economic policy-making and as such it is important but also somewhat dated. In comparison, the paper by Grilli et al. [1991] provides a more detailed description of the institutional environment. They collected new material on the institutions of the industrialized OECD countries. In particular, they collected data on the political conditions of budgetary policy decisions, as for example the frequency of government changes, the degree of proportionality of a country's electoral laws[21] or the fractionalization of the party system[22] and political extremism[23].

The first part of their analysis is purely descriptive. Their main observations are that a lack of fiscal discipline coincides with a high degree of proportionality of the electoral system, a high degree of fractionalization (in-

---

to enforce, because the stream of benefits for the vote traders is noncontemporaneous (one of the traders will benefit earlier than the other) which gives room for reneging on the deal. Also, the "fulfillment" of the deal is likely to be noncontemporaneous (one trader must support the other on the promise that the latter will support him at a later date.)

[21] In the political science literature a main distinction is between presidential (France, US) and parliamentary democracies. In the latter category one distinguishes again according to the *degree of proportionality of the electoral laws.* According to Bingham Powell [1982], a suitable indicator is the number of representatives per district in the parliament. Systems with more than five representatives, as for example Belgium, Italy or Greece, are labelled representational parliamentary democracies, whereas countries with less than five representatives (as for example Germany, UK, Japan, New Zealand) are called majoritarian parliamentary democracies (see table 5 in Grilli et al.[1991], p. 351).

[22] Grilli et al. follow Rae [1967] in defining fractionalization as the probability that two legislators chosen at random belong to different parties.

[23] A party is called extremist if one or more of the following applies: a well-developed non-democratic ideology, a proposal to change the boundaries of the nation, diffuse alienation and distrust of the existing political system (see Bingham Powell [1982]).

dicator of the number of parties participating in the government), political extremism and short-lived governments.

They then run a regression estimating debt accumulation as a function of the extent of government support in the legislature (majority, coalition, minority), government durability and a political instability index (frequency of swings between legislative majorities with very different preferences). Their findings are quite surprising: Whereas, as expected, debt accumulation is negatively correlated to government durability, it is not related to the number of parties in the government or to political instability. The fact that durability matters whereas political stability does not, indicates that deficits are related to the frequency of *any* government change, not only to changes which transfer power from one ideology to another.

Nevertheless, Grilli et al. [1991] do not let go of the idea that government size and political stability matter. They suggest (without testing it) that even though the degree of government fragmentation and the political stability index seem to have no direct influence on public debt, they may play an indirect role via the electoral system. They argue that the highly indebted countries are those governed by representational democracies and that these are in turn the systems with large coalitions, with more extreme parties in the government and with short average tenures of governments. Moreover they estimate a positive correlation with government size and durability, which may suggest that short-lived governments are a proxy for a fragmented political system (see for example Italy).

The empirical literature on the relationship between politics and institutions is still at its beginnings and as Persson/ Tabellini [1994b], p. 9, put it, it "poses more questions than it provides answers". As Malinvaud [1991] points out, a major drawback is still the database. Drawing data on the institutional conditions of economic policy is much more difficult than calculating economic indicators such as unemployment rates or growth rates of GDP. In order to properly identify institutional features a knowledge of history and political science is necessary. A difficulty for the data collector then becomes that "one cannot expect any author, or even any team of authors, to know all historical circumstances that mattered for each of the countries considered. This is why attention should be devoted to improve the data bases and to put on record any hidden national specificity that may exist or may have occurred", [1991], p.377[24]. Pagano [1991], p. 381, criticizes the authors' dis-

[24] Malinvaud is surprised about certain data concerning France as for example the number of significant government changes (3) between 1960-69 when actually de Gaulle had strong power until 1969 (table B1, [1991], p.384).

Their estimate of two years for the average durability of the executive in Germany (table 6,[1991] p. 356) (1950-90) is wrong. The minimum number of years that an executive lasted in the Federal Republic of Germany was three years. Between 1950 and 1990 there have been two government collapses (the Brandt and Schmidt governments in 1972 and 1983 respectively) both after the first three (out of four) years of the parliamentary term. In 1990 elections were

regard for non-political factors in shaping choices about fiscal or monetary policies. "In their effort to make a case for the importance of political facts the authors neglect other likely sources of international debt accumulation" as for example structural differences or import price elasticities of oil.

We want to leave the discussion of the statistical results at that. We have learned in this section that weak governments indicated by a large number of government members and/ or short durability have a tendency for excessive debt accumulation. Throughout this section we have regularly referred to empirical examples for our suggestions. We can conclude that this stream of the literature on the political economy of budget deficits scores quite well when it comes to explain the differences in macroeconomic performance. Why exactly the debt accumulation happened after the oil price shock and not before is left open.

3.5 Debt as a Strategic Instrument

In this section we introduce models that have directly influenced our own work. Unlike the papers of government fragmentation where fiscal inefficiencies were explained as a result of the political conflict between different decision-makers at the same point in time, a feature of the papers in this section is that although the current and future decision-makers may differ, it is always a single policy-maker that is in charge at each point in time. These papers investigate the fiscal behaviour of governments with different ideological preferences in a competitive political environment, i.e. the incumbent policy-maker has to take into account that the voters may replace him in the future with another policy-maker with different preferences. These political pressures may force the government to use debt as a strategic instrument. The literature distinguishes between two strategic aspects of debt:

1. Any fiscal decision that has long run consequences, as for example taking on a debt which has to be served and repaid in the future, affects the future policy-makers. Thus, by leaving debt, the incumbent government influences the policy choices of its successor and can thus tie the future government's hand strategically in its own favour.
2. Moreover, an incumbent can use debt in order to improve its relative standing in the eye of the voter, thus inducing the voter to give him his vote. This way he can influence the electoral outcome strategically in his favour ("election manipulation", see the introduction, page 3, for a discussion of how we use this term here).

---

called one year early due to revolutionary (or better evolutionary) political events (German reunification), see Neumann [1995], p.131. Apart from these cases, all governments since the existence of the Federal Republic of Germany have fulfilled the whole four years of the legislative period.

What exactly an incumbent party will choose to do depends on its objective function: A crucial feature of the models on the strategic role of debt is that parties have ideological ("partisan") preferences, i.e. each party has given preferences about which policy to implement. A reason could be that each party represents the interests of a different constituency[25]. An alternative approach, following Downs [1957], is to assume the parties to be "opportunistic", i.e. their sole objective is to stay in power. As a result, for a given distribution of voters' preferences and a given structure of the economy, in a two-party system both parties will propose the same platform to the voters, which is equivalent to the median voter's position. Thus, both implement the same policies if elected (policy convergence hypothesis)[26].

In the political economy literature the partisan approach is by now more widely used (see for example Cukierman [1992], Wagner [1990] or Wittmann [1983]). According to Alesina [1989], p.60, the following reasons speak against the policy convergence hypothesis:

1. In order to be elected as their party's candidate a politician has to take the party's median position. For credibility and reputation reasons he cannot change this position later.
2. If parties can choose their ideology, new parties may form to suit a group which is currently not represented and political fragmentation will ensue.
3. Unhappy voters can abstain from voting.

The papers we now present have further developed the literature on credibility or time-consistency in macroeconomics[27]. There, the identity of the government is the same over time (there are no political battles) but governments at different dates face different incentive constraints. Thus, a policy which is currently optimal may prove to be sub-optimal at a later date which gives the policy-maker an incentive to deviate from it. Time consistency or credibility requires that a government only announces plans from which it will not wish to deviate later[28]. A similar situation occurs when the decision-maker tomorrow is different from today. In order to announce a credible/time

[25] The "partisan" approach was first formalized by Wittmann [1977] and has been applied in particular in the literature on political business cycles (Hibbs [1977], Alesina [1988]).

[26] The most important macroeconomic application of this approach is probably the "political business cycle" of Nordhaus [1975] and McRae [1977].

[27] In the macroeconomic literature these two terms are used interchangeably, see Persson [1988], p.520, or Alesina/Tabellini [1988], p.543.

[28] In macroeconomics the analysis of the policy-makers' incentives originated with the work of Kydland/Prescott [1977] and Calvo [1978] and was applied to the problem of the maturity structure of government debt by Lucas/Stokey [1983] and Persson/Persson/Svensson [1988]. For short but comprehensive overviews over the literature on credibility in macroeconomics in general and on these papers in particular see Persson/Tabellini [1994a], pp. 3-8 and 22-25 or Persson/ Tabellini [1990], pp. 1-18. Short surveys on credibility and politics are Alesina/Tabellini [1988] and Persson [1988].

consistent policy the decision-maker today has to take into account the future decision-maker's (re)action in response to his policy.

We now present some of the main papers of the literature in more or less chronological order. The time-inconsistency problem in these models stems from the fact that the identity and hence the preferences of the government change over time. This creates incentive constraints for the current incumbent that emanate from the optimal policy choices of future governments. Thus, by manipulating its fiscal variable the incumbent "creates facts" that

1. induce the future government to act in a way favourable to his predecessor and/or
2. that may change the consumers' voting behaviour.

The first two papers by Persson/ Svensson [1989] and Alesina/Tabellini [1990a] focus on the first aspect only, whereas the next two papers by Aghion/Bolton [1990] and Milesi-Ferretti/Spolaore [1994] integrate both of these aspects.

3.5.1 Persson/Svensson [1989]: Why a Stubborn Conservative Would Run a Deficit: Policy With Time-Inconsistent Preferences

Persson/Svensson analyze a simple two-period, two parties model where parties, a left- wing and a right-wing, differ in their desired level of public consumption and where there is no uncertainty about the electoral outcome. They assume a small open economy (the world interest rate is given and equal to 0). There is a known government in each period which can raise taxes each period to finance a public good. Part (or all) of the tax revenues from the first period can be transferred to the second where it will be used for supplying the public good. Taxes are assumed to be distortionary, hence they induce a dead weight loss to the society. The government gets utility out of providing public goods. On the other hand the dead weight loss of taxation causes the government disutility. (This assumption means that there are consumers in the background and the government cares about the losses to society. Thus, one can alternatively describe the model with consumers who enjoy the public good and suffer from the taxes but since they play no active role in the model we can "drop" them describing the model using only the government preferences.)

The results of the paper and their intuition can best be explained in a simpler set-up in which there is public consumption only in the second period. Hence, all tax revenues from the first period get transferred to the second. Note that from a tax-smoothing point of view it would be optimal to raise half of the revenue in each period. (Total income in the economy is the same in both periods).

The authors first notice that the model has an intrinsic time-inconsistency problem. Assume a party to be in power in the two periods. In period 1 it will set a plan of taxes (for the two periods) and government expenditure for the second (which equals the sum of tax revenues of the two periods). In choosing the optimal plan it will equate the marginal cost of the tax distortions (of the two periods) with the marginal benefits of the public good. When coming to the second period, the government may revise its plans. In choosing the optimal ex-post plan (given the possible tax revenues transferred from the first period) it will equate the marginal benefits of the public good with the marginal cost of the tax distortions caused by the tax raised in the second period (all costs of the first period are now sunk). The ex-post optimal plan will in general differ from the ex-ante one for although the marginal benefits of the public good are the same the distortion costs are different. However, it can be assumed that the government will choose a time-consistent plan. That is, when choosing its first period tax it takes into account that the rest of the plan will depend on its past actions and it will choose its first period action such that it will not wish to deviate from it later on.

The time consistency problem becomes sharper as there may be another government in the second period whose preferences differ from those of the first period government. Persson/Svensson analyze the fiscal behaviour of a conservative government that prefers low government spending and that knows that it will be replaced by a government which is in favour of a larger level of public spending. The conservative government would have preferred to have a low level of public good in the second period and would have raised some tax in the first period to be transferred to the second. However, once it knows that the liberal party will be in power it will choose to leave less money to the second period. By leaving less, the government of the second period will have to raise more taxes in order to supply a certain level of public good. Thus, by raising less taxes in the first period the conservative government constrains the liberal expansionary government that follows. Note also that this behaviour of the conservative causes increased tax distortions: Taxes are too low in the first period and too high in the second as compared to tax smoothing.

Now, the exact degree of constraining done by the conservative government will depend on how important the public goods are to it relative to the disutility it suffers from the tax distortions. If it is more "stubborn", i.e. its disutility from too much public good is high relative to the disutility of tax distortions then it will constrain the second period government more by leaving less revenues. On the other hand, a conservative government that is not stubborn sets the first period tax rate according to tax smoothing. It anticipates the level of future spending (time consistency constraint) and is willing to bear the future government's spending choice because even though it would rather spending be less the tax profile is less distorted than in the above case.

Note that we have presented the model so far as a model without any government borrowing (debt), i.e. the whole reasoning of the model "works" with taxes only. The conservative constrains the succeeding liberal government simply by raising less taxes than possible. Nevertheless, Persson/Svensson call their paper "Why a stubborn conservative would run a deficit" and they describe government behaviour inclusive of government borrowing: The first government can not only constrain its successor by raising less taxes than possible but also by taking on an external debt, which the second period government then has to repay. However, the authors do not tell the reader what exactly the first period government does with the externally borrowed money in the case where there is government consumption in the seond period only. If it simply transfers the whole amount to the second period the second period government can then simply take this amount to repay this debt and it will not be constrained in its actions (the world interest rate is assumed to be 0). The only possible intuition is that the first government divides the money among the consumers. Then, indeed the taxes (and the corresponding distortions) in the second period will be higher.

The results can now be summarized: A more stubborn conservative government may end up taking less than optimal taxes (or borrowing more) when it knows that it will be succeeded by a high-spending (liberal) government compared to when it knows that it will remain in power. Moreover, the larger the conflict between the two policy-makers, the greater the deviation from tax smoothing (or the greater the debt issue).

Persson/Svensson give a number of empirical examples for their model. They claim that the fact that fiscal policy is used with a strategic motive is reflected in the discussions in the (first) Reagan administration that the only way to lower government spending in the future was to lower current taxes. Thus, they would create "facts" for future congresses and administrations. Other examples are the privatization policy of the Thatcher government in Britain or the settlements policy of previous (and the current) Likud governments in Israel. These policies will change (or have changed) the constraints for succeeding governments with possibly very different preferences.

We finally point at what we consider another shortcoming of this model. The only political aspect in this model is that there are two different parties with different policy preferences. However, there is no electoral uncertainty. Persson/Svensson themselves mention this (p.342): "Another very interesting expansion, although as far as we can see a very complicated one, would be to make the probability of being reelected depend upon the policy pursued."

3.5.2 Alesina/Tabellini [1990a]: A Positive Theory of Fiscal Deficits and Government Debt

Alesina/Tabellini independently developed a model similar to the one by Persson/Svensson [1989] from the previous section. They consider a situation where two different parties have preferences for combinations of two public goods (defense and welfare say) rather than for different levels of the same public good as in Persson/Svensson. The two parties are ideological, in the sense that they represent the interests of different constituencies. The government in power provides the public with a combination of the two goods. These can be financed by tax revenues (proportional tax on labour income) and/or by issuing government bonds. The economy is closed, thus the interest rate is internally determined. Alesina/Tabellini analyze both the two-period and the infinite horizon case. In each period the government has to repay the debt of the previous period (no default assumption). As in Persson/Svensson, elections are not explicitly modelled: Governments alternate in power according to an exogenously given probability distribution of being elected. There is a large number of consumers who consume, work and save. They are all born at the beginning of the first period and have the same time horizon (two periods or infinite). Individuals are identical except for their preferences for the two public goods. Their utility in each period is given by

$$U(c_t) + V(x_t) + \alpha h(g_t) + (1-\alpha)h(f_t)$$

where c is private consumption, x is leisure, g and f are the two different public goods, α parameterizes the individual's preferences over the composition of the public good bundle (α is distributed in [0,1]) and t indicates the period. Their total utility (over their time horizon) is the discounted sum of the single period utilities and Alesina/Tabellini use an expectations operator to indicate the uncertainty about future policies. Each period each consumer is endowed with one unit of time to be shared between work and leisure. Work is transformed into goods according to a one to one technology. The labour tax influences the labour supply decision and thus private consumption. Since consumers are identical except for their preference for public good and because of the additivity of the utility function, all consumers will choose the same level of private consumption and leisure for a given tax policy.

In this set-up Alesina/Tabellini first analyze the two-period, then the infinite horizon case, contrasting the outcome with the outcome a social planner would have generated. The social planner remains in power all periods and hence maximizes the weighted average of all consumers' utilities. His optimal choice is to balance the budget in every period. In the political set-up, however, the government in power chooses the level and the composition of public goods and the portfolio of financing this bundle (taxes, deficit) in order to maximize the long run utility of its constituency (represented by a representative agent). In doing so it has to consider that it may be replaced by a government with different preferences. In order to simplify the analysis the authors assume the parties' preferences to be rather drastic: One party when in power will only provide good g (welfare say, $\alpha = 1$), the other will only provide good f (defense, $\alpha = 0$).

Alesina/Tabellini analyze the two period case by backward induction. The second period problem is for the policy-maker in power to choose the tax rate and the level and composition of public goods given the debt inherited from the first period which has to be repaid. Then, the first period government, knowing how its deficit decision will affect the future, decides on taxes, deficit and level and composition of public goods in the first period. Because of the simplifying assumptions the solution to the second period problem is perfectly symmetric: for a given level of inherited debt both parties would choose in the second period the same tax rate and the same level of public consumption, although one party spends all on good g and the other spends all on good f.

The long run decision of the first period government (it has to optimize its constituency's long run utility and thus to consider the effects of its actions on the second period) depends on its reelection probability. From the first order condition of the optimization problem it follows that the incumbent chooses the deficit by equating the marginal cost of inheriting debt in the future (this depends on whether he is reelected or not) and the marginal utility in the first period of leaving debt to the future (and thus being able to provide more of the desired good in the first period). The result is that the lower is the probability of being reelected (and thus having to cope with the inherited debt) the higher the optimal level of government borrowing. As a consequence the future government is less flexible: in order to repay the outstanding debt it has to cut back on public spending.

The intuition is that a policy-maker who takes on a debt faces an asymmetry. When he borrows he can spend the extra sources of finance in the way he wants. But when the debt becomes due the spending cuts are not necessarily "his business", since he may be out of office. Consequently, he fully internalizes the benefits of the additional spending in the first period but only partially (according to his reelection probability) internalizes the future costs of the spending cuts. A government that wants to spend a lot on defense, expecting with a high probability that it will lose the the elections will use debt strategically. It provides a lot of defense today and ties the future government's hands by the future debt repayments. The latter who would not spend much on defense anyway will then moreover not be in a position to provide much of the undesired (by the first period government) welfare.

The infinite horizon case proves more complicated. The policy-maker at one point in time can take into account the past and has to weigh the consequences of his actions for a long future time path. There are many possible ways to deal with the past, as for instance to behave to one's opponent as he behaved towards oneself in the past. (Note that with each period the past "increases".) In order to rule out these so called "reputational equilibria", Alesina/Tabellini restrict the incumbent governments to react only to the debt they inherit. They are looking for a stationary equilibrium, i.e. a strategy that is the same at any point in time. This strategy describes a government's reaction (fiscal policy) to any level of inherited debt. Alesina/Tabellini assume further that the parties are symmetric, i.e. that the strategy of one is the mirror image of the strategy of the other. If one party reacts to debt by producing amount x of good f, the other will react by producing x of good

g. Note that an incumbent party has to take into account an infinite time horizon when solving his fiscal optimization problem, in doing so he has to consider all possible future sequences of events (histories). This type of dynamic programming problems can be solved by using the Bellmann equation.

The result (and the intuition) are the same as in the above case: Alternating governments which disagree about the composition of public consumption issue more debt than a social planner and they issue more debt the higher the probability of being "voted" out of office.

For the two period model, Alesina/Tabellini then offer a weak attempt to "endogenize" the electoral outcome. Voters vote for the party whose policy makes them better off in the second period. This of course depends on which party is closer to his political tastes (α), i.e. all voters with $\alpha < 1/2$ vote for one and all voters with $\alpha > 1/2$ for the other party. But there is uncertainty concerning the consumers' preference distribution and thus concerning the elections' outcome. (Are there more voters with $\alpha < 1/2$ than with $\alpha > 1/2$?) In particular there is uncertainty about the position of the median voter. Alesina/Tabellini now "endogenize" the electoral outcome by stating that a party's probability (P) of being elected is $P(\alpha_{median} \geq 1/2)$ for the party with the high α (welfare party) and $P(\alpha_{median} \leq 1/2)$ for the defense party. Note that voting behaviour is totally independent of the parties' policies for the second period. Since they have not offered any model of the voting process their use of "endogenizing" is somewhat exaggerated.

In an extension Alesina/Tabellini analyze the case in which both parties care about both goods, i.e. $0 < \alpha < 1$. They still keep the problem symmetric by keeping α the same for the two parties only that one party attaches weight α to one good (and $(1-\alpha)$ to the other) and the other party attaches weight $(1-\alpha)$ to the good (and α to the other). They then derive that - under certain strict assumptions on the utility function (available from the authors(!)) - the greater the degree of political polarization between the parties (the further α is from $1/2$) the larger is the deficit bias as compared to the balanced budget policy of the social planner).

To summarize, the basic insight of the paper is that in the presence of disagreement between current and future policy-makers, public debt is used strategically by each government to influence the choices of its successors. Since each government knows that with some probability it will be succeeded in the next period by a government that will spend taxes on a kind of public good that the current government does not like, it perceives a low expected marginal utility of next period's public consumption. This provides an incentive to restrict next period's public consumption by borrowing more in the current period compared with a situation in which the current government would remain in power next period with certainty. The reason for this is that both the disagreement amongst alternating policy-makers and the uncertainty about who will be in power in the future prevent the current government from fully internalizing the cost of leaving debt to its successor. As a result debt accumulation is higher than it would be under a social planner and it increases with the degree of polarization between alternating governments and with the likelihood of the other party winning the elections. Contrary to Persson/Svensson [1989] debt accumulation does not depend on the parties' political "couleur". Both right-wing (defense) and left-wing (welfare) parties take on deficits of exactly the same amount.

Linking debt to reelection probabilities seems rather sensible but a point to criticize here is to link debt to the degree of polarization of alternating governments. There have not been many significant government changes in the last two decades and debt has accumulated also in countries in which the same party has been ruling for many legislative periods. And even if there were significant government changes, party polarization is not that high in many OECD countries. The major parties are quite close in their political ideas (SPD and CDU in Germany, ("New") Labour and Tories in the UK or Republicans and Democrats in the US). Moreover, as in Persson/Svensson [1989] there are no proper elections in the model and consumers are as homogeneous in this model as in Persson/Svensson's (only here consumers vary in their tastes and in Persson/Svensson they vary in their income). Moreover, the strict symmetry in all results is somewhat limiting. In order to obtain the results the authors cannot take any two different parties but they need to assume that the parties are symmetrically opposed to each other.

We would just like to mention another paper by Alesina/Tabellini [1990b] ('Voting on the Budget Deficit') which is very similar to the one we discussed and which for this reason we will not deal with at great length. In a two period model public expenditure can be financed by taxes and external debt in the first period and by taxes in the second. The debt from the first period has to be repaid in the second. But whereas in the above model the fiscal decision was taken by a political party, here all voters decide directly on fiscal policy. Any two policy proposals are voted upon in pairwise comparisons. A crucial feature of the model is that there is uncertainty about the identity of future majorities (in particular about the future median voter) and hence about the future composition of public spending. Then, under certain conditions, the first period political majority runs a deficit: The political asymmetry prevents the current majority from fully internalizing the future costs of servicing the debt, the more so the greater is the difference between its preferences and the expected preferences of the future majority, i.e. as in Alesina/Tabellini, [1990a], the greater the economy's degree of political polarization the larger is the budget deficit.

3.5.3 Aghion/Bolton [1990]: Government Domestic Debt and the Risk of Default: A Political Economic Model of the Strategic Role of Debt

We now present papers that also take into account the second strategic aspect of debt: Not only can debt be used to influence the actions of a future government but also to influence the election's outcome. The first paper that derives conditions under which debt is overaccumulated due to strategic manipulation of elections is the one by Aghion/Bolton [1990]. Since this paper is closely related to our model we describe the paper in great detail.

Aghion/Bolton present a closed economy, two-period, two-party model with elections held between the periods. In each period there is a government which provides a public good. In the first period the public good can be financed by a non-distortionary, proportional income tax or by issuing government bonds to the public (deficit financing). The interest rate is endogenously determined. In the second period, only taxes are available to finance both debt repayment and expenditure on the public good. The rate of transformation of public and private goods is equal to one, i.e. one unit of private goods produces one unit of public goods. Aghion/Bolton analyze two variations of this model. In the first, the entire debt has to be cleared at the end of the second period (no-default assumption). In the second the government can decide whether and how much of the inherited debt to repay. The consumers in the economy live for two periods. Each period they earn a fixed income according to a given income distribution. So consumers vary in their income. Public goods, on the other hand, enter the utility function of all consumers in the same way. They derive utility in both periods from private and public consumption, c and g respectively, according to the utility function

$$U(c_1, c_2, g_1, g_2) = \log(c_1 + g_1) + \beta \log(c_2 + g_2)$$

where β is the intertemporal discount rate. Note that this is a very specific utility function which implies that private and public goods are perfect substitutes. Consumers choose their consumption levels in the two periods and their savings in the first period subject to budget constraints in each period in order to maximize the above intertemporal utility function.

Between the two periods the two parties compete for office. A left-wing party who represents the interests of a representative consumer with an income below the average income, and a right-wing party whose representative consumer is richer than the average. Voters are forward looking and vote for the party that guarantees them the higher utility in the second period. The party that gathers the majority of votes wins.

Aghion/Bolton first solve the model under the no-default assumption. They start by contrasting the optimal fiscal policies in both periods of a right-wing and a left-wing "dictator" with a social planner. By "dictator" they mean a party that is guaranteed to remain in power in both periods. They then analyze the case of a change of regimes.

The model is solved by backward induction. First the second period optimal fiscal policy is derived for a given level of inherited debt. Then the first period government decides on the optimal level of debt (as well as of course on the tax and the level of public good in the first period.)

The social planner maximizes the intertemporal utility function of a representative average consumer (the one with the average income). Aghion/Bolton first find that given a certain debt to repay, the planner is indifferent between any feasible level of expenditure on public goods: He is indifferent between a policy where he sets the tax rate in the second period, τ_2, just to repay the debt without providing any public good g_2 or a policy where he sets a higher τ_2 so as to provide also some public good in the second period. The reason is straight forward. Since private and public goods are perfect substitutes and the average consumer pays exactly the share of public goods he gets, he derives the same utility from any combination of private and public consumption. As we will see later that does not hold for consumers whose income is different from the average: A poorer consumer's tax payments are less than average outlay for the public good whereas a rich consumer pays relatively more. A similar result holds for the first period. With non-distortionary taxes and the two goods being perfect substitutes, the social planner is not only indifferent between the portfolio of tax- and debt financing some given level of public good in the first period but also between any feasible level of debt (and therefore between feasible level of period one expenditure on public goods). Aghion/Bolton [1990] call this "Ricardian superindeterminacy", p.321: The indeterminacy is not only in the financial structure for a given expenditure level (as in the Ricardian equivalence theorem) but also in the optimal level of government expenditure. For the average consumer a high debt today induces him to save more in order to make up for the income loss due to higher taxes tomorrow. Moreover, a high debt today implies a high level of public good today so he can derive his utility from that rather than from his private income (perfect substitutes), whereas he can substitute the utility loss from less private good tomorrow (high debt repayment) by a utility gain from private income (high savings).

These results do not hold, however, for a left- or a right-wing dictator. We first state the results for both dictatorships and then discuss them. Let us look at the second period solution given some level of inherited debt. A right-wing government will choose not to provide any public good at all in the second period and set the tax rate just to repay the inherited debt, whereas a left-wing party wants to maximize expenditure, sets $\tau_2 = 1$ and provides as much public good as possible after debt repayment. In the first period, a right-wing dictator wants to minimize expenditure, he does not provide any public good and thus does not have to levy any taxes or take on a debt. Consequently, there will be no savings. A left-wing dictator, on the other hand, wants to maximize government expenditure, he thus sets the maximum possible tax rate ($\tau_1 = 1$); moreover, he can take on any debt below a certain boundary (discounted total income in the second period). This seems to be a rather odd result: Taking on a debt implies that people save (buy government bonds). But how can they do so when the left-wing dictator taxes all their income away? In a footnote (p.341) Aghion/Bolton offer the following explanation: "This is possible since we allow for negative consumption. (...) this unpleasant feature of our model is simply the result of normalization (tax rates are normalized to be in the set [0,1]). A tax rate such as $\tau_1 = 1$ should not be interpreted too literally. In practice governments have upper bounds (less than 1) on how much they can effectively tax income."

Let us sum up: A world with a right-wing dictator can be described as a total laissez-faire world. The government does not interfere at all. There will be no public goods in either period and hence no taxes and no debt. The consumers are left with all their income to spend privately. A left-wing dictator, on the other hand, sets taxes equal to 1 in both periods. If we abstract from negative consumption, then there will be only public consumption in the economy. This could be described as total equality (or total communism). The government takes all the consumers' income away and divides it equally among consumers in the form of a public good. The intuition is the following: If one shared the costs of a public project evenly among consumers each would have to pay the average cost. If one pays for the public good by a proportional income tax then consumers with different incomes pay different amounts. A rich consumer pays more than the average cost, the average consumer pays exactly the average cost whereas the poor consumers pay less. Hence, the rich would rather enjoy their private income than pay for public goods of which they pay a higher share than poor consumers and thus avoid redistribution to the poor (or subsidizing the poor).

Aghion/Bolton now analyze the cases in which there are changes of regime, i.e. they derive the optimal fiscal policies in the first period of a left-wing government followed by a right-wing ($L \rightarrow R$) and the reverse case ($R \rightarrow L$). Solving by backward induction we look at the second period first. The results are the same as above: For a given level of inherited debt, a right-wing party will not provide any public good and set the tax rate just to repay the debt. A left-wing party will set the maximum possible tax ($\tau_2 = 1$), repays the debt and spends the rest on the public good.

Which party will win the elections and actually govern in the second period is entirely determined by the income distribution. It can be shown (and it follows from the intuition we gave above) that the voter indifferent between the two parties is the the voter with the average income: all voters poorer than him are better off under (and thus vote for) the left-wing party, whereas voters richer than the average vote for the right-wing party. Then it depends on the skewedness of the income distribution which party wins. If the median voter is poorer than the average the left-wing party wins and in the opposite case the right-wing party wins. There cannot be any manipulation of elections in this model. The electoral results are entirely determined by the position of the median voter.

Let us now assume that the left-wing party is in power in the first period in an economy whose income distribution will generate an electoral victory for the right-wing party. The left-wing party is in favour of high public expenditure whatever party will govern after him. But now matters are even worse, since its right-wing successor will not provide any public debt at all. The left-wing party then chooses to set $\tau_1 = 1$ and also decides to constrain the future government's hands by taking on a high debt, thus borrowing from the second period. This increases the first period utility of the consumers poorer than the average since their private income could not buy them the amount of public good provided. Moreover, it redistributes from the rich to the poor in the second period since the rich bear a relatively higher tax burden of servicing the debt.

A right-wing government followed by a left-wing, on the other hand, will not gain from constraining the future government through debt. It will not collect any taxes in the first period and since in the next period under the left-wing regime all income will be taxed away anyway the right-wing party is indifferent between the sustainable levels of debt. This follows from Ricardian equivalence. For example, if the right-wing government takes on a high debt the succeeding left-wing government will have to repay that amount and has to cut back on public expenditure. This reduction in public goods is made up for by increasing the private consumption from repaid savings. (A high debt induces high savings to make up for future income losses due to tax increases.)

So far deficits had no strategic effect on the elections' outcome. Aghion/ Bolton now introduce the possibility of costlessly defaulting on part of or on the whole debt in the second period. Their first observation is that a social planner is indifferent between defaulting and repaying the debt. If the social planner defaults in the second period he can set lower taxes and leave its average consumer with more private income. If he does not default and repays the debt the consumer gets his savings back which increases his private income. The average consumer is as well off in either case.

Both left-wing and right-wing governments, however strictly prefer default. As we have seen before, the structure of the utility function leads to the left-wing party always preferring the highest possible level of public expenditure. Thus, by refusing to pay the outstanding debt, the left-wing party can do exactly that. The intuition is that the left-wing party redistributes income in favour of their poorer clientele. Since savings are an increasing function of income the rich are supposed to get a relativley high amount back, as opposed to the poor whose private income will not be significantly boosted by savings repayments. They will be better off with more public good. What is more surprising is that even a right-wing party will choose to default.

We have seen that a right-wing party raises taxes in the second period only to repay inherited debt and that it will not provide any public good. If one now allows the government to partially[29] or fully default on the debt,

[29] When choosing to default partially on the debt, the government has to repay every saver the same percentage. The government cannot for example choose to repay only its clientele.

fully defaulting on the debt maximizes the second period utility of the voter represented by the right-wing party. This follows from the mathematics of the model. The right-wing party does not take any taxes ($\tau_2 = 0$) and totally defaults on the outstanding debt. The intuition Aghion/Bolton give is that from the point of view of the rich voter the cost of higher taxes to finance the savings repayment outweigh the benefits of increased private income due to the savings repayment. (For each dollar they get back, they have to pay more than a dollar in taxes.)

So neither party will repay inherited debt. Hence, there does not exist a rational expectations political equilibrium where a government finances public expenditure through debt. No one would lend to the government if he anticipates default in the second period.

All the simplifying assumptions so far (non-distortionary taxes, goods being perfect substitutes, one to one technology) have led to the model generating rather extreme results which are not robust against small changes in the model. Changing any of these assumptions will as we now show change the results drastically. Aghion/Bolton vary the production function: instead of a one to one technology (one unit of private goods produces one unit of public goods) they increase the rate of transformation, so that now more than one unit of private goods is needed to produce one unit of public goods. The production of public goods has thus become more expensive. This alters the results of the model, in particular a right-wing government in the first period will now use the debt strategically to manipulate elections in order to stay in power.

First of all the new technology has effects on the income distribution: It creates a "middle class" which is strictly in favour of debt repayment in the second period. Moreover, the size of this middle class depends on the level of inherited debt. Due to the change in technology there is a new marginal (indifferent) consumer . With the one to one technology the marginal voter was the one with the average income. This average voter was indifferent between the two choices in the second period ($\tau_1 = 1$ under the left regime or $\tau_2 = 0$ under the right, default in both cases) because one unit of his income could buy him exactly one unit of public good. Now that the production of the public good has become more expensive the average voter feels differently: If all his income is taxed away the public good he gets in return is less than what he could have bought with his private income. Consequently, he now feels better off under the right-wing party. The new indifferent voter is thus poorer than the average. This is demonstrated in figure 3.3. The group in the income range between the new indifferent voter and the average voter is called the middle class. They are distinct from the rich voters (above the average income) in one respect though. Whereas as before the very rich still feel better off with no taxes and default in the second period the middle class - even though it does not want any public goods in the second period - is in favour of honouring the debt. They hence want the tax rate to be

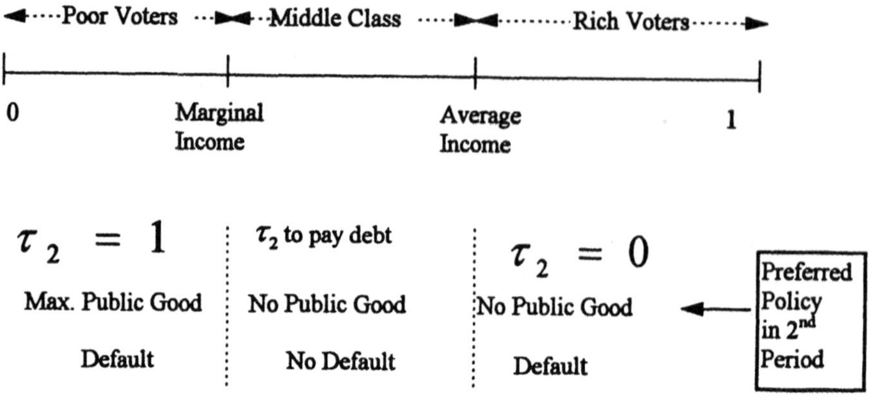

Fig. 3.3. Optimal Default Policies

just about high enough to repay the savings. For them the benefits of higher private income outweighs the corresponding tax they have to pay. So if the representative voter of the rich party is in the middle class the party will honour the debt. Also, as before, the very poor would rather have all their (small) income taxed away, be compensated with a high level of public goods and default on the debt.

The new marginal voter is sensitive to the level of inherited debt which makes it potentially possible to manipulate elections. The lower the debt the closer to the average the new marginal voter is. A low debt implies little saving in the first period so that the middle voters will probably not get much back in the second. They may thus prefer public goods and vote for the left-wing party. With this feature the debt becomes a strategic instrument that influences the size of the middle class and thus - as we will now show - the elections.

As before the elections' outcome depends on the position of the median voter. Aghion/Bolton now assume that both parties represent voters around the new marginal voter, the left-wing party represents a voter poorer and the right-wing party represents a richer voter (but close) to the average voter. Moreover, they assume the median voter to be in that region too, so that for a sufficiently large debt the median is richer than the marginal voter and votes for the right-wing party, while for a sufficiently low debt he is poorer than the marginal and votes for the left-wing party. Aghion/Bolton now show that an incumbent right-wing government in the first period takes on a debt for strategic reasons in order to get reelected. It still would prefer not to provide any public goods and sets the tax rate accordingly ($\tau_1 = 0$), but this would lead to an electoral victory of the left opposition party. But by taking on a sufficiently high debt (which can only be used to provide public goods) the right-wing party "moves" the marginal voter to the left of the median so as to be reelected. It will then honour this debt in the second period.

Aghion/Bolton have thus shown how a right wing government accumulates excessively large amounts of debt solely for electoral purposes. The intuition is that by creating a majority of voters holding a substantial fraction of their income in government bonds the left-wing party - who is known to default on inherited debt - loses support.

What first of all strikes the reader is that the model hinges on very many simplifying but restricting assumptions (i.e. the results are not robust) as for example one-to-one technology, non-distortionary taxes, goods are perfect substitutes). The results for the no-default case are hence quite extreme (a left-wing party always takes the highest possible tax and provides the highest possible level of public good, wheras the right-wing party sets the tax at ist lowest possible level (preferably equal to 0) and never provides any public good. This is very extreme and does not allow for qualitative results. Also, the right-wing parties in the OECD economies do not give the impression that they strictly dislike public spending.

Moreover, the paper shows that giving debt a strategic (electoral) role requires a richer set-up than the original left-right polarization. Aghion/Bolton need to relax the no-default assumption and further assumptions on the income distribution. In particular they need the median voter to be from the "middle class". This leads to the next remark. The economy now consists of three "constituencies" only two of which are represented by a party, namely the poor and the middle class.

3.5.4 Milesi-Ferretti/Spolaore [1994]: How Cynical Can an Incumbent Be? Strategic Policy in a Model of Government Spending

Milesi-Ferretti/Spolaore [1994] present a political model of government spending where the incumbent party can use its fiscal instruments strategically in order to get reelected. There are two - assymmetric - parties, party A (the incumbent in the first period) and opposition party B. Party A can spend its budget "productively" for the benefits of all consumers in the economy (for a public good say) or "unproductively" for the exclusive benefits of its own constituency. Party B, on the other hand, spends the whole budget productively.

The consumers in the economy belong to either of two groups: To the constituency of party A or to the larger group of unattached voters. So there is no explicit constituency of party B. The authors now derive three utility functions for party A and its constituency, for party B and for the unattached voters. Party A and its constituency derive utility from the public good (productive expenditure), from unproductive public expenditure as well as directly from A being in power. Party B gets utility from the public good and directly from being in power and the unattached voters enjoy the public good and to a certain extent (measured by q^i) from party A being in power. This exogeneous preference parameter q^i is uniformly distributed across the unattached voters with zero mean and support $[-q; q]$.

Milesi-Ferretti/Spolaore investigate the second period and the longer horizon case. Both cases start with party A being the party in power in the first period. An incumbent government decides on two issues: It decides on how to allocate the tax revenues at its disposal which were actually raised in the previous period and it determines the total amount of resources available for public spending in the following period. (Tax revenues raised in one period become available only in the next.) This latter assumption, borrowed from Cukierman et al. [1992], is justified by explaining the government decision as determining the efficiency of the tax system. The economy is equipped with a given tax system that can extract resources equal to a certain amount M at maximum efficiency or less according to the incumbent's decision.

The two period model is solved by backward induction: First, the optimal spending decisions in the second period of the two parties given the inherited amount of resources are derived. Then, given the two policy programs to choose from the elections outcome is derived and finally the optimal "efficiency" decision of the first period is investigated.

In the second period party B will spend the whole inherited budget productively whereas party A will spend the budget in part productively and unproductively. Given these two possible policies to choose from the rational forward looking voters now vote for the party that brings them the higher utility. The voter of party A's constituency vote (of course) for A. More interesting is the behaviour of the unattached voters. As we will now show this depends on the degree of tax efficiency. Consider the extreme case where incumbent A in the first period decides on zero-efficiency, thus leaving no resources to spend in the second period. Party B will not be liked (or voted for) without resources. Party A, however, is voted for by its constituency and by those unattached voter who simply derive utility from A being in power ($q^i > 0$). When the first period government (A) now gradually increases the degree of the efficiency of the tax system, i.e. tax revenues approach M, more and more voters will vote for B: The higher the level of available resources for the second period government the larger becomes its weight in the voting decision as compared to the voters' exogeneous preferences (q^i). In principle, the unattached voters prefer party B's expenditure decision. At maximum efficiency most of them would vote for B (all those whose q^i is not too high) and thus vote B into power (this result follows from the assumptions of the model), since as mentioned above the fraction of unattached voters is larger than A's constituency. From this it also follows that the median voter is an unattached voter and as is usually the case in this kind of models the behaviour of the median is the key to the electoral result. The assumptions of the model guarantee that the median has a positive q, i.e. in the absence of resources in the second period, he would still vote for A.

Given these considerations concerning the economy's voting behaviour the incumbent government (A) in the first period now chooses the level of resources for the second period (by deciding on the degree of efficiency of the tax system). It faces a trade-off: On the one hand it would like the highest degree of efficiency so as to maximize available resources for productive and unproductive expenditure in the second period. But this would lead to an electoral victory for B. On the other hand, in order to win the elections it has to set a lower degree of efficiency at the cost of lower available resources in the second period. As to be expected, party A chooses the degree of efficiency just about low enough to make the median vote for A. The degree of inefficiency is higher the higher B's comparative advantage in allocating spending and the smaller is the "incumbency bias" (i.e. the smaller is A's constituency).

We have introduced a model where an incumbent policy-maker intentionally chooses an inefficient tax system, even though this imposes not only a cost on society as a whole but also on himself in the form of lower spending in the future. Nevertheless, this guarantees his staying in power. The intuition is that the strategic manipulation of the degree of tax inefficiency alters the relative position of the two parties in the eyes of the voters: "In so doing A 'ties the hands' of any future policy-maker, making the allocation of public spending less relevant for unattached voters. Consequently the other aspects taken into account by the voters (exogeneous preferences) become more relevant and determine the results of the election", Milesi-Ferretti/Spolaore [1994], p.130.

As the time horizon becomes longer the strategic inefficiency caused by A increases. This is the only way of preventing B from gaining power and staying there forever (B always behaves fully efficiently). The reason is that the unattached voters anticipate A's inefficient future behaviour, so in order to make them vote for A, the party has to act even more inefficiently. This implies that both voters and parties have an (infinitely) long time horizon. This seems to be a rather unreasonable assumption that voters and parties do think so far ahead when taking their voting and fiscal decisions. Moreover, it is questionable whether agents actually think to the end of time as required here. And why should they continue voting for A if they do foresee that there will be inefficiencies with A all the time?

Another point to criticize is the extreme assymmetry between the parties and the strong assumptions on the consumers' distribution in the model; there are people who like party A per se but none who like party B per se. But why should rational voters like a party independent of this party's actions? Also, party A's constituency has to be smaller than the group of unattached voters in order for the median voter to be an unattached voter. Otherwise there would be no room for election manipulation or even elections, the electoral outcome would be given and A would never be voted out of power. Moreover, there is no decision that influences both periods. A party inherits some amount of resources to spend today. This spending decision does not "carry over" to the next period. The decision on the degree of tax inefficiency, on the other hand, does not influence the current period at all. With most fiscal decisions, however, the policy-maker finds himself in a more elaborate environment as benefits and costs spread over a number of periods.

We would finally like to mention that there are two "variations on the theme" of the strategic use of policy instruments for electoral purposes by Milesi-Ferretti. In his paper "Do Good or Do Well", [1995a], he analyzes incentives for strategic manipulation in the context of a debt management model in which two parties with different inflation aversion compete in elections. The incumbent in the first period decides not only on the level of debt to leave to the next period but also on whether this debt should be nominal (will be eroded by inflation) or indexed to the price level (is immune to inflation). The debt has to be cleared in the second period. It is shown that the inflation-averse party may issue nominal debt in order to make its opponent "look bad" in the eyes of the voters, whereas an inflation-prone government may issue indexed debt in order to increase chances of reelection.

In "The Disadvantage of Tying Their Hands", [1995b], the incumbent chooses between alternative exchange rate regimes. It is shown that an inflation-averse party may avoid a binding commitment to fixed exchange rate because in doing so it would solve the incentive problems of its more inflationary opponent and make the latter look better in the eyes of the voters. Conversely, a more inflation-prone party may choose fixed exchange rates and thus give away possible future stabilization instruments (as for instance devaluation of the domestic currency) in order to remove inflation from the political agenda and score points among the voters.

3.5.5 A Critical Evaluation of the Models and Implications for this Thesis

In this section we give a brief critique of the models we described and we show how they motivated our work.

The first two of the models, Persson/Svensson [1989] and Alesina/Tabellini [1990a], have no election manipulation. They deal only with the possible use of fiscal instruments to constrain the future government's actions. Both models assume an exogeneous change of government. In Alesina/Tabellini [1990a] the change is with an exogeneously given probability, in Persson/Svensson [1989] it is simply assumed that a conservative is followed by an expansionary government. Thus, all discussion of politics and the role of voters' political preferences is excluded from the model.

Elections and manipulation of elections are present in the other two models we described at length, Aghion/Bolton [1990] and Milesi-Ferretti/Spolaore [1994]. Both hinge on strong assumptions that are either unrealistic as in Aghion/Bolton (non-distortionary taxes, private and public goods are perfect substitutes, one to one technology) or counterintuitive as in Milesi-Ferretti/Spolaore (asymmetric parties): Due to its assumptions, Aghion/

Bolton's model has strong neutrality properties that leave no room for manipulation. To rescue election manipulation they have to introduce default. Even so, default appears extremely as either no default or complete default. Milesi-Ferretti/Spolaore obtain election manipulation at the cost of simplifying the model and introducing great asymmetry between the competing parties: one has a fixed constituency of faithful voters to which it allocates public resources while the other party has no constituency and it will create public good to all when in power.

Given these, what we consider shortcomings of the existing literature, our goal is to develop a model whose structure is as simple as in the described papers (two periods, two parties, elections in between, see section 4.3 for an explanation), but whose political dimension is explicitly modelled and whose assumptions are not too far-fetched. By keeping the model's structure as simple as possible we aim to obtain an undistracted view of the interrelation of fiscal behaviour and the political pressures emanating from the voters.

The election's outcome in our model will not be exogeneous but contingent on the voters' political tastes. These are not fixed but dependent on the parties' actions. Thus, an incumbent party can influence the electoral outcome. We believe that parties are not entirely opportunistic in the sense that all their fiscal policy actions are guided by the sole desire to stay in power. Rather, parties care about ideology, i.e. they care about the utility of a particular voter they choose to represent, and they will do everything in their power for this voter. This may include manipulating the elections in order to stay in power as this may be better for the representative voter. When this happens it usually is accompanied by overspending. On the other hand, if this is too costly the party will choose not to manipulate and will give up power. By departing from the exogeneity of the electoral outcome we will also be able to explain fiscal "misbehaviour" when an incumbent party can generate its reelection. In contrast to Persson/Svensson and Alesina /Tabellini, we can then explain debt even when there are no (significant) government changes.

Since we believe that a main constraint for political parties is the electorate's political heterogeneity we want to put special emphasis on the latter. We therefore describe our consumers with two attributes instead of only one as in the existing literature. We will thus have to depart from the median voter model which all the literature uses. We consider it as one of the main contributions of this Ph.D. thesis to the political economy literature that we can indeed solve the model going beyond the rather simplistic median voter model; see section 4.2.1 for a lengthy discussion of this point.

Our assumptions about the parties and the voters' distribution are as basic as possible. We want to obtain strategic use of fiscal instruments for election manipulation without allowing default as in Aghion/Bolton and without assuming strong asymmetry between the parties and a group of faithful voters who vote one party irrespective of its actions as in Milesi-Ferretti/Spolaore. Our parties will represent a given clientele (representative voter) each; we only assume that the voter represented by the left-wing party is poorer than the average and the voter represented by the right-wing party is richer. Only when we derive the electoral outcome as a function of the actions of the first period government will we have to restrict the voters' distribution slightly. In section 4 we will introduce the structure of the model in great detail and we will discuss all our assumptions at length.

To summarize, the contribution of the models reviewed in this section (3.5) is that they suggest a dependence between the political institutions, differences between parties, polarization of preferences and electoral uncertainty on the one side and fiscal policies on the other. Since these variables vary between countries the theory suggests that the fiscal policy will be different. Moreover, these variables can in principal be measured and they are quite likely to vary across countries and time periods. Thus, in principle, these models are testable and may be able to provide explanations for our observations in section 2, namely increased debt accumulation after 1972 and the different debt behaviour in the OECD countries. Although testable, not much has been done in this direction: "However, the empirical work based upon these models has thus far been sketchy and at best suggestive", Alesina/Perotti [1995] p.15. The theory has only paved the way for better understanding fiscal decisions based on political institutions. There is now need for extensive empirical studies of these effects.

4. Introduction to the Model

We now come to present our model. Before we explain it with all the technical details we will describe it in this section only verbally and intuitively. This allows the reader to get a thorough picture of the model without being overwhelmed by technicalities. Moreover, we discuss the assumptions and the main novelties of the model, showing similarities and differences from the existing literature as described in section 3.5.

4.1 The Model's Time Structure

The model is a two-period model with elections held between the periods. The economy we describe consists of a - possibly different - government in each period and a fixed number of consumers who all live in both periods.

The government provides a public good by raising taxes in both periods. In the first period in addition to tax revenues it can raise money by selling bonds, i.e. by taking on an (internal) debt. The government repays its debt in the second period with interest[1].

Consumers have two attributes, the income they earn each period, m, and their relative preference for private versus public good, α. They pay taxes in both periods and given the fiscal policy in the first period, decide how much to save (how many bonds to buy). In the second period they get their savings back with interest.

Between the two periods elections are held, the consumers can vote for one of two parties, a left-wing and a right-wing party. A party is assumed to represent some consumer and choose the policy variables to maximize this consumer's utility. The party that gathers the majority of votes wins and runs the government in the second period. The model's time structure is depicted in figure 4.1.

What do the different players want to do? All agents in our model aim to maximize some utility: The parties aim to maximize the utility of the

[1] Our results will also hold for the case where the government repays only a certain percentage of the debt. We want to exclude though it being a policy option that the government may choose whether or not to default on the debt; see Aghion/Bolton [1990] (as presented in section 3.5.3) for a model that allows the government to choose whether or not to default.

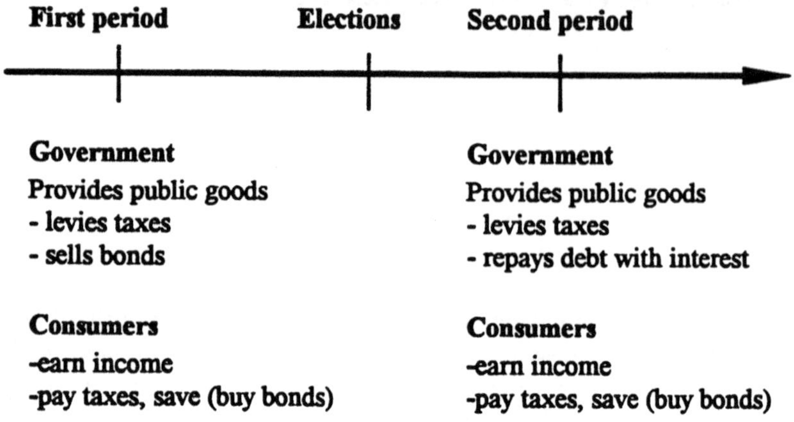

Fig. 4.1. The Model's Time Structure

particular voter they represent and the consumers aim to maximize their individual utility. Let us look at the government first: The government in power in the first period chooses the debt level and the tax rate in order to maximize its representative consumer's long run utility (this will depend on who is in power in the second period) and the government in power in the second period chooses the second period tax rate to maximize its representative consumer's utility in the second period, given the debt inherited from the first period. At the beginning of the first period consumers decide how much to save so as to maximize their individual long-run utility. They are forward-looking and thus, in the elections they give their vote to the party that promises them the higher utility in the second period.

4.2 The Main Novelties of the Model

Before we take a closer look at the interdependencies of the model, we would like to draw the reader's attention to the special features we introduced to the set-up we just described. First of all, we describe the consumers by two attributes; moreover, we endogenize the elections' outcome. We also show how the model is related to the papers described in the literature survey, chapter 3.

4.2.1 The Two-Dimensionality of Voters

In all the models in this literature voters differ in one variable only. This variable is usually taken to be either voters' income or their preferences for public goods. These - one-dimensional - models are designed in such a way that they have a single median voter. The authors justify this by saying that this makes these models technically easy to handle. Why is that so?

In a Median Voter Model political issues are linearly ordered in some way (left to right policies, higher/ lower taxes, etc.). Consumers are also linearly ordered by some parameter (income, tastes, etc.) The orders agree in the following sense: Given two policies $l < r$, if a particular consumer prefers r to l then all consumers ranked above him in the consumers' order prefer r to l. In such a model, given two issues it is sufficient to know what the median voter prefers in order to get the outcome of the vote.

In the next two paragraphs we give a short review of the median voter model with ideological parties. The reader who is familiar with it is thus welcome to jump these paragraphs. The median voter is defined as the voter who divides the voters' distribution in half, i.e. 50% of the voters are on the left side, the other 50% are on the right side of the median voter. Let us look at the example of figure 4.2 where the attribute voters differ in is taken to be their income. Income is denoted by m. Half of the population is at least as poor as the median and half is at least as rich. Let us now introduce two

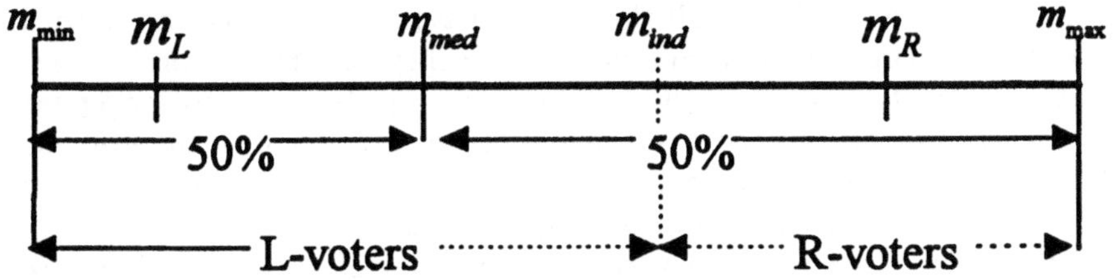

Fig. 4.2. The Median Voter Model With Ideological Parties

parties, a right-wing party R and a left-wing party L . The latter represents some (fixed) poor voter with income m_L, the former represents some rich voter with income m_R[2]. All the voters poorer than m_L vote L and all the voters richer than m_R vote R. But what about the voters in between? Voters richer than m_L but still close to m_L will quite likely still vote for L, voters on the left of m_R probably still vote for R. The median voter will be located somewhere on this line dividing the population in half. Thus, as soon as we know which party the median voter prefers we know the elections' outcome. If for example the median voter votes for the L-party then the L-party has at least the 50% poor voters on its side plus the median voter and it thus wins with at least $(50 + \epsilon)\%$ of the votes.

[2] Note that this is not the Hotelling, [1929], location choice model, where the parties can choose which voter to represent. For a discussion of the assumption that parties have fixed representative voters see page 29 as well as section 4.3.2.

Another way to show this is to introduce the indifferent voter. As shown before, all the voters vote for the party that guarantees them the higher utility. The one voter who is as well off under either party and is thus indifferent between the two, is called the indifferent voter. Whereas the median voter divides the population in 50% poorer and 50% richer voters, the indifferent voter divides the population in R- and L-voters. All voters poorer than the indifferent voter vote for L and all voters richer than him vote for R. In figure 4.2 the indifferent voter has an income larger than the median voter. It is easy to see that the electoral outcome is known as soon as we know where - relative to the median voter - the indifferent voter is located. Here, he is located on the right side of the median, which implies that even some voters richer than the median vote for L and the L-party wins with a comfortable margin.

The importance of the median voter in these types of models becomes now obvious. In order to know the electoral outcome it suffices to answer either of the following questions: Which party does the median voter vote for? Or, where relative to the median voter is the indifferent voter located? This boils down to the median voter determining the whole economy's politics: It is enough to know what a *single* voter prefers in order to determine who wins the elections. Hence, all the parties have to concentrate on is to win over the median voter and thus choose the policy variables according to this single voter! If the set of issues now changes, eg. they are no longer taxes but pension plans, but the new ranking of issues agrees with the ranking of consumers as above then we still need to ask the median in order to know who wins the elections (or alternatively which issue will win).

We believe that this is a very restricted view of the world. There exist many more relevant issues in which voters vary. Therefore, in our model, each consumer is described by two attributes: his income and his preference for private versus public goods[3]. This allows for the fact that two voters with the same income may still be significantly different in their ideas concerning the provision of public goods. Instead of a one-dimensional distribution the voters are now distributed in the two-dimensional space as in figure 4.3. In such a distribution there is no single median voter anymore. Elections are now determined by a set of indifferent voters. In our model, given two policies for the second period there is a curve of indifferent consumers splitting the population according to their vote into left-wing and right-wing voters. This is

[3] The reader may think that this choice of attributes is rather arbitrary. However, we have just combined the two attributes which appear separately in the one-dimensional models. Also, in some countries data on our taste-income distribution is gathered. The Economist [1995], pp.41-42, reports on the British Social Attitudes survey of November 23rd, 1995. This survey asked citizens in different income groups whether taxes should be cut, left at the current level or raised. (An interesting result is that in Britian in 1995 only 4% of the voters wanted tax cuts, whereas 58% are in favour of tax increases. Even a majority of high-income voters were in favour of the latter.)

demonstrated in figure 4.4. Indeed, we can, for each population distribution, identify a group of consumers whose role is analogous to the median voter's: Given two tax policies (derived from the first period policy) if any of these pivotal consumers prefers one policy, that policy will win the election.

However, there is one crucial difference between the median voter model and ours. It is important to notice that in the (one-dimensional) median voter model for *any* issues linearly ranked independent of the precise utility function it is the median voter who will determine the outcome. In the two-dimensional plane, however, one cannot order consumers. Thus, in our two-dimensional model the political issues agree with the partial ordering of the consumers in the following "partial" sense: If a consumer (α, m) prefers r to l $(r > l)$, then all consumers with higher α and higher m agree. Here, for each utility function describing the political issues one can find a group of consumers that play the role of a median voter, i.e. if one of them prefers issue r to l then at least 50% will vote for r. However, when one changes the utility functions or the issues this pivotal group of consumers changes. Thus, we no longer have a single person (or group) whose views determine the election whatever the political issues.

The most important result of this two-dimensionality assumption is that politics have now to be done according to the global distribution of voters and as a working hypothesis we may derive that the large differences in public debt in the OECD economies may result from different characteristics (distributions) of the populations in these countries.

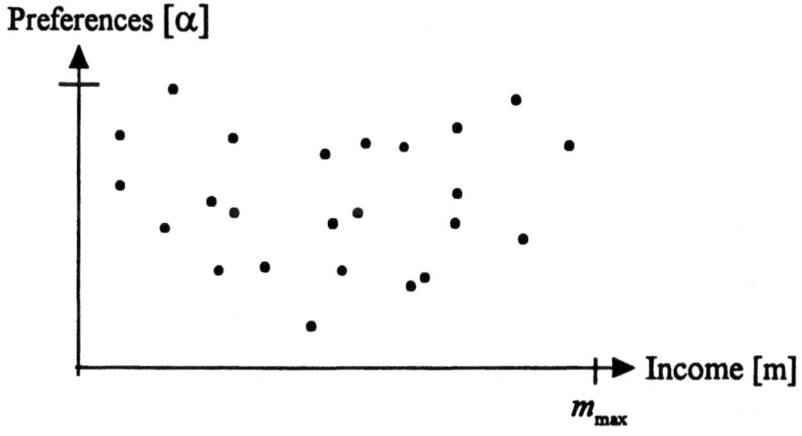

Fig. 4.3. A Two-Dimensional Distribution

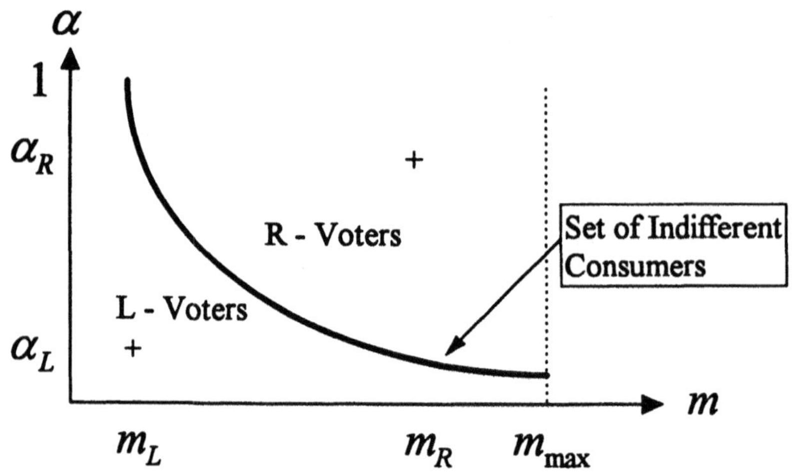

Fig. 4.4. The Set of Indifferent Consumers in Taste-Income Space

4.2.2 Endogenizing the Electoral Outcome: Debt as a Strategic Instrument

As mentioned in the literature survey, section 3.5, we can distinguish between two strategic aspects of public debt: A government takes on a debt in order to finance government expenditure. Since the debt usually has to be repaid at some point in the future it forms an additional budget constraint for the future policy-makers. Thus, a government can strategically use this fiscal instrument in order to tie the hands of its successor and thus influence the future in its own favour. This is the strategic aspect most of the papers of the literature focus on.

We believe that there is another relevant aspect when it comes to the strategic role of debt: In addition to tying a future government's hand debt can be used to influence voters and thus to "manipulate" elections[4]. In most of the models described in the previous chapter this aspect is left out: In Alesina/Tabellini [1990a], elections are determined according to a given probability distribution, in Persson/ Svensson [1989] a conservative government knows for sure that it is followed by a left-wing government. Aghion/ Bolton [1990] get election manipulation, but only once they introduce the additional choice variable of defaulting on the debt.

Why is that? How does election manipulation work? A government's debt decision constrains what the parties running for office can do in the next period and thus what they can offer in the elections as their policy programs. So if a change in the debt decision of the government in power at some point in time leads to different policy programs offered by the parties and if this

[4] See the detour in the introduction, page 3 for a discussion of the use of this term in the political economy literature.

in turn alters the voters' decision, the government in power can use debt strategically to influence the electoral outcome. As Milesi-Ferretti [1995b], p.1381, puts it, all the government in the first period needs to do is to alter the relative standing of the two parties in the eyes of the voters (see section 3.5.4).

Let us verify this by looking at the models described above. Let us first look at the one-dimensional case of figure 4.2. Here, the government in power in the first period has fixed its policy choice such that the electoral programs indicating what the L- and R-parties wish to do in the next period lead to a victory of the L-party. Let us assume the R-party to be the party in power in the first period. Can the R-party manipulate the elections' outcome in its favour? Yes, if it changed its debt policy such that the two parties change their electoral programs in such a way that more people (in particular the indifferent voter plus some voters to his left) feel better off under the right-wing party under these new alternatives. In the one-dimensional model of figure 4.2 the right-wing party could alter the electoral outcome in its favour if it offered a policy program such that the voter who was indifferent between the parties before now feels definitely better off under the right regime. If the right-wing party offered a program of the form that the voter indifferent between the two parties is poorer than the median voter, the right-wing party would even win the elections.

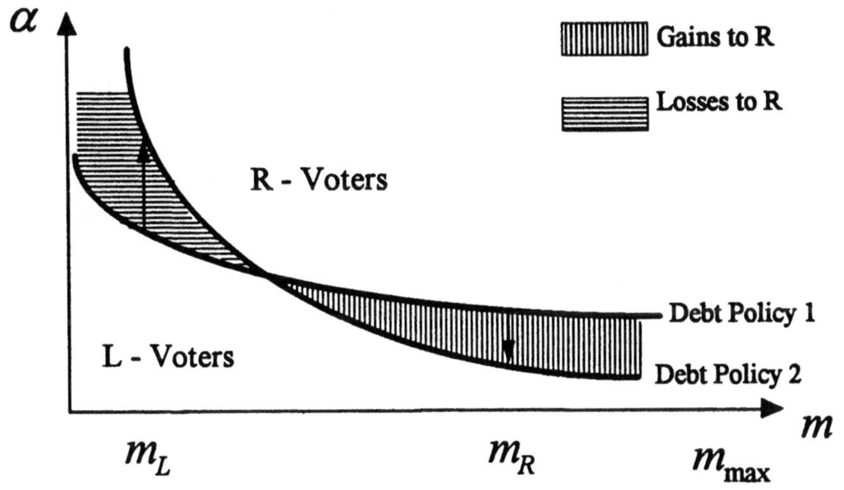

Fig. 4.5. Election Manipulation in the Two-Dimensional Model

In our two-dimensional model elections' manipulation is equivalent to moving the curve that represents the indifferent voters in figure 4.4. We then get a different set of indifferent consumers as a function of the government's politics (again via the parties being forced to change their elections programs). This is demonstrated in figure 4.5.

Note also, that contrary to the one-dimensional case, here the voters' reaction to a change in politics is not unambiguous. This is another interesting and more realistic feature of our model: When a government or a party decides to alter its politics it is usually the case that some voters approve of this while others are opposed to it. Hence, the electorate's reaction is not as clear-cut as the one-dimensional case suggests. In the example of figure 4.5, again assuming that the right-wing party is the party in power in the first period, a change in politics is approved of among richer voters but the right-wing party looses votes among the poorer voters.

Before we continue we have to discuss one more issue: What do we mean by "a voter's reaction to policy changes"? The message so far is that all we require in order to get elections manipulation is that the voters react to changes in politics. In the language of our model this means that the voter is sensitive to changes in the government's policy variable. If a policy variable is changed the consumer may vote for another party. However, studying the papers by Alesina/Tabellini [1990a, b], Persson/Svensson [1989] or Aghion/Bolton [1990] as in section 3.5 we find that their choice of utility functions and tax systems preserves neutrality and voters are insensitive to policy changes. Politics are neutral: Voters react to policy changes in such a way that their utility levels in the second period remain the same. Thus, there is no change in voting behaviour and for whatever the two parties offer in the elections the indifferent voter remains the same, elections cannot be influenced. We adopt the feature of a homothetic utility function from the papers described in the previous chapter[5] but by modifying the tax system slightly we depart from neutrality and enrich the model decisively: We introduce a progressive tax system: Only income above some tax-free amount (one may call it subsistence level) is taxed. This tax scheme is progressive in the sense that the percentage of tax paid from total income increases with pre-tax income as in figure 4.6. The fact that voters with different income have different fractions of taxable income makes them react differently to tax changes.

4.3 Further Assumptions of the Model

We now briefly discuss the other important assumptions of our model. These assumptions are of course simplifying, if we relax them the model becomes more complicated. We show what the complications are and discuss whether the simplifications are justified.

---

[5] Homothetic preferences can be mathematically represented by a utility function of the form $f\big(U(x,y)\big)$, where $f' > 0$ and U is homogeneous of degree h ($h > 0$), i.e. $U(\lambda x, \lambda y) = \lambda^h U(x,y), \forall x, y, \lambda > 0$, see Chiang [1984], pp.423-425.

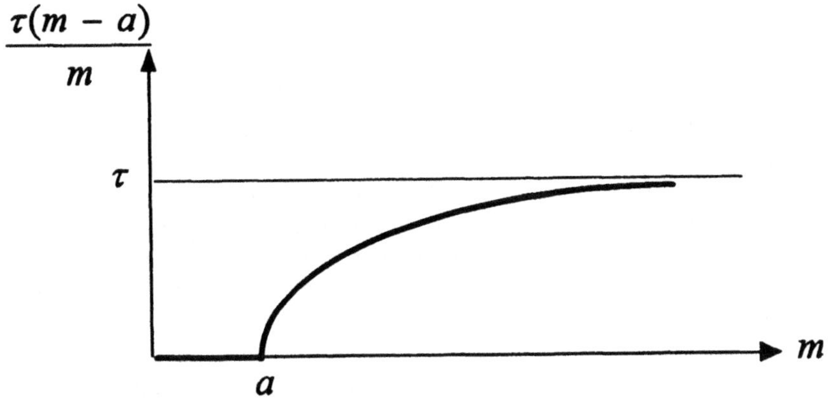

Fig. 4.6. A Progressive Tax Scheme

4.3.1 Two Periods

In our model we assume that all agents (consumers and parties) are rational and fully informed. Introducing more than two periods and still maintaining the rationality of the agents will raise serious modelling problems: Consumers' beliefs have to be very elaborate. When taking their savings and voting decisions they will have to take into account the long run effects of their actions on all the periods to come. The same with the parties: When taking any action today they will have to take into account all the effects this action will have on the future. It is not likely that voters or even longer thinking parties do take all their horizon into account. So a long horizon model requires deviation from full rationality, i.e. some bounded rationality. Although this problem is well known there are no satisfactory models describing such boundedly rational decision-making[6]. Therefore we stick with two periods where these problems are not that sharp. Most of the models in the literature also avoid this problem and remain with two periods. In a two period model there is only one election between the periods and beliefs are simply about the next period. The few models that introduce a longer horizon, do so by simplifying the model drastically and at a cost of ignoring the political-economic problem which they came to solve, Alesina/Tabellini, [1990a], assume that the elections are exogenously determined and Milesi-Ferretti/Spolaore, [1994], assume very simple preferences of the voters, see sections 3.5.2 and 3.5.4.

[6] See for example Rubinstein [1995], chapter 0, p.5.

4.3.2 Two Ideological Parties

It is well known that if parties are allowed to choose their ideological platform ('opportunistic parties') they will all converge to the "median ideology" and in fact there will be two identical parties, see page 29 for a discussion of this point. If however, the number of parties is not fixed new parties may emerge representing extreme voters and the result may be fragmentation, i.e. a large variety of parties. If a large number of parties exists coalitions are possible and the model will have to determine which coalitions will form. Some of these problems have been dealt with in a related literature (Cooperative Game Theory) but unfortunately they did not come up with any operational models. Since our model wants to emphasize the strategic effects on the future of an action a government takes today we avoid these problems by assuming that there are only two parties and that their ideologies are different from each other and fixed.

4.3.3 No Default

Total default or even partial default where people do not get all their investment back cannot be part of a rational expectations equilibrium because consumers will not save; we have already discussed this problem in section 3.5.3 where we introduced the model by Aghion/Bolton. A fixed partial default is equivalent to a lower rate of interest and can be dealt with in the framework of our model. Choosing the degree of default strategically has been analyzed by Aghion/Bolton [1990]. Our model finds that government expenditure has a strategic role even in the absence of default which seems to be more suitable to OECD countries since there is no evidence of governments defaulting on internal debt. According to Alesina/Prati/Tabellini [1990], p.100, this possibility seems very remote even for Italy. "In the current (1990) Italian situation it would probably have very high political costs, by disrupting the system of financial intermediation and causing arbitrary wealth redistribution". In order to avoid a confidence crisis which would result from the possibility of a government defaulting on its debt and an associated reluctance of investors to hold this debt, most highly indebted European countries shorten the maturity of their bonds, as for example Belgium, Italy Greece or Portugal, see Giavazzi/Pagano [1990], p.128[7].

[7] Note however, that shorter maturities may on the other hand cause a financial crisis: If the maturing debt is concentrated at few dates the government (treasury) may find itself in the critical situation of having to refinance a large portion of its debt at these dates through the capital market on unfavourable terms. The only evidence for a country that ran into a serious financial crisis because the public refused to hold government debt was Italy in 1987. Investors had suffered substantial capital losses in the 1970s due to rising inflation and they were not willing to hold debt at the low risk premium against default the Italian treasury offered. At times, the market bought even less than 50% of the amount offered

4.4 The Interdependencies of the Model

In this section we analyze the model's time structure as described in section 4.1 and depicted in figure 4.1 in great detail and we derive its interdependencies as presented in figure 4.7. Moreover, we show how we go about solving the model.

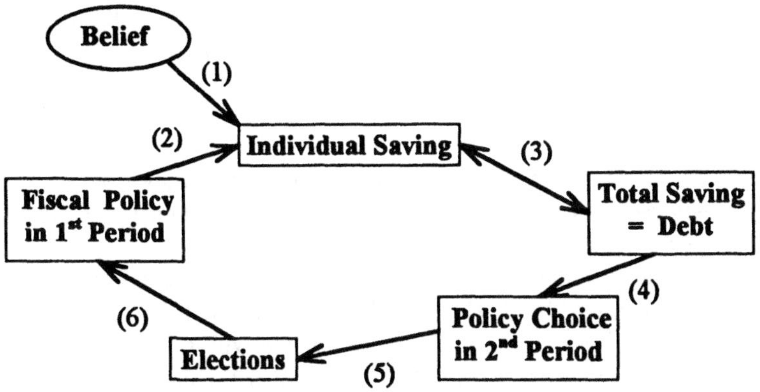

Fig. 4.7. The Interdependencies of the Model

We start by analyzing the individual consumer's savings decision. When saving, people transfer money from today to tomorrow. The saver foregoes consumption today in order to consume more at some point in the future when he gets his savings back with interest. Thus, he needs information on what he can gain from saving in the next period and on what he is deprived of today: the parameters that influence the savings decision are the interest rate, ρ, the consumption alternatives, i.e. the level of public goods, in the two periods, y_1 and y_2, and the tax rates in both periods, τ_1 and τ_2. So at the beginning of the first period, when people decide how much to save, they need information about the current and the future period.

Acquiring information about public consumption in the current (first) period does not pose a problem since the government in power announces its fiscal policy (tax, debt) for that period. But the level of public consumption in the second period is determined by the future policy-maker and in the first period when the savings decision is taken, consumers do not know yet who will be in power in the second period and will determine the level of public consumption then. Thus, consumers have to form some kind of

and "since the summer of 1987 the sales of CCT's [Treasury Credit Certificates] to the public have never been fully subscribed", Alesina/Prati/Tabellini [1990], p.99.

belief about which party will win the elections and determine the second period's fiscal policy. Throughout the model we will assume that the beliefs are exogenously given, that all consumers have the same beliefs and that the government knows these beliefs[8]. So, the government's fiscal policy choices in the first period together with the consumers' beliefs determine the individuals' savings decision (arrows 1 and 2 in figure 4.7). Individual savings add up to total savings (amount of government bonds) as announced by the first period government. This is ensured by the interest rate which adjusts so that all government bonds will be bought by the savers (arrow 3 in figure 4.7). Total savings form the debt to be repaid by the second period government. This debt in turn determines the two parties' policy programs for the second period, one of which the consumers vote for in the elections (arrows 4 and 5 in figure 4.7). It is thus that the consumers' beliefs in the first period determine the second period government. If the beliefs are such that they are verified, i.e. the party believed to win the elections actually wins, then the outcome is a rational expectations equilibrium.

In what follows we will denote by P the party in power in the first period, by Q the opposition party, by T the "true" party that will be in power in the second period and by B the party people believe will gain power in the second period. (When the party people believed to win the elections actually wins $T = B$.) At the beginning of the first period the party in power, P, announces $\tau_1(P)$ and the debt level S, the interest rate ρ will be determined by the equilibrium. The consumers form beliefs about the future government and about the tax rate expected to be set by this government, $\tau_2(B)$. The consumers then decide how much to save on the basis of $(\rho, \tau_1(P), \tau_2(B))$[9].

We can think of different stories of how the savers can get the information concerning τ_2 at the moment when they take their saving decision: Since we assumed the agents to be fully rational and well informed, they could calculate $\tau_2(B)$, $B = L$ or R, themselves once they know the policy plans

[8] In order not to complicate the model further, we assume that all consumers have the same beliefs concerning the electoral outcome. Of course, one could also assume that consumers vary in their beliefs. However, we do not consider our assumption to be too far-fetched. Belief is not to be confused with the voters' wishes concerning the electoral outcome and opinion polls which are published regularly, especially close to elections' time, usually give quite a reliable forecast about the elections' outcome and may thus influence peoples' expectations.

If we assume that the population has different beliefs about the future, some believe that the right-wing party will win, some that the left-wing party will win, then another factor comes into consideration. Beliefs influence the savings decision and so it is necessary to specify how beliefs are distributed among the income levels; for example the beliefs could be uniformly distributed or alternatively the rich may have different beliefs than the poor. If this distribution is known then one could solve the model.

[9] In general, consumers need to know the levels of public goods in each period before deciding how much to save. In this model we take utility functions in which the public good enters additively and hence the decision to save depends only on ρ and the two tax rates, see section 5.2.2.

of the first government. This is equivalent to Subgame Perfection in Game Theory. Another story could go like this: The two parties announce at the beginning of the first period the tax rate for the second period they would set should they win the elections. (The reigning government starts with its announcements since the opposition party needs to know the level of debt that has to be repaid in the second period.) Of course, these announcements have to be credible, i.e. the two parties announce at the beginning of the first period tax rates for the second ($\tau_2(\cdot)$) they will not (wish to) deviate from in the second period (credibility constraint). Consumers, being fully rational, would detect a "wrong" policy announcement, i.e. they will recognize when a party announces a tax rate that is insufficient to repay the debt.

In addition we impose an equilibrium constraint. The first period government is assumed to announce the parameters in such a way that when the consumers react to them (by deciding how much to save) this decision will be compatible with the total debt announced by the government, i.e. the individual savings add up to the total debt announced by the government (individual savings, the bonds sold by the government, form tomorrow's debt). This is our equilibrium requirement and as mentioned above, the interest rate will adjust to equate the two.

Given the credibility/subgame perfection and equilibrium constraints, the government in power in the first period should choose only the level of total debt, S, and τ_1, all other variables, namely individual savings s, the interest rate ρ and the tax rates the two parties will set in the second period, $\tau_2(P)$ and $\tau_2(Q)$, are determined by the constraints. In fact we shall see later that the only relevant variable will be the level of public goods in the first period, y_1[10].

Consumers are allowed to vote and choose between two parties. We assume that the two parties are a left-wing party L, representing a consumer (α_L, m_L) and a right-wing party R, representing a consumer (α_R, m_R), where $m_R > m_L$ and $\alpha_R > \alpha_L$: The R-party represents a richer consumer who cares more about private goods.

Given the two policies (tax schemes of the two parties) for the second period consumers split according to their preferences. Some prefer to vote for the first policy and some for the second. Due to the two-dimensionality of the voters, in this model there is no single indifferent consumer but a group of them. We find that the indifferent consumers lie along a curve in the two-dimensional taste-income space and we find that this curve is a decreasing function of income m (see section 5.3.1). All consumers above the curve vote

[10] As we will show in section 5.2.4, the model has one degree of freedom. Since we want to analyze the (strategic) behaviour of the first period government we choose the variable that this government can influence, namely y_1, as the exogeneous policy variable.

Moreover, in section 5.2.5 we will identify a neutrality in the model: Consumers are indifferent to the portfolio of tax or debt financing a given level of public good. Their utility is affected though, as the level of public good, y_1, changes.

for the R-party and all below vote for the L-party. This is shown in figure 4.4. What we can also see from figure 4.4 is a very intuitive result: The left-wing party is more popular among the poorer population with a lower preference for private relative to public goods, whereas the right-wing party is more popular in "the other corner" of the populations' distribution. Given a distribution of consumers in this space, the position of the indifferent consumers' curve determines which party will win the elections.

To sum up the model's structure as depicted in figure 4.7, the two alternative policies offered by the parties for the second period will be entirely determined by the policy of the first period government. The policy of the first period determines the debt to be repaid in the second period, this in turn determines the optimal tax (and the corresponding level of public goods) each of the two parties wishes to set in the second period. These tax rates are the two policies among which consumers have to choose in the elections.

The question that now arises is, whether a change in the optimal choice of the first period fiscal policy has any influence on the elections' outcome. Consider what happens when the government of the first period announces another fiscal policy, a higher y_1 say, i.e. a different program (τ_1, S) - this program like the first one should satisfy the equilibrium and credibility/subgame perfection constraints. This higher level of public goods will have to be financed by either higher taxes, τ_1, or higher debt, S, or both. As a result the interest rate ρ will adjust at a higher level[11]. The intuition is straightforward. Neutrality ensures that the composition of y_1, i.e. the portfolio of tax or debt financing it, does not matter (see section 5.2.4). All combinations of τ_1 and S leading to the same y_1 will also lead to the same ρ. If the policy-maker now increases y_1 he will have to adjust his portfolio; for example by taking on a higher debt and leaving the tax at its old level. In order for the additional bonds to be sold the equilibrium interest rate will have to be higher.

Let us now return to our question how this change in politics affects the electoral results: Does the curve of indifferent consumers react to the increase in y_1, i.e. in ρ and if so, how? In section 5.3.1 we show that the curve of indifferent consumers changes with increasing ρ as in figure 4.9: The curve shifts up for low incomes (at the left end) and shifts down for higher incomes (at its right end). Thus, voters react to changes in the fiscal policy of the first period government and the latter can use its fiscal instruments in order to influence the electoral outcome.

The intuition for the way the curve reacts to fiscal policy changes is as follows. The described movement of the curve implies that in the low income groups indifferent voters feel definitely better off under the left-wing party as ρ, i.e. y_1, increases. The reverse holds for the high income groups. Why is that? A higher level of public consumption in the first period, y_1, leads

[11] We will show in section 5.2.5 that - given beliefs - for each level of public goods y_1 there exists a corresponding, endogenously determined, interest rate ρ, which increases with y_1.

to a higher interest rate, ρ. Then, for a given τ_1 the debt that has to be repaid in the second period, ρS, is higher. Thus, both parties will (have to) set higher tax rates in the second period, but the left-wing party increases its tax by more than the right-wing party (for proof see appendix A.10). Moreover, the left-wing party increases taxes in such a way that it provides even more public goods in the second period whereas the right-wing party even though it increases $\tau_2(R)$ provides less public goods than it would have done under the lower ρ (see figure 4.8). Let us look at this from the point of view of a poor voter with an income barely higher than the tax free amount who was indifferent between the two parties under the low ρ. He now - after the increase in ρ - votes for L. By providing even more public goods, $y_2(L)$, than before the left-wing party tries to make up for the loss of private income due to the tax increase. The poor voter with hardly any taxable income is, however, scarcely affected by a tax increase. So whether taxes increase by little (as under an R-regime) or by a lot (as under an L-regime) does not make that much of a difference to him. But he profits from the higher level of public goods under the L-party. He now feels definitely better off under the L-party. This is not the case for some rich indifferent voter, almost all of his income is taxed. He thus suffers from the tax increase under any government but he suffers even more under the left-wing party, even so that his utility loss from higher taxes cannot be outweighed by higher public consumption. He now votes for R.

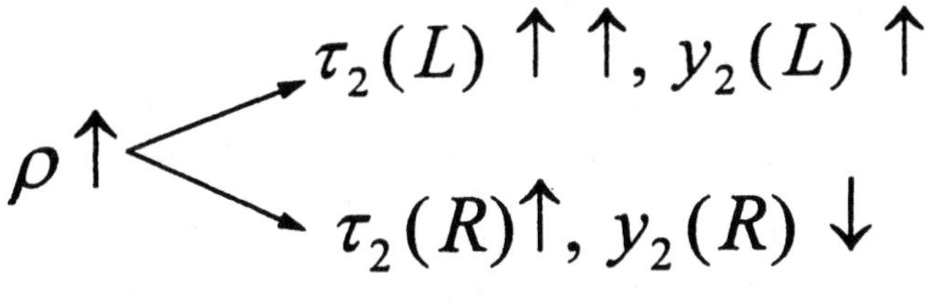

Fig. 4.8. Parties' Reactions as ρ Increases

Moreover, one can show that there exists a region to the left where the curves of indifferent consumers always shift up with ρ and a region to the right where the curves always shift down with ρ. These regions are depicted by A and B in figure 4.10. If the distribution of voters has most of its weight in region A (type A economy) then the party representing poorer voters, the L-party, gains votes from increasing ρ, whereas the R-party, representing a richer voter, loses votes. If on the other hand voters are mainly distributed in region B (type B economy) the L-party will need to decrease the interest rate in order to gain votes, the R-party will have to increase ρ. (Bear in mind that the policy-maker actually sets y_1 and that ρ adjusts endogenously.)

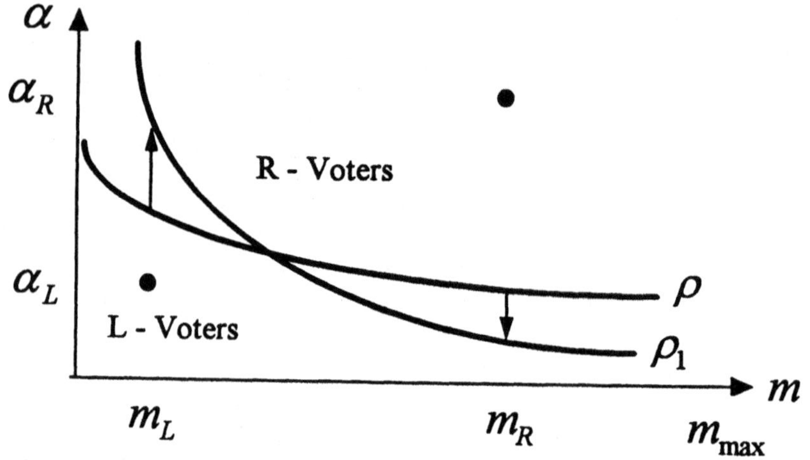

Fig. 4.9. The Curve of Indifferent Consumers for Different Interest Rates, $\rho_1 > \rho$

The class of populations of type A (or B) is huge. The only restriction to be a population of type A (or B) is that the individuals of this population are located in a certain area in the taste-income space. It is not possible to compare all populations within such a big class. Hence, to be able to do comparative statics we identify some groups of populations all of type A (or all of type B) which can be ordered in some way. We introduce a measure for the political attitude of a society which to a certain extent is the analogue of the median voter in one-dimensional models[12]. We identify a ρ for which the curve of indifferent voters splits the population in half: exactly half will vote for each party. Populations with the same average income (mean preserving change) have the same indifferent consumers' curves and can therefore be compared according to the value of this critical ρ[13]. In a type A economy the higher this ρ, the more conservative or the more right-wing the population, in a type B economy the reverse holds.

We have now fully analyzed the model: We have seen how the first period's fiscal policy determines the debt to be repaid in the second period and how this in turn influences the elections. We have traced the voters' reactions to policy changes and seen that the electoral outcome can indeed be influenced by the first period government. Finally, we have introduced a measure for the political attitude (or conservativeness) of a society, which enables us to compare at least some distributions out of the vast group of population distributions.

---

[12] In section 4.2.1 we explain the difference between our model and the median voter model. See section 5.3.2 for a formal and intuitive presentation of our measure of 'political couleur'.

[13] Note that this is a partial ordering. Not all populations can be compared according to their critical ρ, see section 5.3.2 and appendix A.11.

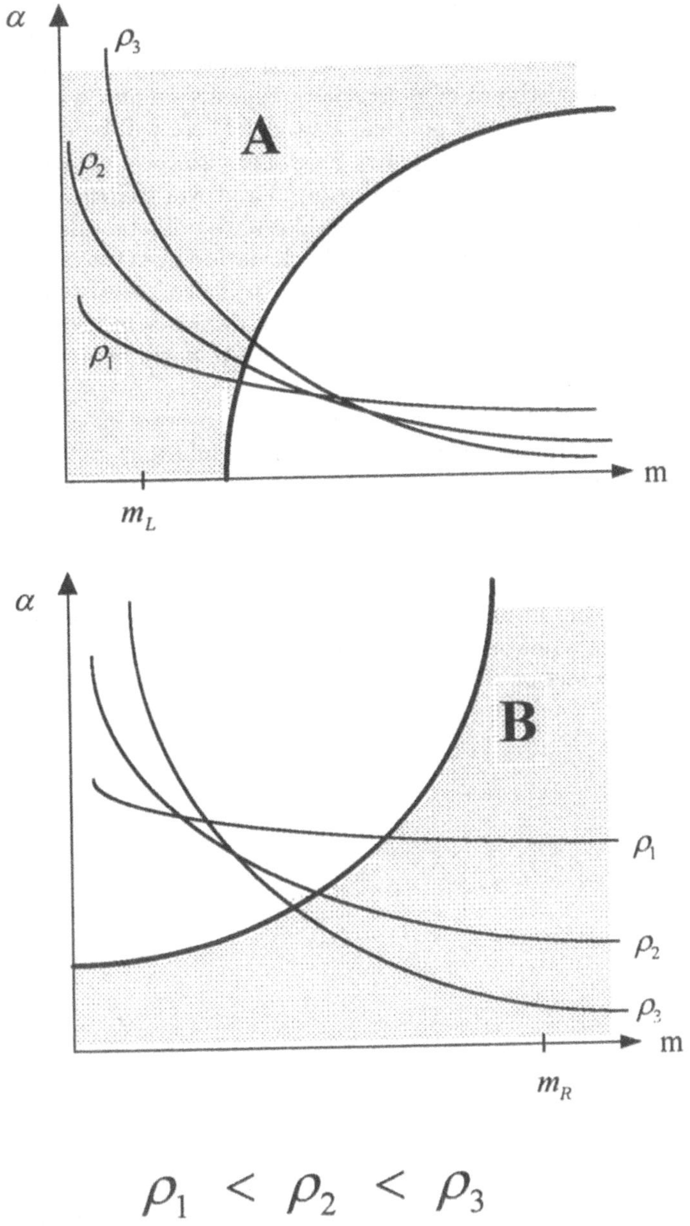

Fig. 4.10. The Curve of Indifferent Consumers in Type A and B Populations

The last question that remains is how the first period government will actually choose to set its fiscal variables. In section 6 we derive the results for a given type of population (A or B) and for a given party (L or R) in power in the first period. We also analyze whether, and if so how, the government's optimal decision changes as the society's degree of conservativeness changes. We will see that the optimal choice of y_1 crucially depends on the type of population as well as on the society's political attitude: There will be cases, where the incumbent can set the fiscal policy he would also have chosen if his staying in power was guaranteed ("dictatorship") and win the elections easily. In other populations (of a different type and/or with a different degree of conservativeness) he may have to compromise by deviating from the policy under "dictatorship" in order to be reelected. Last, we will also identify cases where deviating is too costly and where the incumbent decides - in the best interest of the voter he represents - to give up power. All this will be derived and explained in detail in section 6.

Furthermore, we find that the actions taken by the government of the first period need not be continuous as a function of the populations' political attitude. Small changes in conservativeness may cause drastic changes in policy. These discontinuities are inherent to the problem and cannot be removed by smoothing out the model, for example by introducing a small uncertainty about the electoral outcome[14].

Since expectations of the future are present in the model, one can look for Rational Expectations equilibria. We identify the rational expectations equilibria in our model in section 6.

[14] The issue of uncertainty will be discussed in section 6.6.

5. The Model

In the previous chapter we have fully described the model and its results verbally. We now present the model formally and we derive all the results.

The model is a two-period model with elections held between the periods. The economy consists of a - possibly different - government in each period and a large number of consumers.

5.1 The Agents and their Decisions

5.1.1 The Consumers

There is a continuum of consumers of measure N . All consumers live during the two periods. The population is described by a joint distribution of income and tastes, (α, m), where m denotes a consumer's income and the taste variable α his relative preference for private versus public goods, $\alpha \in [0,1]$. The higher the α, the less interested the consumer is in public goods. This two-dimensional distribution allows for a higher degree of heterogeneity among consumers as it for example allows for two consumers with identical income to have opposite ideas concerning the provision with public goods. In what follows a consumer is characterized by (α, m).

The consumers' utility function is given by the product of two Cobb-Douglas functions linked by an intertemporal discount rate, δ, written in log form:

$$\alpha \log x_1 + (1-\alpha)\log y_1 + \delta[\alpha \log x_2 + (1-\alpha)\log y_2] \tag{5.1}$$

where $x_1, x_2, (y_1, y_2)$ are the private (public) goods for periods $1, 2$. Consumers act (save and vote) in order to maximize that utility function[1].

5.1.2 The Government

The government provides public goods in both periods (y_1, y_2). Public good is produced from money using a $1-1$ technology: One unit of revenue provides

[1] Here we have taken $\log(\cdot)$ to be the 'common' utility function. In fact all our results hold for a large class of utility functions $U(x) = x^h, (0 < h < 1)$.

one unit of the public good. Public goods can be financed by tax revenues and by an (internal) debt, the latter possibility only being open in the first period. The debt has to be repaid in the second period with interest. Let us discuss these two financial means one at a time.

The Tax System. There is a given tax-free amount, a. Only income above a is taxed according to a proportional income tax τ_t (the subscript indicates the period, $t = 1, 2$). A consumer with income m will then be left with $m - (m - a)\tau_t$ net income after tax to spend on private goods. As mentioned before to get the possibility of manipulating the elections it is important that $a > 0$ and that the tax system is progressive.

Total tax revenues are given by $(K - aN)\tau_t$, where K denotes the total income in the economy and N the number of consumers in the economy.

Internal Debt. In the first period the government can - in addition to taxes - take on an internal debt by issuing government bonds to the public. This debt has to be repaid with interest in the second period. The interest rate is denoted by i, ($\rho = 1 + i$). We rule out default here[2]. Thus, individuals can decide to spend part of their net income on government bonds. A consumer with income m buys $s(m)$ bonds (s for savings, since buying bonds is equivalent to reducing consumption in order to save more) and will be repaid $\rho s(m)$ in the second period.

Integrating over all individual savings gives the total savings (total debt) S to be repaid in the second period.

We can now derive the equations for private and public goods in the two periods: Public provision in the first period is determined by tax revenues plus the revenue from bonds sales (debt) taken on:

$$\begin{aligned} y_1 &= \text{tax revenues} &+& \quad \text{debt} \\ y_1 &= (K - aN)\tau_1 &+& \quad S \end{aligned} \tag{5.2}$$

In the second period the debt has to be repaid, hence public provision has to be paid out of the tax revenues left after the debt repayment:

$$\begin{aligned} y_2 &= \text{tax revenues} &-& \quad \text{repaid debt} \\ y_2 &= (K - aN)\tau_2 &-& \quad \rho S \end{aligned} \tag{5.3}$$

In the first period consumers save, thus an individual with income m is left with his after-tax-income reduced by the amount he saves.

$$\begin{aligned} x_1 &= \text{after-tax-income} &-& \quad \text{savings} \\ x_1 &= m - (m - a)\tau_1 &-& \quad s(m) \end{aligned} \tag{5.4}$$

In the second period the government repays the debt, the individual with income m can spend his after-tax-income plus the returned savings on private consumption

---

[2] For a discussion of this assumption see page 58.

$$x_2 = \text{after-tax-income} \quad + \quad \text{repaid savings}$$
$$x_2 = m(m-a)\tau_2 \quad + \quad \rho s(m) \tag{5.5}$$

5.1.3 Elections

Elections take place before the second period. There are two parties running for office, a left-wing party, denoted by L , and a right-wing party, denoted by R. Both parties attend to some fixed clientele, each represented by a "representative" voter: The left-wing party represents the consumer (α_L, m_L) whereas the right-wing party represents the consumer (α_R, m_R), where

$$\alpha_L < \alpha_R \quad \text{and} \quad m_L < \frac{K}{N} < m_R$$

The right-wing party represents a voter (a clientele) with a higher preference for private income as opposed to public provision than the left-wing party. Moreover, the voter represented by the left-wing party has a lower income than the one represented by the right-wing party and his income is below the society's average income (K/N), whereas the income of the voter represented by the right-wing party is above average. These assumptions are in line with the conventional public finance models, where right-wing parties usually represent rich voters with a high degree of tax aversion and hence a high degree of aversion to public goods and left-wing parties represent opposite interests. Figure 5.1 shows a society's joint taste-income distribution with the consumers represented by the two parties being highlighted.

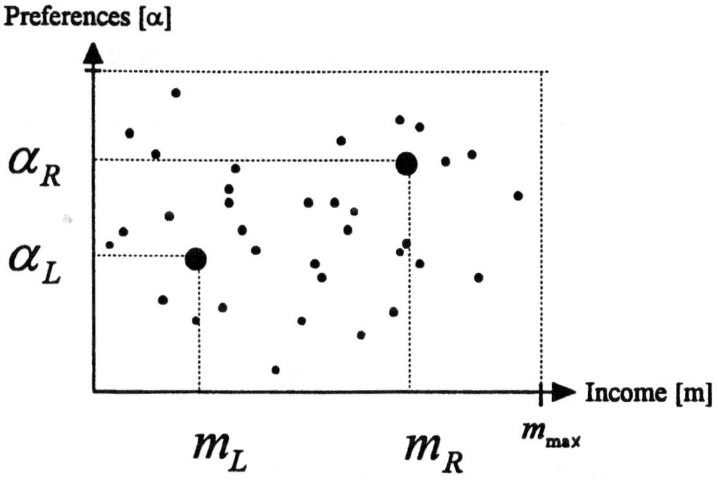

Fig. 5.1. The Economy's Distribution and the Two Representative Voters

We assume here that voters are forward looking, when elections take place the first period is past for them. They vote for the party that guarantees them the higher utility in the second period. An alternative way to model voters would be to assume that it is the past and not the future that determines how a person votes, as for example in learning models, adaptive expectations models or in case-based decision theory (Gilboa/Schmeidler [1994]). Here, decisions are influenced by past satisfaction or disappointment rather than by foresight. However, we follow the tradition of modelling agents as rarional. They therefore consider the future only and whatever happened in the past does no longer matter.

5.2 Solving the Model

5.2.1 The Problem to Be Solved

The problem we want to analyze is the following: Given an economy with the agents and the voting system we just described, what is the optimal fiscal policy for a government to choose in the first period?

Recall the model's information structure: First period politics (together with the beliefs) determine savings which enter as debt in the second period budget constraint. This in turn determines the parties' election programs and the electoral outcome which in turn enters - as a side constraint - in the first period government's fiscal policy optimization problem. All events are interrelated in a well-defined way as was demonstrated in figure 4.7.

Before we actually solve the first period's optimization problem we want to derive all the neccessary information from the model we can get: How - as a function of the first period fiscal policy choice - do voters save? How - as a function of the total debt to be repaid - will the two parties propose to set the fiscal variables of the second period? How does the society vote, given the two policy alternatives to choose from? With this information we can precisely solve the first period optimization problem. We will see later that this actually boils down to solving a system of simultaneous equations.

Let us start by solving the consumers' savings problem.

5.2.2 The Consumers' Savings Decision

Saving (by buying government bonds) is equivalent to reducing ones' disposable income now in order to profit from better consumption possibilities at some point in the future. Whether one wants to transfer income to the future depends of course on the consumption alternatives now and the ones in the future. In our model, these are described by the levels of private and public consumption in both periods, x_1, x_2, y_1 and y_2. In order to be able to calculate these the consumer needs to know τ_1, ρ, S and τ_2. Where do they get this information? The government announces τ_1 and S at the beginning of the first period[3]. The interest rate ρ will be determined in equilibrium and

[3] See section 5.2.4 for a discussion of this choice of fiscal variables.

will be assumed to be known to the consumers. The second period tax rate τ_2 is to be determined by the party which will be in power after the elections and is not currently known to the consumers. Thus, they have to form beliefs about who will be in power (and will set the tax rate in the second period). As mentioned above, we assume that all consumers believe that the same party $B(B = L$ or $R)$ will be in power in the second period (see footnote 8) and that it will set the tax rate at $\tau_2(B)$.

Based on this information about the first period's fiscal policy and the beliefs about the future government, consumers choose their individual level of savings, $s(m)$, as a function of their income in order to maximize their long-run utility function, i.e. their utility over the two periods.

In order to obtain the long run utility of consumer (α, m) we substitute the levels of private and public goods of the two periods $(y_1, y_2, x_1, x_2,)$ from equations (5.2), (5.3), (5.4) and (5.5) into the long run utility function given in equation (5.1). A consumer (α, m), who saves $s(m)$ (i.e. buys s bonds) will then have the long run utility

$$\begin{aligned}\alpha\log\Big(m-(m-a)\tau_1-s(m)\Big)+(1-\alpha)\log\Big((K-aN)\tau_1+S\Big)\\+\delta\Big[\alpha\log\Big(m-(m-a)\tau_2(B)+\rho s(m)\Big)\\+(1-\alpha)\log\Big((K-aN)\tau_2(B)-\rho S\Big)\Big]\end{aligned}\tag{5.6}$$

Note that this utility is influenced by beliefs: the second period's utility is influenced by $\tau_2(B)$.

In order to simplify calculations, it will be useful to introduce the following variables:

$$\tilde{m}=\frac{m}{m-a}\qquad \tilde{s}(m)=\frac{s(m)}{m-a}$$
$$\tilde{S}=\frac{S}{K-aN}\qquad \tilde{K}=\frac{K}{K-aN}$$

These give the individual's variables income (m) and savings (s) as well as the economy's variables total debt (S) and total income (K) over taxable private $(m-a)$ and taxable total income $(K-aN)$ respectively. Note, that

$$\tilde{m}>1\qquad 0<\tilde{S}<1\qquad \tilde{K}>1$$

We can now simplify the optimization problem by eliminating some constants from the utility function. This will change the absolute level of the utility but leaves the maximum points unchanged. The long run utility of consumer (α, m) can then be written as[4]

[4] For later use we note that we subtracted $(1+\delta)[\alpha\log(m-a)+(1-\alpha)\log(K-aN)]$ from the utility.

$$U = \alpha \log \left(\tilde{m} - \tau_1 - \tilde{s}(m) \right) + (1-\alpha) \log \left(\tau_1 + \tilde{S} \right)$$
$$+ \delta \left[\alpha \log \left(\tilde{m} - \tau_2(B) + \rho \tilde{s}(m) \right) + (1-\alpha) \left(\tau_2(B) - \rho \tilde{S} \right) \right] \quad (5.7)$$

(See appendix A.2 for a derivation of this.)

Consumer (α, m) will choose $\tilde{s}(m)$ so as to maximize the above utility. We assume that the amount an individual saves is very small compared to total savings in the economy. Then, the influence of the individual savings on the level of total debt is negligible, i.e. $\partial S / \partial s \to 0$. Hence, the individual saver can take the total level of savings and the levels of public goods as given. Note that the additivity of the utility function ensures that the saving decision is independent of the levels of public goods in both periods (the marginal utility of income is independent of y_1 and y_2). This gives the first order condition

$$\frac{\partial U}{\partial s(m)} = - \frac{\alpha}{\tilde{m} - \tau_1 - \tilde{s}(m)} + \frac{\delta \rho \alpha}{\tilde{m} - \tau_2(B) + \rho \tilde{s}(m)} = 0$$

Solving for the optimal level of savings gives:

$$\tilde{s}(m) = \frac{1}{\rho(1+\delta)} \left[\tau_2(B) - \delta \rho \tau_1 + \tilde{m}(\delta \rho - 1) \right] \quad (5.8)$$

From this it also follows that all consumers with income m save the same amount irrespective of their α.

Summing (integrating) over all consumers gives

$$\tilde{S} = \frac{1}{\rho(1+\delta)} \left[\tau_2(B) - \delta \rho \tau_1 + \tilde{K}(\delta \rho - 1) \right] \quad (5.9)$$

(see appendix A.3 for calculation of this).

From equation (5.8) we see that the consumers need to know only τ_1, ρ and $\tau_2(B)$ in order to know how much to save. The tax rate of the first period, τ_1, is announced by the government in power. The fiscal policy of the second period, i.e. $\tau_2(B)$, will be discussed in the next paragraph. What about ρ? We have said earlier, that the government in the first period decides on the portfolio of financing the level of public goods it wants to provide, i.e. on the taxes, τ_1, and on the debt, S: the fiscal announcement of the first period comprises τ_1 and S, the supply of government bonds. The savers then decide on their demand for government bonds; the interest rate ρ adjusts in order to clear the market.

5.2.3 The Government's Constraints

In this paragraph we want to analyze the tax rate of the second period, τ_2, for the two alternative parties, L and R.

As we have shown in the previous paragraph the consumers need information on the fiscal policy in the first period as well as the second period in order to take their saving decision. The policy of the first period is announced by the incumbent government. The second period's fiscal policy enters into the consumer's optimization problem through $\tau_2(B)$, the tax rate set by the party consumers believe to be in power then. This can be either the left-wing or the right-wing party. Our rationality assumption ensures that the government of the second period will choose τ_2 so as to maximize its representative voter's utility of the second period. The consumers who are also rational can put themselves in any parties' place and calculate this optimal rate as well and so can foresee what each party will do in the future (this is equivalent to subgame perfection and to what is sometimes known in the literature as credibility constraint). Moreover, either party has to set τ_2 in order to repay the debt inherited from the previous period: The feasibility constraint is given by

$$\tau_2(\cdot)(K - aN) > \rho S$$

i.e. τ_2 has to be such that the tax revenues are sufficient to repay the debt in the second period.

We now calculate the tax rate a party would set in the second period should it win the elections and given the debt inherited from the first period (credibility constraint): If a party P represents consumer (α_P, m_P) it will choose $\tau_2 = \tau_2(P)$ in order to maximize (after the first period) the utility of the second period:

$$U_2^P = \alpha_P \log\left(\tilde{m}_P - \tau_2 + \rho\tilde{s}(m_P)\right) + (1-\alpha_P)\log\left(\tau_2 - \rho\tilde{S}\right) \qquad (5.10)$$

(Here we have already substituted $\tilde{m}, \tilde{s}(m_P)$ and $\tilde{S}$ and subtracted the constants, see footnote 4.) Note that $\tilde{S}, \tilde{s}(m_P), \rho$, the variables inherited from the first period are now - after the first period - taken as given.

The first order condition is

$$\frac{\partial U_2^P}{\partial \tau_2} = -\frac{\alpha_P}{\tilde{m}_P - \tau_2 + \rho\tilde{s}(m_P)} + \frac{1-\alpha_P}{\tau_2 - \rho\tilde{S}} = 0 \qquad (5.11)$$

This yields:

$$\tau_2(P) = \alpha_P \rho \tilde{S} + (1-\alpha_P)\left(\tilde{m}_P + \rho\tilde{s}(m_P)\right) \qquad (5.12)$$

The tax rate is influenced by the total level of debt to be repaid and the individual income and savings of the party's representative voter.

Note that our assumptions ensure that the poorer the representative voter of a party the higher the tax rate. Hence, $\tau_2(L) > \tau_2(R)$, (proof see appendix A.4).

5.2.4 The Model's Mathematical Structure

Now the order of choosing the policy parameters can be made explicit. The government has the freedom to choose τ_1 and S . These two variables together with the belief about which party will hold office in the next period determine private savings $\tilde{s}(m)$ and hence total savings $\tilde{S}$. Knowing $\tilde{s}$ and $\tilde{S}$ the voters can then calculate the optimal $\tau_2(\cdot)$ either party will set should it win the elections. The variables $\tilde{s}, \tilde{S}$ and τ_2 for all income levels m and for all parties P are determined by equations (5.8), (5.9) and (5.12). (Equations (5.8) and (5.9) represent the consumers' optimal savings decision and (5.12) the government's optimal tax choice.) These in turn determine the levels of public goods provided in the two periods: $\tilde{y}_1 = \tau_1 + \tilde{S}$ and $\tilde{y}_2 = \tau_2 - \rho\tilde{S}$. (The feasibility constraint guarantees that the latter is positive.)

We have thus identified three simultaneous equations, (5.8), (5.9) and (5.12), for the five (interdependent) variables of the model. (τ_1, s, S, ρ and $\tau_2(\cdot)$). This leaves us with two degrees of freedom: The system is well defined once we determine two of these five variables. We choose τ_1 and S as the exogeneous variables. This is in line with most macroeconomic models where among others the tax and debt levels are political variables in the governments' hands to pursue their fiscal policy plans.

5.2.5 Neutrality

We have now fully analyzed the interdependence problem of the fiscal variables which has to be solved in the first period. We know for any announcement (τ_1, S) how much each individual saves and what the society's savings level and hence the debt to be repaid in the second period will be. We also know for any level of debt to be repaid, the policy choices for the second period of the two parties, $\tau_2(L)$ and $\tau_2(R)$. In the following sections we will analyze the electoral outcome for any two such policy programs. And as shown before, it is in fact the fiscal announcements (τ_1, S) of the government in power in the first period that in the end determines the electoral outcome. Thus, the elections' outcome is another endogeneous variable in the first period policy-maker's optimization problem.

Before we proceed to solve this optimization problem, we would like to draw the reader's attention to an important neutrality property of this model.

The model can be written and solved in terms of the variables relevant to the consumers' election behaviour. The policy-maker has to choose the optimal fiscal policy and for this choice he needs information on the political consequences of his actions. The variables relevant for the government are $x_1(m), y_1, x_2(m, P), y_2(P), \rho$ and B, the private and public goods in both periods (where the second period variables depend on the party P in power then, $P = L$ or R), the interest rate and the consumers' beliefs. These determine not only the indifferent voters and thus the outcome of the elections but also the long-run utility of the party's representative consumer: In order to solve the political problem the policy-maker needs to know what the individuals relevant for the political structure of the economy, namely the indifferent voters and the two representative voters, get under alternative policy choices. He does not need to know what every single consumer in the economy exactly does.

The above variables are related to the savings and tax variables via the following definitions:

$$\begin{aligned}\tilde{x}_1(m) &= \tilde{m} - \tau_1 + \tilde{s}(m)\\ \tilde{x}_2(m,P) &= \tilde{m} - \tau_2(P) + \rho\tilde{s}(m)\\ \tilde{y}_1 &= \tau_1 + \tilde{S}\\ \tilde{y}_2(P) &= \tau_2(P) - \rho\tilde{S}\end{aligned}$$

These are equations (5.4) and (5.5) divided by $(m - a)$ and equations (5.2) and (5.3) divided by $(K - aN)$. The second period variables are influenced by the (in the first period unknown) party parameter P, $(P = L, R)$.

When we solve the model in these variables we get the following equations, the first three of which are equations (5.8), (5.9) and (5.12) rewritten with the above variables, the fourth is an additional equation which is a budget constraint and stems form the fact that the four variables x_1, x_2, y_1 and y_2 are not independent:

$$\begin{aligned}\tilde{x}_2(m,B) &= \rho\delta\tilde{x}_1(m)\\ \rho\delta\tilde{y}_1 &= \tilde{y}_2(B) + \tilde{K}(\rho\delta - 1)\\ (1-\alpha_P)\tilde{x}_2(m_P,P) &= \alpha_P\tilde{y}_2(P)\\ \tilde{m}(1+\rho) &= \rho\tilde{x}_1(m) + \rho\tilde{y}_1 + \tilde{x}_2(m,P) + \tilde{y}_2(P)\end{aligned}$$

The first equation is derived from the optimality of the consumers savings decision, the second from integrating over optimal individual savings and the third equation from the optimal tax choice of party P in the second period. The fourth equation is the budget constraint for the first and second periods jointly (for a derivation of these equations see appendix A.5). Note that we have now identified four equations for five variables. Thus, we here have only one degree of freedom. Taking y_1, the level of public goods in the first period, as the first government's policy variable, these equations should then be solved for given values of $\tilde{y}_1$ and B to find $\rho, \tilde{x}_1(m), \tilde{x}_2(m,P)$ and $\tilde{y}_2(P)$.

This shows the neutrality in this model. Deciding on $\tilde{y}_1$, the level of public good provided in the first period, determines the variables in the second period and hence the election's result. Voters do not react to changes in τ_1 or S unless the level of y_1 is affected[5]. If the first period government fixes

[5] Our model exhibits Ricardian neutrality in the sense that when the government changes its way of financing y_1 (by moving from debt to taxation) then the consumers readjust and maintain the same utility levels. Thus, changing τ_1 and S, holding y_1 fixed, does not change the consumers' utility under future govern-

the amount of public good but sets the variables so as to finance it by debt rather than taxation the consumers will respond by adjusting their savings decisions so that both private and public consumption in the second period and hence their long run utility level remain constant. Therefore, they will not alter their election behaviour[6]. It is however crucial to our model that the voters decision is sensitive to changes in y_1. It then suffices to check responses to changes in y_1 in order to get information on the political development in our model society. So we actually have here a political-economic model of government expenditure. The model becomes a political-economic model of government debt if we assume τ_1 to be fixed.

Note that y_1 as a function of ρ is

$$\begin{aligned} \tilde{y}_1 &= \frac{(1-\alpha_B)\tilde{m}_B}{1+\delta}\left(1+\frac{1}{\rho}\right)+\frac{\alpha_B+\delta}{\delta(1+\delta)}\tilde{K}\left(\delta-\frac{1}{\rho}\right) \\ &= \frac{(1-\alpha_B)\tilde{m}_B}{1+\delta}+\frac{(\alpha_B+\delta)\tilde{K}}{1+\delta}+\frac{(1-\alpha_B)\tilde{m}_B-\frac{\alpha_B+\delta}{\delta}\tilde{K}}{(1+\delta)}\rho^{-1} \end{aligned} \quad (5.13)$$

From the second expression one can easily see that some simple assumptions will guarantee that $\partial\tilde{y}_1/\partial\rho > 0$, i.e. there is a monotonic relation between y_1 and ρ[7], (see appendix A.6). It therefore does not matter whether we solve the political problem as a function of ρ or of y_1. Instead of taking $\tilde{y}_1$ as the decision variable, we will indeed solve the model in terms of ρ. We do this for two reasons:

1. The interest rate ρ determines the second period variables (y_2, x_2) and the electoral outcome independent of the beliefs and
2. it simplifies the algebra.

When solving for all variables as functions of ρ (see section 6.3) we observe that the two variables of the second period $\tilde{x}_2(m, P)$ and $\tilde{y}_2(P)$ are independent of the belief B while $\tilde{x}_1(m)$ and $\tilde{y}_1$ depend on B (see equations 6.1 to 6.4, page 92 below). Thus, for a given value of ρ the election result which is influenced by the second period variables is determined independently of the beliefs B. However, when the first period government comes to choose $\tilde{y}_1$ so that ρ will (say) guarantee its reelection it will have to take beliefs into account. It is therefore easier to take ρ as the government's decision variable, but whatever the results with ρ we can interpret them in terms of y_1 . Note that this relation depends on B: A given level of public goods y_1 together with

---

ments and hence will not change their voting decision. Since, as will be shown later in this chapter, our consumers are sensitive to changes in the level of public provision, however, our model does not exhibit what Aghion/Bolton [1990], p.321, labelled Ricardian superindeterminacy, see section 3.5.3.

6 As before the results and the neutrality can be extended to utility functions U for which U' is a homogeneous function. Here U is $\log(\cdot)$ and U' is homogeneous of degree -1, see footnote 1.

7 We require that α_L is not too close to 0.
For the intuition that a higher y_1 leads to a higher ρ see page 62.

the beliefs B determine ρ, but ρ then determines the second period variables independent of the beliefs. Intuitively, this makes perfectly good sense. The only role the beliefs play is in determining the interest rate (via the equilibrium condition). After that, ρ determines the second period independently. Consumers know exactly how to save for some given expected ρ. But which ρ to expect depends on which party they believe to be in power. However, the reader should bear in mind that we assume the government to decide on $\tilde{y}_1$, the level of public good, and that ρ the interest rate is endogeneously determined.

5.3 Elections and the Economy's Taste-Income Distribution

In the previous paragraph we have identified the level of public goods in the first period, y_1, as the government's policy variable that determines the whole system. We have also shown that given beliefs for any y_1 there exists a unique corresponding ρ and that we can - by analyzing the whole problem in terms of ρ - eliminate the influence of the beliefs for the second period subgame.

In this section we analyze the elections issue in terms of ρ. We first introduce the curve of indifferent consumers and we analyze how this curve reacts to changes in the policy decision. We then investigate how the electoral outcome hinges on the economy's taste-income distribution. In particular, we define a measure for the political attitude of the economy. This enables us to compare different economies and we can check how the politics of the model are affected when the society changes, becomes more conservative say.

Thus, in this section we cover all the issues related to elections: We will be able to predict for some given political attitude and given beliefs, who will win the elections for any choice of fiscal policy by the reigning government in the first period, y_1 and for any type of society.

5.3.1 Voting and the Indifferent Voters

In this paragraph we analyze the question whether elections can be influenced by the government in power in the first period and if so, how this can be done.

We have shown earlier that manipulating elections is tantamount to changing the minds of those voters relevant to the electoral outcome, namely the indifferent voters. Thus, we first identify the indifferent voters before we then proceed to ask whether they are sensitive to the government's politics.

After the first period, elections take place. The debt to be repaid in the second period, ρS, has been determined and the two parties running for office can formulate their policy programs, $\tau_2(\cdot)$, on the basis of ρS. Consumers choose between the left-wing party L, representing the consumer (α_L, m_L) and the right-wing party R, representing the consumer (α_R, m_R). Both parties set the tax rate $\tau_2(\cdot)$ according to equation (5.12). Voters vote for the party that guarantees them the higher utility in the second period. A consumer (α, m) will be indifferent between the two parties if the utility levels in the second period under the two possible regimes are the same. (The different regimes enter through the tax rate $\tau_2(\cdot)$.)

$$\begin{aligned} \alpha \log\left(\tilde{m} + \rho\tilde{s}(m) - \tau_2(L)\right) &+ (1-\alpha)\log\left(\tau_2(L) - \rho\tilde{S}\right) = \\ \alpha \log\left(\tilde{m} + \rho\tilde{s}(m) - \tau_2(R)\right) &+ (1-\alpha)\log\left(\tau_2(R) - \rho\tilde{S}\right) \end{aligned} \qquad (5.14)$$

In one-dimensional models as described in paragraph 4.2.1 there exists a single indifferent voter such that all voters poorer than the indifferent voter vote for the left-wing party and all voters richer than the indifferent voter vote for the right-wing party. We will now show that in contrast to these one-dimensional models of voting here there is a curve of voters indifferent between the two parties. Thus, not a single voter but a set of voters divides the society into right-wing and left-wing voters.

We now show that for any fiscal policy choice of the first government, y_1 (or ρ), there exists a set of indifferent voters and that this is a decreasing curve in the two-dimensional taste-income space as shown in figure 5.2.

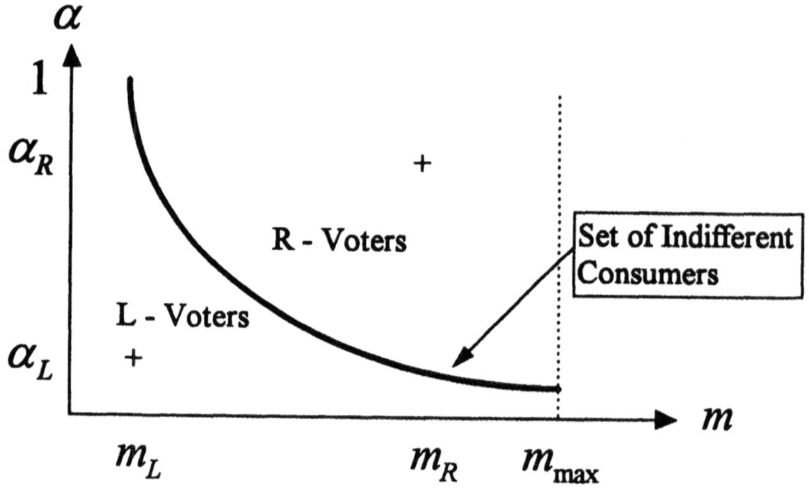

Fig. 5.2. The Set of Indifferent Consumers

We first calculate for each income group m the preference level in which the consumer is indifferent between the two parties by solving equation(5.14) for α. (Note that (5.14) can be seen as an equation defining α as a function of m). We denote the α that solves this equation for income group m by $\alpha^{ind}(m)$:

$$\alpha^{ind}(m) = \frac{\log \frac{\tau_2(L)-\rho\tilde{\bar{S}}}{\tau_2(R)-\rho\tilde{\bar{S}}}}{\log \frac{\tau_2(L)-\rho\tilde{\bar{S}}}{\tau_2(R)-\rho\tilde{\bar{S}}} + \log \frac{\bar{m}+\bar{s}(m)\rho-\tau_2(R)}{\bar{m}+\bar{s}(m)\rho-\tau_2(L)}} \tag{5.15}$$

(See appendix A.7 for derivation of this equation.)

Let us now check the derivative of $\alpha^{ind}(m)$ in equation (5.15) with respect to m. We find that

$$\frac{\partial \alpha^{ind}(m)}{\partial m} < 0 \tag{5.16}$$

(Proof see appendix A.8)

The former equation, (5.15), gives the curve of indifferent consumers as demonstrated in figure 5.2, the latter equation, (5.16), shows that $\alpha^{ind}(m)$ as a function of m is decreasing in the taste-income space, with all consumers above the curve voting for the right-wing party while all those below vote for the left-wing party. In order to find out the winner of the elections one has to check on which side of the curve the majority of voters is located.

The intuition for the shape of the indifferent consumers' curve is straightforward. Let us look at this from the point of view of a very wealthy consumer. It is usually the case that rich consumers have a very high preference for private goods. But even if we have the classical case of a *Salonkommunist*, a rich consumer whose preferences resemble those of a poorer voter, only if his preferences are really extreme ($\alpha \to 0$) does he vote the left-wing party. Analogous for a poor voter: His tastes have to be extreme ($\alpha \to 1$) in order for him to be better off under an R-regime. The R-party is more popular among richer voters whereas the L-party is more popular among poorer voters.

Now that we have identified the set of indifferent consumers for any policy, we want to investigate whether in our model the elections' outcome can be manipulated: Does the set of indifferent consumers react to changes in the first government's policy programme y_1, i.e. in ρ? It is obvious that this is a neccessary requirement for elections to be manipulable. If the indifferent consumers do not react to changes in the policy variables then policy cannot change the elections' outcome. We find that in our model the indifferent consumers indeed do react to the government's politics: We can show that the curve of indifferent voters shifts upwards on the left side and shifts downwards on the right side when ρ increases. This is demonstrated in figure 5.3.

We will here just sketch the rather tedious proof for the reaction of the set of indifferent consumers to policy changes in the first period; for a detailed presentation of the proof see appendix A.9. By differentiating the equation for the indifferent consumer in some income group m, $\alpha^{ind}(m)$ in equation (5.15), we find that

1.

$$\text{at } m = m_L: \quad \frac{\partial \alpha^{ind}}{\partial \rho} > 0$$

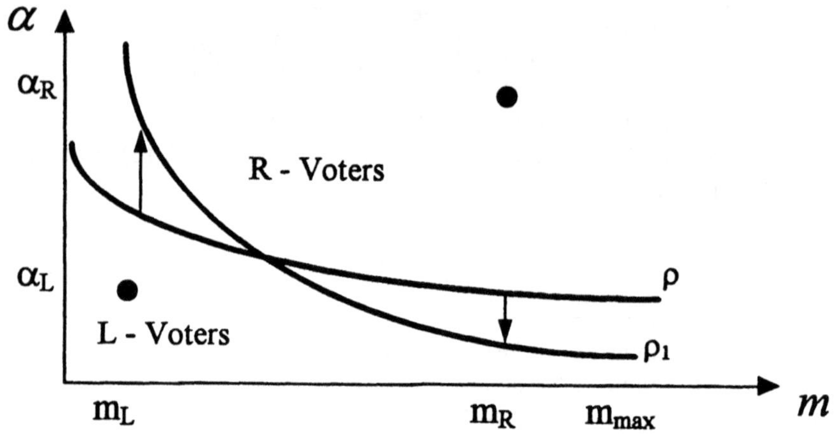

Fig. 5.3. The Curve of Indifferent Consumers as a Function of ρ, $\rho_1 > \rho$

$$\text{at } m = m_R: \quad \frac{\partial \alpha^{ind}}{\partial \rho} < 0$$

After an increase in ρ , i.e. an increase in y_1, the new indifferent voter in income group m_L is a voter with a higher preference for private goods: The higher the level of public provision y_1 and thus ρ, the more voters in income group m_L vote for the L-party. Analogous for the right-wing party.

2.

$$\frac{\partial \alpha^{ind}}{\partial \rho} > 0 \quad \forall m < m_L$$
$$\frac{\partial \alpha^{ind}}{\partial \rho} < 0 \quad \forall m > m_R$$

The curve of indifferent consumers shifts up on its left end and shifts down on its right end: A party gains votes among the poorer voters and looses votes among the richer voters from increasing y_1, i.e. ρ.

3. Any two curves of indifferent voters corresponding to two different ρ, i.e. to two different fiscal policies, y_1, have exactly one intersection point between m_L and m_R as shown in figure 5.3.

Thus, as sketched in figure 5.3, as a reaction to a change in ρ the curve shifts up for all m less than a certain income and it shifts down for all m larger than that income. Note that this - crucial - income changes with ρ. In figure 5.4 we present the sets of indifferent consumers for three different fiscal policy choices represented by ρ_1, ρ_2 and ρ_3. If we compare for example the fiscal policies 1 and 2 (ρ_1- and ρ_2-curves) we find that m_A is the crucial income in the sense that $\forall m < m_A$ a party gains votes from choosing ρ_1

instead of ρ_2 and $\forall m > m_A$ it looses votes. When we compare policies 1 and 3 and 2 and 3 these crucial incomes are given by m_B and m_C respectively.

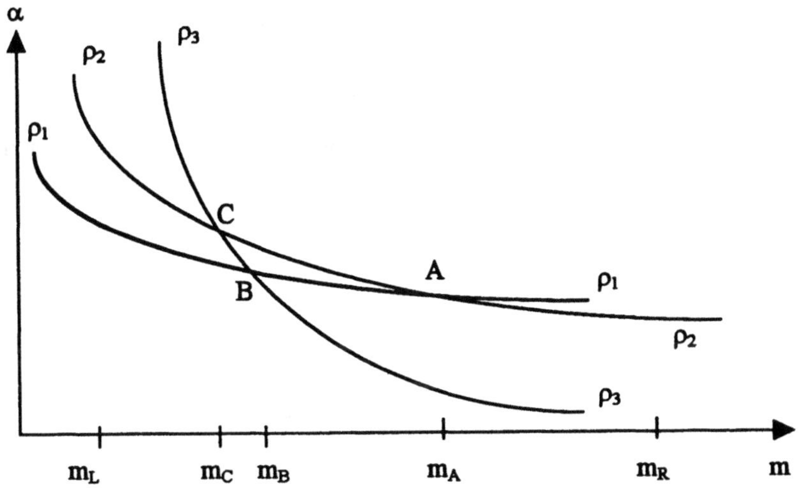

Fig. 5.4. The Sets of Indifferent Consumers for Different Fiscal Policies

Let us repeat the important result here: Voters react to changes in the fiscal policy of the government in power in the first period. Thus, elections can be influenced and the reigning government can use its fiscal policy strategically in order to manipulate elections! (The intuition for the way the curve behaves was described at length on page 62.)

5.3.2 The Role of the Economy's Taste-Income Distribution

Type A and Type B Distributions. The previous section shows that by increasing ρ the left-wing party gains votes of the poorer consumers and loses votes of the richer ones. But as we can deduce from figure 5.4 from this it does not neccesarily follow that the higher (lower) the ρ, the higher the electoral victory for the left-wing (right-wing) party: In figure 5.4 as ρ increases from ρ_2 to ρ_3, a party will lose some of the votes it won when it increased ρ from ρ_1 to ρ_2 (the voters in the area $[ABC]$). That is, as long as voters are distributed in the messy part between m_L and m_R where the ρ-curves intersect, we will have a hard time evaluating the exact political consequences from changing a ρ, as ρ increases the elections' outcome could then switch back and forth between the parties as in figure 5.5.

But we can bound this indeterminate part so that we can get clear-cut results: This is demonstrated in figure 5.6: Simple continuity arguments ensure that there exist two values $\underline{m} < \overline{m}$ such that $\forall m < \underline{m}$ the indifferent

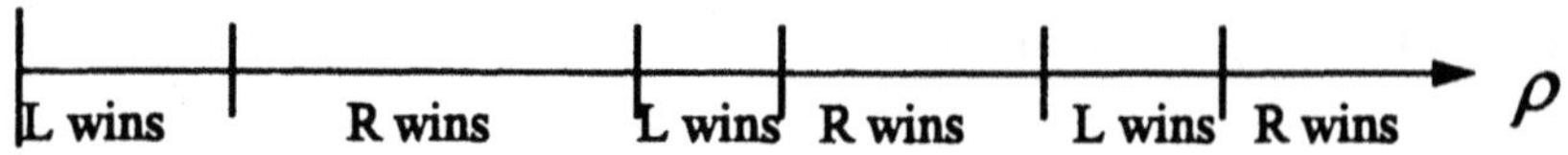

Fig. 5.5. Discontinuous Elections' Outcome Function

consumers' curve shifts upwards with ρ whereas $\forall m > \overline{m}$ the curve strictly shifts downwards as ρ increases, see A.9.

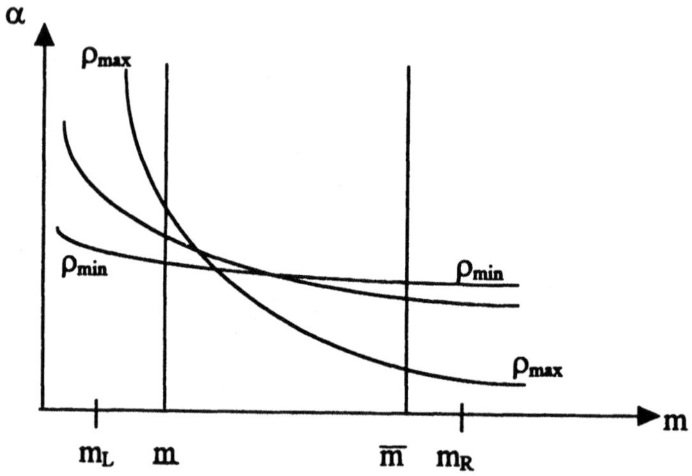

Fig. 5.6. Areas With Ordered ρ-Curves

In the following we will thus assume that the population is concentrated in either of these areas. Let us be a bit more precise and introduce two different types of populations that we will work with for the remainder of this thesis, a type A distribution as in figure 5.7 and a type B distribution as in figure 5.8.

In a type A society preferences for private consumption increase rapidly with income, whereas in a type B economy the reverse holds. One could interpret the type A economy as an example for societies like the USA where the lower and middle classes believe in American individualism and are in their preferences much like the upper class. As an opposite example the type B economy could represent countries like Sweden where even the middle and upper middle classes used to believe strongly in a strong and active state.

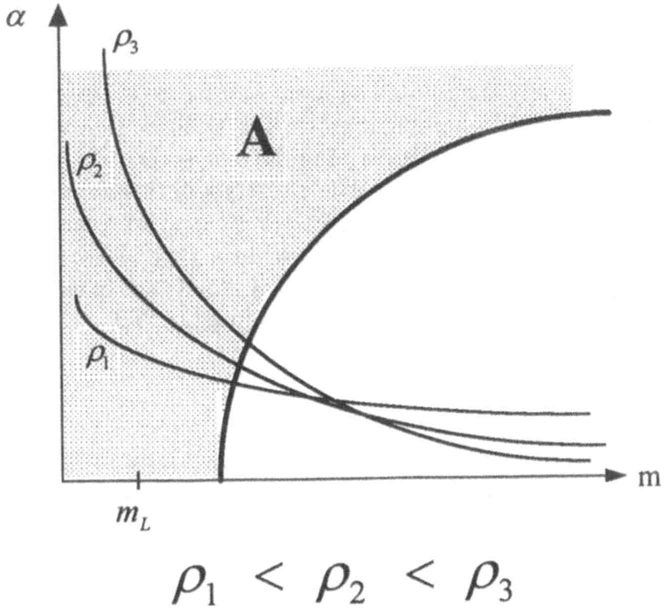

Fig. 5.7. Curves of Indifferent Consumers in a Type *A* Economy

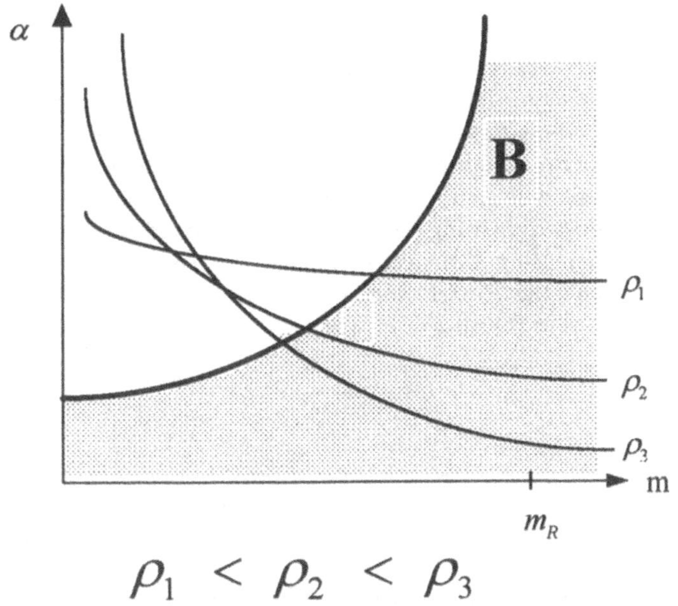

Fig. 5.8. Curves of Indifferent Consumers in a Type *B* Economy

The Elections' Outcome as a Function of the First Period Policy. We are now in a position to derive the elections' outcome as a function of ρ. If we assume that consumers are only distributed in area A of figure 5.7 (type A economy), then increasing ρ will unambiguously bring additional votes to the left-wing party. The area below the curve of indifferent voters where the L-voters are located increases as ρ increases. The L-party will therefore tend to increase ρ in order to win the elections. A right-wing party, however, will gain from lowering ρ, i.e. from decreasing y_1. Thus, in a type A economy we expect the left-wing party to win for high values of ρ and the right-wing party to win for low values of ρ. This is demonstrated in figure 5.9.

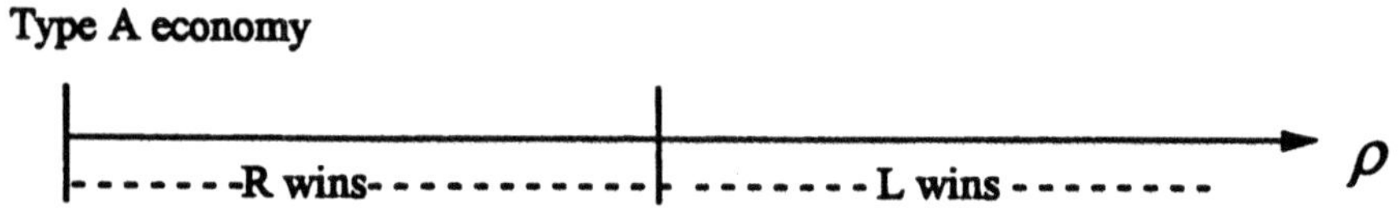

Fig. 5.9. Elections' Outcome Function in a Type A Economy

There will be one fiscal policy choice, y_1, and a corresponding ρ, where the society is undecided and the elections will end in a draw. Let us define μ as the level of interest rate that generates a draw in the elections (μ is a function of the global income-taste distribution and plays the role of the median voter in one-dimensional models.) In a type A economy the R-party wins for all $\rho < \mu$ and the L-party wins for all $\rho > \mu$, see figure 5.9.

In a type B economy as in figure 5.8 the reverse holds. Note that in a type B economy a "low" curve of indifferent consumers, i.e. a curve close to the origin, is associated with a high ρ and vice versa. Hence, in this type of economy an L-government will gain votes by lowering ρ, i.e. by increasing the area below the curve. A right-wing party on the other hand will increase its number of votes by increasing ρ. Hence, in a type B economy the L-party tends to win for low ρ and the R-party for high ρ. This is demonstrated in figure 5.10. The R-party wins for all $\rho < \mu$, whereas the L-party wins for all $\rho > \mu$.

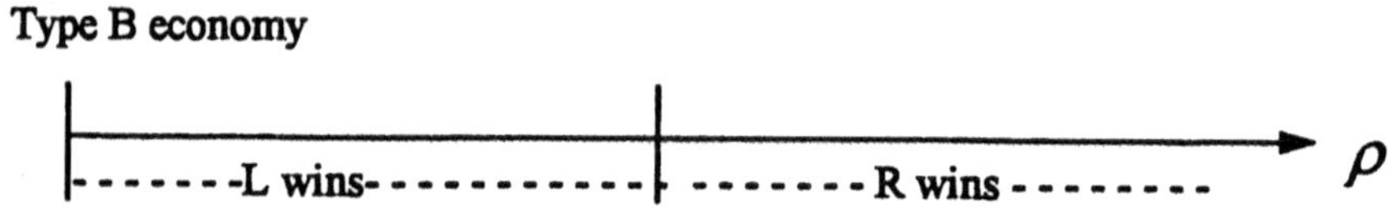

Fig. 5.10. Elections' Outcome Function in a Type B Economy

We get another interesting result here: The population's type affects the direction of the policies a party will wish to take in order to win the elections.

The same party may wish to take opposite measures depending on the global distribution of voters.

What is the intuition behind the kind of behaviour we just described? Why does the right-wing party in a type A economy win for low levels of public goods in the first period, y_1, whereas in a type B economy it wins for high levels (analogous for the left-wing party)? In a type A economy (figure 5.7) voters with low income resemble the richer voters in their preferences. In such a situation a right-wing party can pursue its desired policy (little public good, little debt to repay in the second period and thus a low τ_2). But as y_2 and thus ρ increase, the second period tax rate has to be set at a higher level and contrary to the R-party the L-party even raises the level of public goods in the second period. This makes them more popular among poor voters who are hardly affected by the tax increase, but who enjoy utility from y_2. Thus, the higher ρ the more attractive the L-party becomes to the voters with intermediate income.

In a type B economy on the other hand, only voters with very high income may have strong preferences for private income. The "middle class" resembles in its tastes the lower class. The R-party can only win over the middle class voters by setting a high level of ρ. This induces the L-party to set a high tax rate (and a higher level of public goods) in the second period. This makes the middle class voters who have a considerable fraction of taxable income suffer from the high taxes and this loss in utility cannot be compensated by the higher level of public consumption.

A Measure for Comparing Societies. We are now in a position to determine for given beliefs and given type of society the elections' outcome for any fiscal policy choice of the first period, y_1, i.e. ρ. Before we solve the optimization problem of the first period government we want to take a closer look at μ. The parameter μ divides the society into 50% voters below the curve and 50% voters above the curve. In the following sense, μ can be interpreted as an indicator for the political *couleur* of a society: When we restrict ourselves to type A (or B) economies then the more to the left (the closer to the origin) the μ-curve the more left-wing (or liberal) a society is. Let us verify this by looking at the following example which is depicted in figure 5.11: Here, we compare two type A societies whose first period fiscal policy choices (y_1) that lead to a draw in the elections are reflected by the endogenously determined interest rate μ_{A1} and μ_{A2} for the two societies respectively. In Society $A1$ the 50% voters with the lowest incomes and the lowest preferences for private income are squeezed below the μ_{A1}-curve whereas in the $A2$ society they are scattered in the larger area below the μ_{A2}-curve which also comprises both higher incomes and higher preferences for private consumption. If we call - in accordance with the general assumptions in public finance - a voter more left-wing (more liberal) the lower his income and his preferences for private income are, then society $A1$ consists of relatively more liberal voters as compared to society $A2$ and is thus more liberal. The same interest rate that

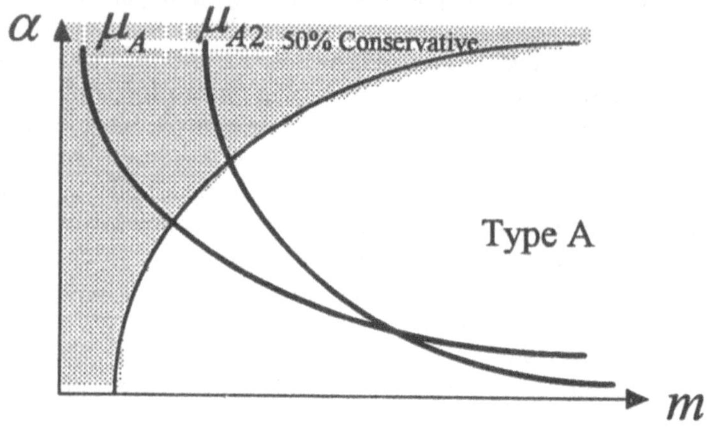

Fig. 5.11. μ as an Indicator for the *Political Couleur* of a Society (Type A Economy)

leads to a draw in the elections in society $A1$ would generate a comfortable victory for the right-wing party in society $A2$. Hence, the latter can be called more conservative. Note that in type A economies a high μ-curve is associated with high values of μ. So for a type A economy we can say that the higher its μ the more conservative the society.

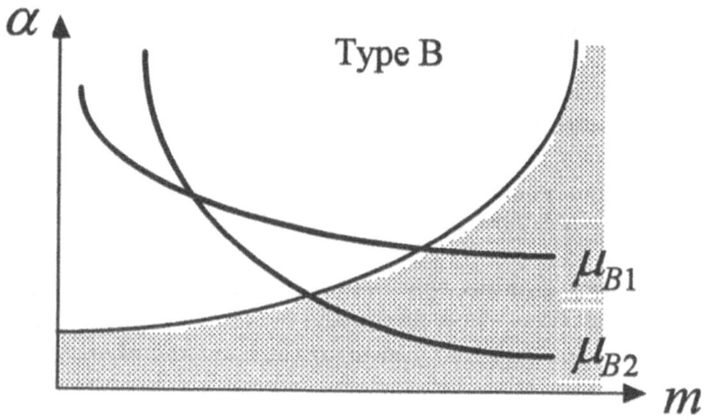

Fig. 5.12. μ as an Indicator for the *Political Couleur* of a Society (Type B Economy)

In a type B economy as demonstrated in figure 5.12 things are slightly different. Here again, we compare two societies with different μ's. Again we find that the closer the μ-curve to the origin the more liberal the society, i.e.

society $B2$ is more left-wing than society $B1$. But remember that in type B economies low μ-curves are associated with high values for μ. Thus, in type B economies the higher the μ the more liberal the economy.

So we can take μ as a measure for the degree of political conservatism in a type A economy, while $(-\mu)$ is a measure of conservatism in type B economies.

However, comparing societies, the way we just did, is possible only if the indifferent consumers' curves are identical. In that case they do not intersect in the relevant area[8]. This happens to be so if the two societies have the same average income (mean preserving change)[9]. Thus, ordering societies by their μ is only a partial ordering. However, there are many possible societies (distributions in the taste-income space) that we should be grateful to be able to compare at least some societies. Societies with the same average income may differ though in their specific μ and we can thus distinguish between two different societies by comparing their μ. For a demonstration of the problem of intersecting μ-curves see appendix A.11.

---

[8] We have already touched this problem in section 5.3.2. There we introduced the types of society (A, B) in order to avoid having to deal with the problem of intersecting indifferent consumers' curves.

[9] This follows from the equation defining the curve of indifferent consumers $\alpha_{ind}(m)$, equation (5.15). If in this equation the values of $\tilde{S}$, (equation(5.9)), and $\tau_2(\cdot)$, (equation (5.12)) remain the same as ρ changes then we get the same set of indifferent consumers' curves for different societies; $\alpha_{ind}(m)$ also depends on $\tilde{s}(m)$ but this in turn is determined by τ_2, see equation (5.8); all the first period variables are taken as given when we calculate the indifferent consumers. We thank Torsten Persson for this observation.

6. The Implications for Fiscal Policy

Before we now finally come to solve the fiscal policy problem of the government in power in the first period, let us recapitulate what we have done in the previous chapter. First we have solved the individual consumers' savings problem, given some fiscal policy announcement (τ_1, S). We then derived the optimal tax rate the parties will wish to set in the second period given the debt inherited from the first period. We have then rewritten the problem in terms relevant for the government's policy decision. We argued that the government is interested in the overall consequences of its actions and not in what each single individual in the society does. Rewriting the model makes it also technically easier to handle and we can even eliminate the influence of the exogeneous beliefs when solving the elections' problem. We then derived ρ as the variable determining the whole system and analyzed the election outcome as a function of ρ. We first restricted our economy to two types of distributions so that we could derive clear-cut results concerning the electoral outcome as a function of ρ. We then derived election outcome functions for both types of society. Finally, we introduced μ as an indicator for the economy's political attitude.

In this chapter we finally solve the long run optimization problem for the party in power in the first period: Given a type of taste-income distribution, what is the optimal fiscal policy y_1, i.e. ρ? Will the first party decide to set its policy variable so as to stay in power? How does the government's optimal policy decision change as the society's degree of conservatism, μ, changes? We will see that the optimal choice of y_1 crucially depends on the type of population as well as on the society's political attitude.

We first want to demonstrate in a very general way and for some given level of society's conservatism, how we derive the optimal policy (ρ) of the first period government. (Recall that all results with ρ can be interpreted in terms of y_1.) We then calculate the optimal fiscal policies for the various cases of our model, namely for a given type of population (A or B) and given some first period government (L or R). Finally, we demonstrate for these special cases how the optimal fiscal policy changes as a society's political attitude changes.

6.1 A General Example

In the following we denote by P the party in power in the first period and by Q the opposition party.

Let us assume that we are looking at a society as in figure 6.1 where the reigning party P wins the elections for high values of ρ while the opposition party Q wins for low values of ρ. The party in power in the first period chooses its fiscal variable y_1, and thus ρ, in order to maximize the long-run utility of its representative voter, denoted by U_P. When calculating this long run utility, the party in power in the first period has to consider which party will be in power in the second period. There could be two possibilities: Either it stays in power or the opposition party takes over. Thus, for each ρ there are two utility levels possible, one denoted by $U_{P \to P}$ when P remains in power and the other by $U_{P \to Q}$ when the other party wins. It is obvious that for the consumer represented by party P the utility achieved when P stays in power (under "dictatorship", $P \to P$) is always higher than if the other party reigns. (A dictator can always imitate the strategies of other players.) Thus, in figure 6.1 the function $U_{P \to P}$ is always above $U_{P \to Q}$. However, the range of ρ's is partitioned into two parts. The party knows that for interest rates higher than μ it will win the elections and the relevant function will be $U_{P \to P}$, while for interest rates lower than μ, $U_{P \to Q}$ is the relevant function. This is illustrated in figure 6.1. The global long run utility function that the party aims to maximize is then given by the thick line, it consists partly of $U_{P \to P}$ and partly of $U_{P \to Q}$. In figure 6.1(a) the maximum under dictatorship $(P \to P)$ is at ρ_P. The party would have preferred to choose ρ_P and win the elections. This, however, is impossible, since if it sets ρ_P the elections' outcome will lead to a victory of the Q-party. In order to win the elections P has to set $\rho \geq \mu$ but in our example this is too far from the maximum of the global long run utility function, ρ^*, and causes a large loss of utility. Thus, in the example of figure 6.1(a) choosing a public good level y_1^* that leads to ρ^* and giving up power is the best -under the given circumstances- the P-party can do for its representative voter.

We here also see that this result hinges essentially on the position of μ. Had μ been closer to ρ^* as in figure 6.1(b), the peak of the global long run utility function would have lead to the P-party choosing its policy variable so as to remain in power. But note that choosing $\rho * = \rho_P$ still leads to a victory for the opposition party. The P-party has to compromise and set $\rho * = \mu > \rho_P$ in order to stay in power.

6.2 Fiscal Policy in Our Model

We now solve the fiscal optimization problem in the first period for the L- and R-parties in the two types of population distributions. In order to find

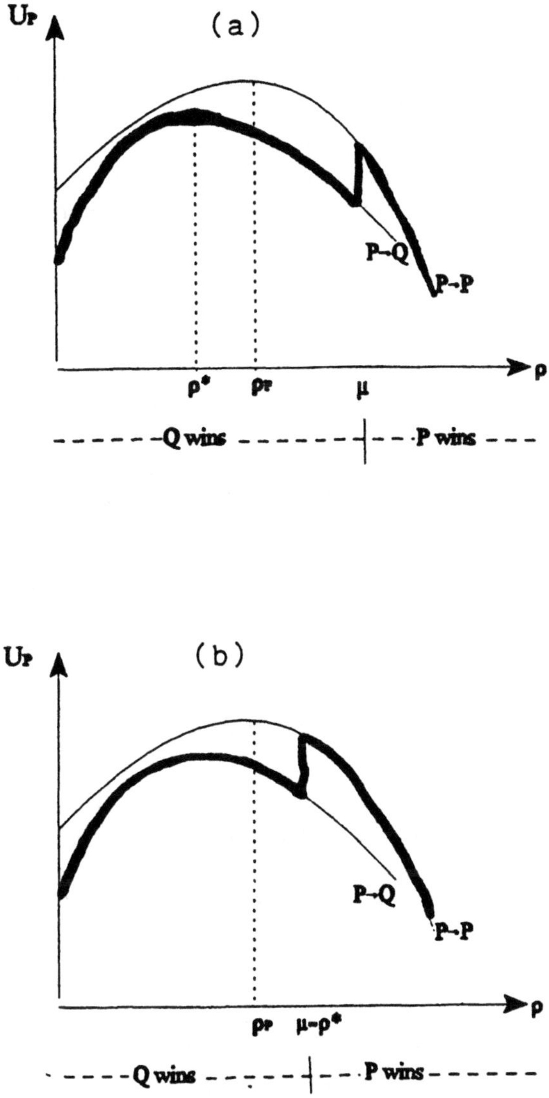

Fig. 6.1. The Global Long-Run Utility Function of a P-Party

the optimal fiscal policy, i.e. the ρ that maximizes the party's representative voter's long run utility for the cases of our model we take the following steps

1. We first specify the long run utility to be maximized in general form, i.e. for any first period government P, beliefs B and "true" party in the second period T.
2. We then take the derivative of the general long run utility function with respect to the policy variable ρ.
3. Next, we make an assumption about the exogeneous variables in our model, namely the party in power in the first period, $P = L$ or R, the party consumers believe to win the elections, $B = L$ or R and the type of economy, A or B. (This determines which party wins the elections for any level of ρ.)
4. We then calculate the long run utility maximized by the first period government U_P as a function of its policy variable (ρ) for the two possible cases, $T = P$ or Q, i.e. the reigning party stays in power or the opposition party takes over. (Since a dictator can always imitate the strategies of his opponent and since the voter represented by a party is always better off if this party stays in power, we note that for any level of ρ the long run utility of the voter represented by the first period government if the party stays in power is at least as high as under a change of regimes, $U_{P\to P} \geq U_{P\to Q}$.)
5. Given the global long run utility function, we are then in a position to identify the optimal fiscal policy for the policy-maker of the first period. Moreover, we now know the elections outcome and whether the first period government decided to stay in power.
6. Finally, we derive the optimal policy choice as a function of the economy's degree of conservativeness, μ.

We denote as before by P the party in power in the first period, by Q the opposition party, by B the party people believe to be in power in the second period ($B = P, Q$) and by T the party that will actually be in power in the second period ($T = P, Q$). When the beliefs turned out to be correct ($B = T$) the outcome is a rational expectations equilibrium.

6.3 The Long Run Utility Function in General Form and its Derivative With Respect to ρ

The long run utility function to be maximized by party P representing the voter (α_P, m_P), denoted by U_P, given society's beliefs is given by equation (5.7):

$$U_P = \alpha_P \log \tilde{x}_1 + (1 - \alpha_P) \log \tilde{y}_1 + \delta \Big[\alpha_P \log \tilde{x}_2 + (1 - \alpha_P) \log \tilde{y}_2 \Big]$$

$$\text{where} \qquad \tilde{x}_1 = \tilde{m}_P - \tau_1 - \tilde{s}(m_P) \qquad \tilde{y}_1 = \tau_1 + \tilde{S}$$
$$\tilde{x}_2 = \tilde{m}_P - \tau_2 + \rho\tilde{s}(m_P) \qquad \tilde{y}_2 = \tau_2 - \rho\tilde{S}$$

In the previous chapters we have derived all the optimal decisions, namely optimal individual savings and thus total savings as well as the optimal $\tau_2(\cdot)$, so we are now in a position to specify all variables in the above utility function. Substituting the optimal variables for $\tilde{s}(m_P)$, $\tilde{S}$ and $\tau_2(\cdot)$ into $\tilde{x}_1, \tilde{y}_1, \tilde{x}_2$ and $\tilde{y}_2$ we get (after rearranging):

$$\tilde{x}_1 = \frac{1+\rho}{\rho(1+\delta)}\tilde{m}_P - \frac{1+\rho}{\rho(1+\delta)}(1-\alpha_B)\tilde{m}_B - \frac{\delta\rho-1}{\delta\rho(1+\delta)}\alpha_B\tilde{K} \tag{6.1}$$

$$\tilde{y}_1 = \frac{1+\rho}{\rho(1+\delta)}(1-\alpha_B)\tilde{m}_B + \frac{\delta\rho-1}{\delta\rho(1+\delta)}(\alpha_B+\delta)\tilde{K} \tag{6.2}$$

$$\tilde{x}_2 = \frac{\delta(1+\rho)}{1+\delta}\tilde{m}_P - \frac{\delta(1+\rho)}{1+\delta}(1-\alpha_T)\tilde{m}_T - \frac{\delta\rho-1}{1+\delta}\alpha_T\tilde{K} \tag{6.3}$$

$$\tilde{y}_2 = \frac{1}{1+\delta}(1-\alpha_T)\Big((1+\rho)\delta\tilde{m}_T - (\delta\rho-1)\tilde{K}\Big) \tag{6.4}$$

(see appendix A.12 for derivation of this)

Substituting these in the long run utility function then gives after subtracting the constants

$$\begin{aligned} U_P &= \alpha_P\left[\log\left((1+\rho)\tilde{m}_P - (1+\rho)(1-\alpha_B)\tilde{m}_B - \frac{\delta\rho-1}{\delta}\alpha_B\tilde{K}\right) - \log\rho\right] \\ &+ (1-\alpha_P)\left[\log\left((1+\rho)(1-\alpha_B)\tilde{m}_B + \frac{\delta\rho-1}{\delta}(\alpha_B+\delta)\tilde{K}\right) - \log\rho\right] \\ &+ \delta\left[\alpha_P\log\left(\delta(1+\rho)\tilde{m}_P - \delta(1+\rho)(1-\alpha_T)\tilde{m}_T - (\delta\rho-1)\alpha_T\tilde{K}\right)\right. \\ &+ \left.(1-\alpha_P)\log\Big((1+\rho)\delta\tilde{m}_T - (\delta\rho-1)\tilde{K}\Big)\right] \end{aligned} \tag{6.5}$$

(see appendix A.13)

In order to find the maximum of that function we take its derivative with respect to ρ:

$$\frac{\partial U_P}{\partial\rho} = \alpha_P\frac{-\tilde{m}_P + (1-\alpha_B)\tilde{m}_B - \frac{\alpha_B}{\delta}\tilde{K}}{\rho\left[(1+\rho)\tilde{m}_P - (1+\rho)(1-\alpha_B)\tilde{m}_B - \frac{\delta\rho-1}{\delta}\alpha_B\tilde{K}\right]}$$

$$
\begin{aligned}
&+ \quad (1-\alpha_P)\frac{\frac{\alpha_B+\delta}{\delta}\tilde{K}-(1-\alpha_B)\tilde{m}_B}{\rho\left[(1+\rho)(1-\alpha_B)\tilde{m}_B+\frac{\delta\rho-1}{\delta}(\alpha_B+\delta)\tilde{K}\right]} \\
&+ \quad \delta^2\left[\alpha_P\frac{\tilde{m}_P-(1-\alpha_T)\tilde{m}_T-\alpha_T\tilde{K}}{\delta(1+\rho)\tilde{m}_P-\delta(1+\rho)(1-\alpha_T)\tilde{m}_T-(\delta\rho-1)\alpha_T\tilde{K}}\right. \\
&+ \quad \left.(1-\alpha_P)\frac{\tilde{m}_T-\tilde{K}}{(1+\rho)\delta\tilde{m}_T-(\delta\rho-1)\tilde{K}}\right] \qquad (6.6)
\end{aligned}
$$

(see appendix A.14)

For later use note that for special cases parts of equation (6.6) can be simplified. When people believe that the first period party P remains in power, $B = P$, the first two terms reduce to

$$
\begin{aligned}
&\alpha_P\frac{-\tilde{m}_P-\frac{1}{\delta}\tilde{K}}{\rho\left[(1+\rho)\tilde{m}_P-\frac{\delta\rho-1}{\delta}\tilde{K}\right]} \\
+&(1-\alpha_P)\frac{\frac{\alpha_P+\delta}{\delta}\tilde{K}-(1-\alpha_P)\tilde{m}_P}{\rho\left[(1+\rho)(1-\alpha_P)\tilde{m}_P+\frac{\delta\rho-1}{\delta}(\alpha_P+\delta)\tilde{K}\right]} \qquad (6.7)
\end{aligned}
$$

When the first period party P remains in power, ("dictatorship", $T = P$), the last two terms can be reduced to

$$
\delta^2\frac{\tilde{m}_P-\tilde{K}}{(1+\rho)\delta\tilde{m}_P-(\delta\rho-1)\tilde{K}} \qquad (6.8)
$$

For any given values of the parameters $\alpha_L, \alpha_R, m_L, m_R, K, N$ and δ we can now in principle and with the help of a powerful computer plot the long run utility function U_P for any party and belief and calculate equation (6.6) to find its maximum. In order to obtain analytical results we introduce some assumptions that ensure that the utility functions $U_{P\to P}$ and $U_{P\to Q}$ are both decreasing over the relevant range. The relevant range is defined by the minimum and maximum values ρ can take: The minimum value $\rho^{min} = 1/\delta$ since $\rho\delta > 1$ is needed to guarantee positive savings[1]. The maximum value ρ can take is given by $\rho^{max} = \tau_2(K - aN)/S$. This follows from the feasibility constraint $\tau_2(K - aN) \geq \rho S$.

---

[1] In a simple intertemporal model where one saves s today and gets ρs back tomorrow, there will be positive savings as long as $\delta\rho > 1$: Take a utility function in log form as we did in the model: $\log(x - s) + \delta\log(x + \rho s)$. Its derivative with respect to s is given by $-\frac{1}{x-s} + \frac{\delta\rho}{x+\rho s}$. If this is positive at $s = 0$ then the utility function's optimum is at some value $s > 0$. At $s = 0$ $\quad -\frac{1}{x} + \frac{\delta\rho}{x} > 0$ if $\delta\rho - 1 > 0$ or $\delta\rho > 1$, q.e.d.

Of course one could also extend our model to cases where the government actually lends to consumers at an interest rate $\rho < 1/\delta$ so that consumers can transfer income from the second period to the first.

So in order to ensure that both $U_{P\to P}$ and $U_{P\to Q}$ are decreasing between ρ^{min} and ρ^{max}, we assume that the voter represented by the right-wing party has rather strong preferences for private income, $\alpha_R \to 1$, and we assume further that the voters represented by the two parties are close in their income: $\tilde{m}_L \sim \tilde{K} \sim \tilde{m}_R$.

6.4 The Optimal Fiscal Policy of an R-Government

We start by deriving the optimal fiscal policy for the R-party in power in the first period. Two cases are possible, it remains in power or it loses the elections. We solve equation (6.6) for $P = R, B = L$ or R and $T = L$ or R. We find that - irrespective of the beliefs[2] - in the relevant range ($\rho^{min} \leq \rho \leq \rho^{max}$) the long run utility function is a decreasing function of ρ:

$$\frac{\partial U_{R\to R}}{\partial \rho} < 0 \qquad \text{and} \qquad \frac{\partial U_{R\to L}}{\partial \rho} < 0$$

(see appendix A.15)

Since the voter represented by R is always better off when R remains in power, $\forall \rho \quad U_{R\to R} \geq U_{R\to L}$. This is demonstrated in figure 6.2. In order to

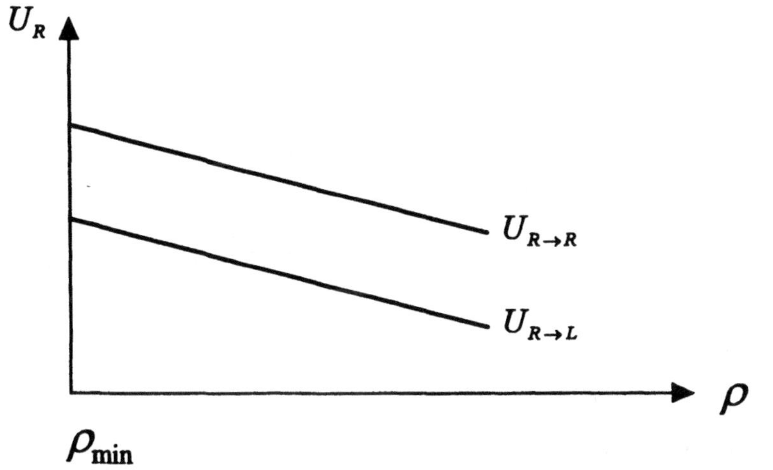

Fig. 6.2. The Long Run Utility Function of an R-Government

identify the global long run utility function we have to make an assumption about the type of economy. In type A economies the R-party wins for $\rho < \mu$, whereas in type B economies it wins for $\rho > \mu$. This gives the global long run utility function for the two types of economies as in figures 6.3 and 6.4.

[2] We will return to the role of the beliefs on page 99.

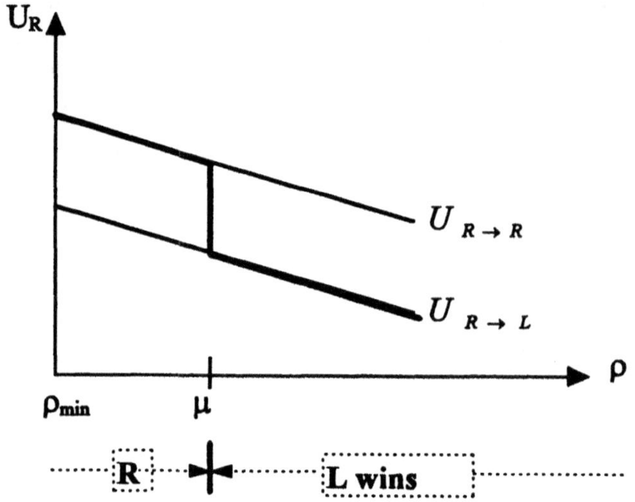

Fig. 6.3. The Global Long Run Utility Function of the *R*-Party in a Type *A* Economy

6.4.1 Type *A* Economy

We have just derived the global long run utility function for the R-government in a type A economy and it is obvious to see that the global optimum is at $\rho^* = \rho^{min} = 1/\delta$. This optimal policy can be pursued by the R-party whatever the position of μ, i.e. whatever the society's political attitude. This is demonstrated in figure 6.5. In a type A economy R will always choose $\rho^* = \rho^{min}$ and will stay in power.

The intuition behind this result is straightforward. Recall the election outcome function in a type A economy as depicted in figure 5.9. In type A economies especially the middle class (those with intermediate incomes) but also some poor voters have preferences like the rich (high α). These voters enjoy their private income, so if the first period government keeps the debt and thus τ_2 low, as is the desired policy of an R-government, then they vote for this government. Only for high levels of public good y_1 (and hence high ρ) does the L-party have a chance in the elections. In that case taxes will be high under any regime in the second period, but under the L party there will also be an considerable amount of public goods. The L party gains popularity among some poor and middle class voters, because their loss in private income is compensated by sufficient public goods. So by keeping the debt to repay low, which is R's preferred policy anyway, R can easily stay in power and prevent L from gaining popularity.

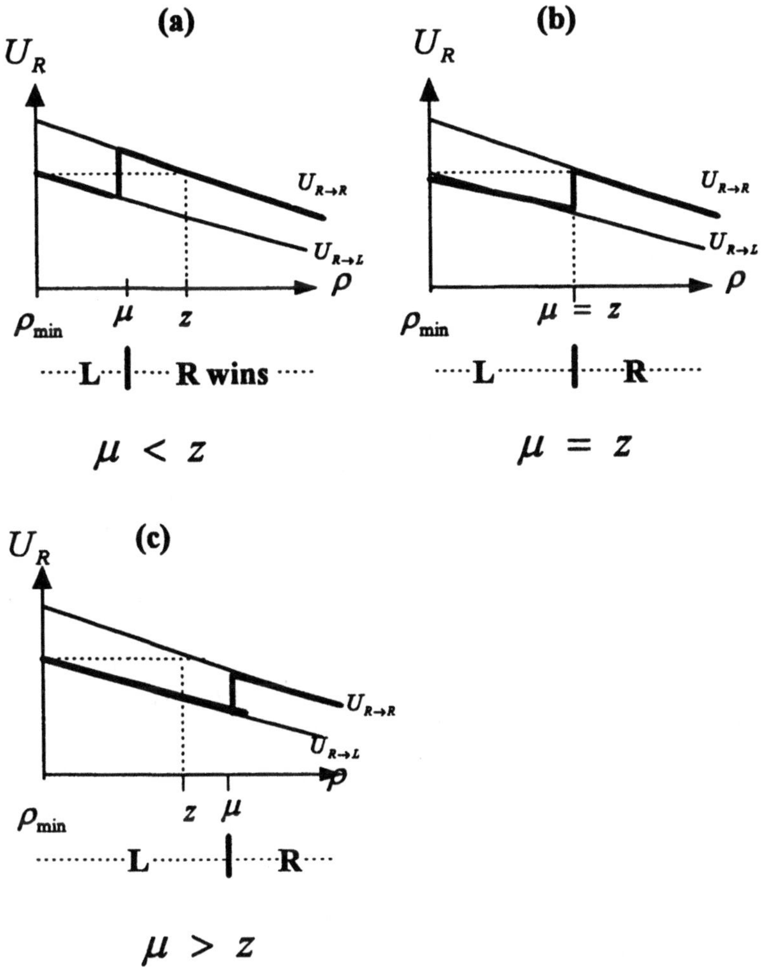

Fig. 6.4. The Global Long Run Utility Function of the R-Party in a Type B Economy

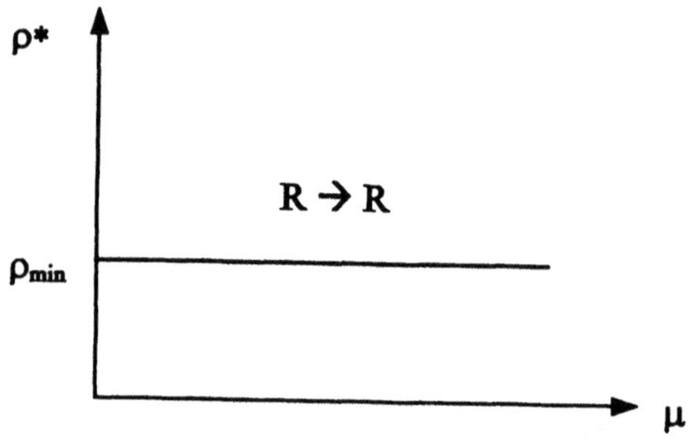

Fig. 6.5. The Optimal Fiscal Policy (ρ^*) of an R-Government in a Type A Economy as a Function of Society's Conservativeness (μ)

6.4.2 Type *B* Economy

In a type B economy the choice of fiscal policy for the R-government is a bit more difficult. If R choses $\rho^* = \rho^{min} = 1/\delta$, which it would like to do were there no elections, R will lose the elections. We will now derive the optimal policy choice for different degrees of society's conservativeness and we will show how it depends on the position of μ whether R chooses to remain in power or not. Let us first define an interest level $\rho = z$ for which the two relevant branches of the global utility function have the same maximum as demonstrated in figure 6.4(b). For $\mu < z$, as in figure 6.4(a), the maximum is reached on the upper branch ($R \rightarrow R$) at μ while for $\mu > z$, as in figure 6.4(c), the global maximum is reached on the lower branch ($R \rightarrow L$) at ρ^{min}.

Figure 6.6 depicts the optimal ρ, (ρ^*), for each level of society's conservativeness μ[3]. For a type B economy, a higher μ represents a more liberal population. So we use $(-\mu)$ as a measure of society's conservativeness as in figure 6.6. In very liberal societies ($\mu > z$ or $-\mu < -z$) the R-party sets $\rho^* = \rho^{min}$ and gives up power. In intermediate societies ($\rho^{min} < \mu < z$) R fights in order to stay in power. It deviates from the policy it would have chosen if its staying in power was guaranteed (ρ^{min}), sets $\rho^* = \mu$ and wins the elections by a slight margin. In conservative societies ($\mu < \rho^{min}$) however, it can win the elections by choosing its globally optimal action ($\rho^* = \rho^{min}$)[4].

Note that the party's optimal policy is not continuous in the society's conservativeness. As the society becomes more conservative, beyond z, the

[3] In order to change μ we have changed K and N. This in turn shifts the two utility functions of figure 6.4 by a constant (see footnote 4). Subtracting that constant leaves the maximum ρ of the two functions unchanged. As a result we may vary μ without changing the two functions.

[4] Note that the value of μ need not be in the feasible range of the interest rate.

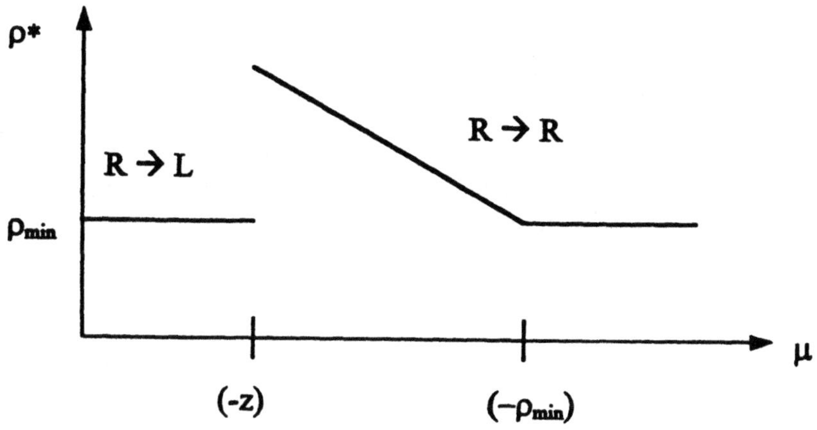

Fig. 6.6. The Optimal Fiscal Policy (ρ^*) of an R-Government in a Type B Economy as a Function of Society's Conservativeness (μ)

right-wing party suddenly raises the interest rate drastically and will win the elections. This discontinuity is inherent to this type of problems. The discontinuity in figure 6.6 is not due to the discontinuity of the global utility function (thick lines in figure 6.4) but rather due to the fact that it is not single peaked. The discontinuity in the latter can be smoothed out by introducing uncertainty of the elections' outcome (see section 6.6). This however, will not remove the discontinuity of figure 6.6.

We have derived the results irrespective of the beliefs. This again shows why it is convenient to solve the model in terms of ρ. But the crucial variable the government decides on is the level of public goods y_1 (see section 5.2.5). Here the beliefs come in: In order to achieve a certain ρ, the corresponding y_1 that generates this ρ, depends on the beliefs.

With our assumptions, in particular that $\tilde{m}_L \sim \tilde{K} \sim \tilde{m}_R$, we get that $\tilde{y}_1$ decreases with α_B for any given ρ (see appendix A.16). Hence, in order to achieve a certain ρ^*, the R-party sets the level of public goods at a higher level when the electorate believes that the left-wing party will take over than when the electorate believes that R remains in power. The intuitive explanation is that when people expect the L-party to win they expect a higher tax rate in the second period and for the same level of ρ they will choose to save more (to have more private income tomorrow, savings are not taxed). This will give the first government more money to spend on the public good (all this is under the assumption that τ_1 is fixed).

For a Rational Expectations equilibrium beliefs should be that R wins in a type A economy and in conserative and intermediate type B economies, while in a very liberal (left-wing) type B economy Rational Expectations beliefs are that L wins.

6.5 The Optimal Fiscal Policy of an L-Government

In order to find the optimal fiscal policy for a left-wing party in power in the first period we solve equation (6.6) for the two possible cases, L remains in power or R takes over ($P = L, T = L$ or R and $B = L$ or R). Again, we find that - irrespective of the beliefs - in the relevant range ($\rho^{min} \leq \rho \leq \rho^{max}$) the long run utility function is a decreasing function of ρ[5]:

$$\frac{\partial U_{L\to L}}{\partial \rho} < 0 \qquad \text{and} \qquad \frac{\partial U_{L\to R}}{\partial \rho} < 0$$

(see appendix A.15); and since the voter represented by the L-party is always at least as well off when L remains in power than when R takes over, $\forall \rho \;\; U_{L\to L} \geq U_{L\to R}$ (see figure 6.7).

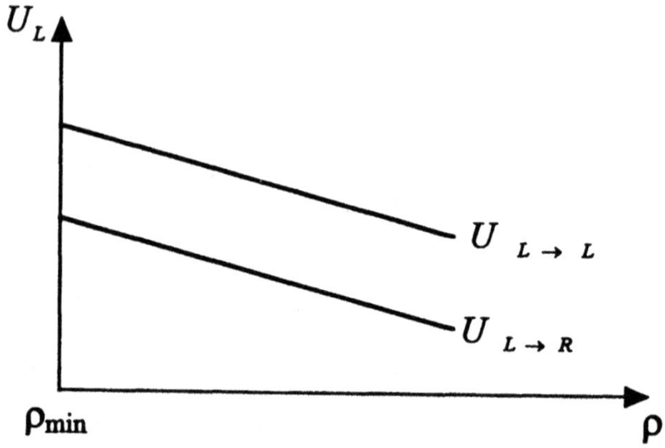

Fig. 6.7. The Long Run Utility Function of an L-Government

We now derive the optimal policy choices for the two types of economies. Recall that in type A economies the L-party wins for $\rho > \mu$, whereas in type B economies it wins for $\rho < \mu$. This gives the global long run utility function for the two types of economies as in figures 6.8 and 6.9.

6.5.1 Type A Economy

If the left-wing party did not have to worry about being re-relected, it would want to set ρ^* at ρ^{min}, thus reaching the maximum possible utility level of its representative voter. But this would lead to a victory of the opposition party.

[5] As we show in the appendix A.15, we here make use again of the assumption that α_L is not too close to 0, see footnote 7. In fact in order to get decreasing long run utility functions for the L-government we need that $\alpha_L \delta \rho > 1$.

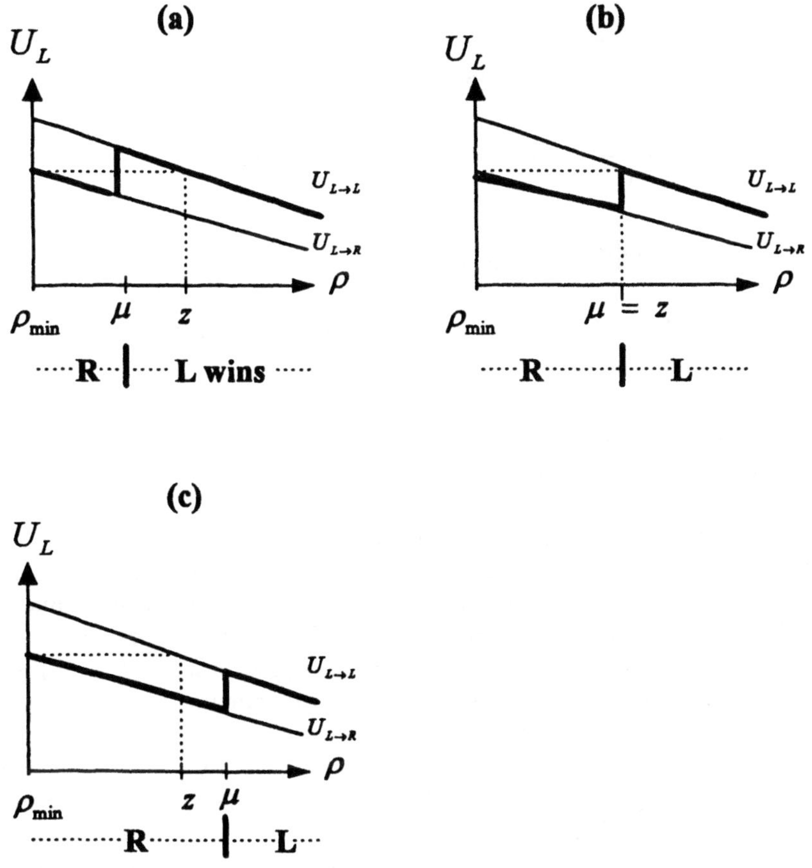

Fig. 6.8. The Global Long Run Utility Function of the L-Party in a Type A Economy

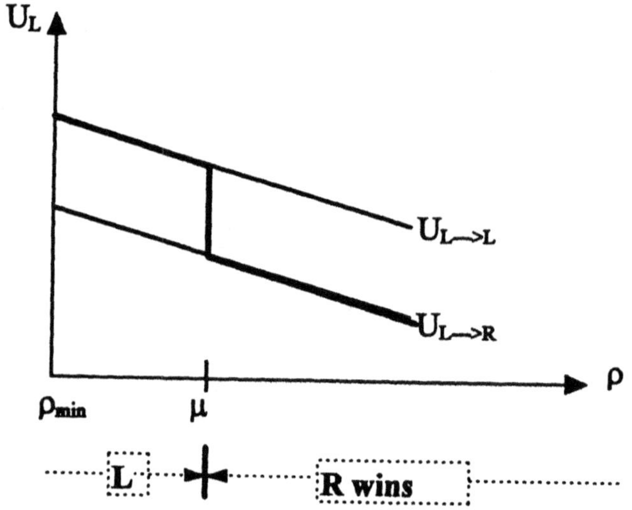

Fig. 6.9. The Global Long Run Utility Function of the *L*-Party in a Type *B* Economy

Similar to an *R*-government in a type *B* economy, the *L*-party's optimal fiscal policy depends on the economy'spolitical attitude.

We will now derive the optimal policy choice for different levels of society'sconservativeness and we will show how it depends on the position of μ whether L chooses to remain in power or not. Again we define an interest level $\rho = z$ for which the two relevant branches of the global utility function have the same maximum as demonstrated in figure 6.8(b). For $\mu < z$, as in figure 6.8(a), the maximum is reached on the upper branch $(L \rightarrow L)$ at μ while for $\mu > z$, as in figure 6.8(c), the global maximum is reached on the lower branch $(L \rightarrow R)$ at ρ^{min}.

Figure 6.10 depicts the optimal ρ, (ρ^*), for each level of society's conservativeness (μ). In a type A economy, a higher μ represents a more conservative population. In very liberal societies $(\mu < \rho^{min})$ the L-party can set its first best, $\rho^* = \rho^{min}$, and stays in power. In intermediate societies $(\rho^{min} < \mu < z)$ L fights in order to stay in power. It deviates from the policy it would have chosen if its staying in power was guaranteed (ρ^{min}), sets $\rho^* = \mu$ and wins the elections by a slight margin. In conservative societies $(\mu > z)$ however, deviating from its first best action and staying in power would be worse for L's representative voter than if L gave up power. So L sets $\rho^* = \rho^{min}$ and loses the elections.

Again the party's optimal policy is not continuous in the society's degree of conservatism. As the society becomes more conservative, beyond z, the left-wing party suddenly lowers the interest rate drastically and loses the elections. As the society reaches a certain degree of conservatism, deviating

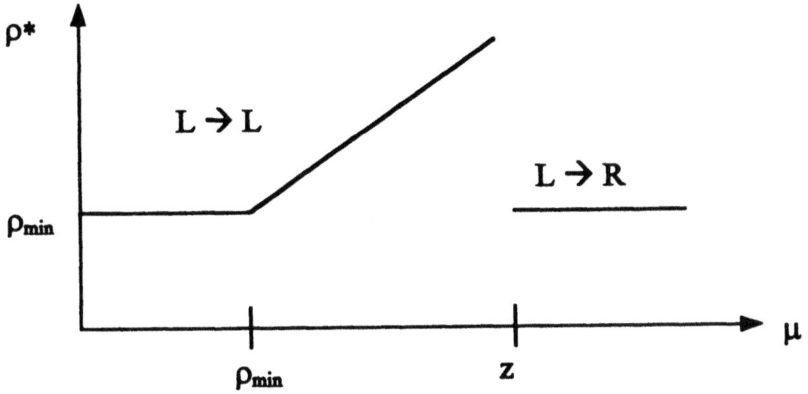

Fig. 6.10. The Optimal Fiscal Policy (ρ^*) of an L-Government in a Type A Economy as a Function of Society's Conservativeness (μ)

from the optimal policy just to stay in power becomes too costly in utility terms.

In order to report the results in terms of y_1 we have to take the beliefs into account. As before, in order to achieve a certain ρ^*, the L-party sets the level of public goods at a higher level when the electorate believes that the left-wing party will win than when the electorate believes that R wins. For the intuition see section 6.4.2.

6.5.2 Type B Economy

In a type B economy it is obvious to see that the global optimum is at $\rho^* = \rho^{min} = 1/\delta$. This optimal policy can be pursued by the L-party whatever the position of μ, i.e. whatever the society's political attitude . This is demonstrated in figure 6.11. In a type B economy L will always choose $\rho^* = \rho^{min}$ and will stay in power.

For a Rational Expectations equilibrium beliefs should be that L wins in a type B economy and in very liberal and intermediate type A economies, while in a conservative type B economy Rational Expectations beliefs are that R wins.

6.6 Uncertainty

So far we assumed the electoral outcome to be known for any ρ. What if we now introduced uncertainty about the elections' outcome? We will show that

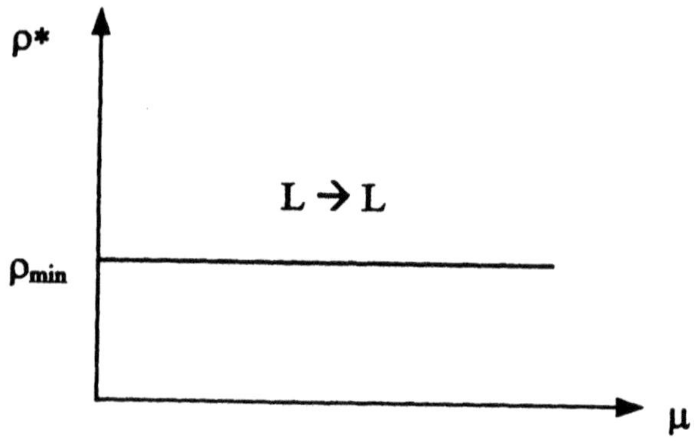

Fig. 6.11. The Optimal Fiscal Policy (ρ^*) of an L-Government in a Type B Economy as a Function of Society's Conservativeness (μ)

the qualitative results, in particular the discontinuity in politics as a function of μ will not be affected.

What do we mean by "uncertainty"? Let us assume that a certain percentage of the population vote at random. In every society there are voters that have a very strong affiliation to a certain party and vote for that same party in every election. But there are also voters who feel more or less equally well off under either party and who thus vote more or less randomly (the so called *Wechselwähler* (floating votes)). These voters will most certainly not affect the electoral outcome for extreme policy measures, i.e. for policy measures ρ which are distinctively different from μ, see figure 6.12. It makes intuitively sense that a society does not have a problem to decide whether it wants an extreme policy or not. In the cases of figure 6.12 the choices ρ_1 and ρ_2 will guarantee a secure victory for the L- and R-party respectively. But what if the incumbent P chooses a ρ close to μ? Let us take the extreme case where P sets $\rho = \mu$.

Let us assume that a proportion c of the population vote randomly. Then, at $\rho = \mu$, a proportion $(1-c)$ are distributed such that half of them are located on each side of the indifferent comsumer curve which in this case coincides with the μ-curve. The electoral outcome and consequently the global long run utility function hinges on the electoral decisions of the floating votes. At $\rho = \mu$, and also for values close to μ, the incumbent will have to take the expected utility, i.e. a weighted average of the utilities if it wins ($U_{P \to P}$) and if it loses ($U_{P \to Q}$),

$$U_P = \pi U_{P \to P} + (1 - \pi) U_{P \to Q}$$

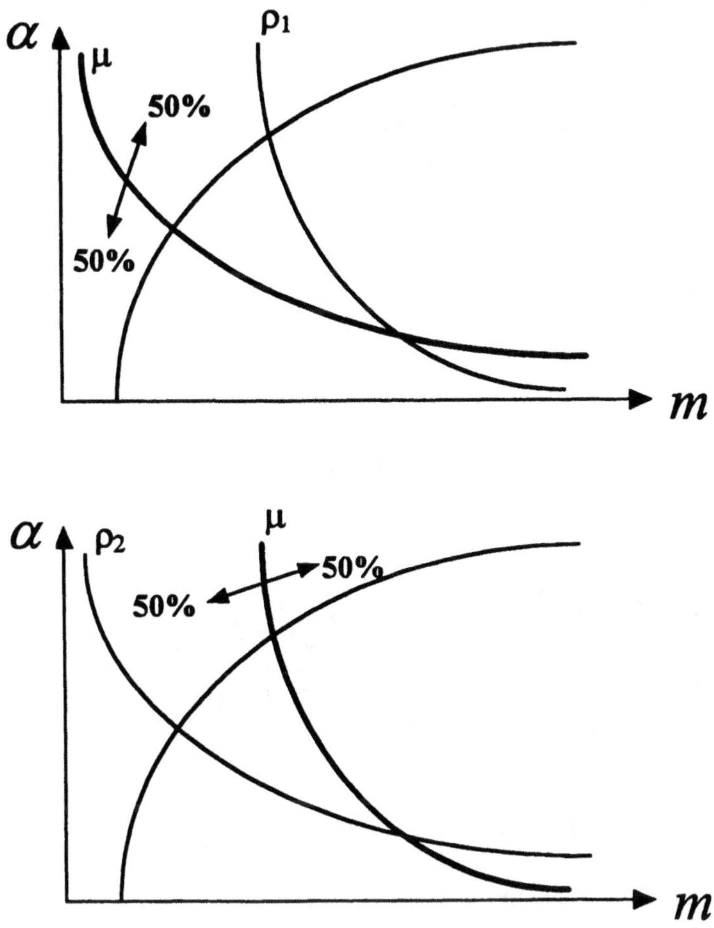

Fig. 6.12. Extreme Policy Choices

where π denotes the probability that P wins the elections (this probability π may depend on the first government's actions). We thus smooth out the long run utility function the P-party maximizes, see figure 6.13.

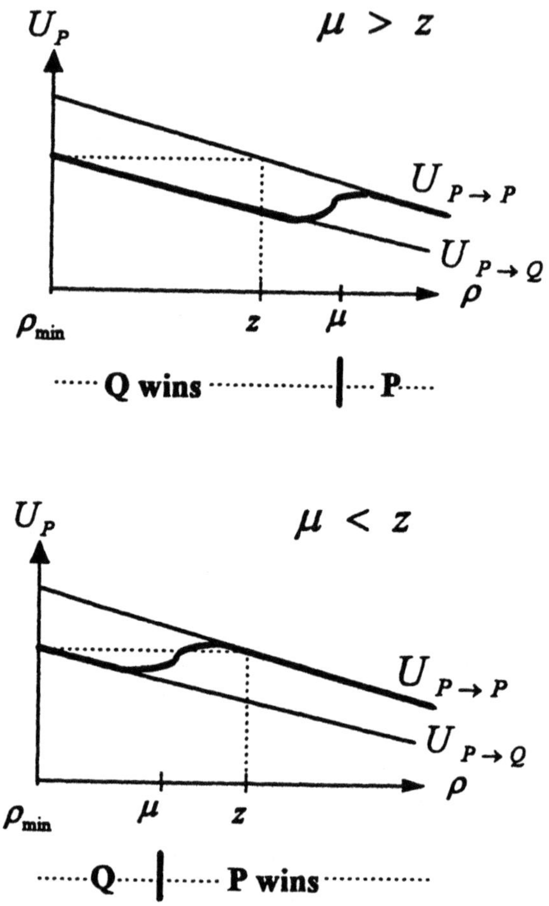

Fig. 6.13. P's Long Run Utility When There is Uncertainty

When we now derive the optimal policy of P as a function of μ it becomes obvious that the discontinuity result is not affected, see figure 6.14. Discontinuity in politics as a function of μ is inherent to this type of problem even if we introduce uncertainty. What is affected though is the (quantitative) choice of ρ^*. For intermediate levels of μ the incumbent does not set $\rho = \mu$ and wins with just $(50 + \epsilon)\%$, but to be on the safe side, he starts fighting earlier and fights longer.

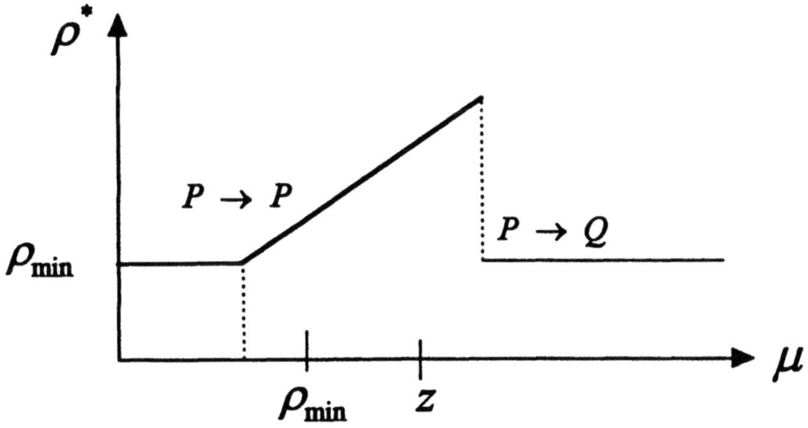

Fig. 6.14. Optimal Fiscal Policy When There is Uncertainty

7. Conclusions

The Model and its Novelties. We have presented a two-period model of political economy in which the government in power in the first period levies taxes and sells bonds to produce a public good. The government in the second period levies taxes to repay the debt to the individual savers and produce some public good. Between the periods consumers are asked to vote the party that will reign in the second period.

Similar models appear in the literature. However, we have eliminated some of the shortcomings of these models. Although the literature claims to present election manipulation very few models of the literature actually do so. Our model is a fully blown model of internal debt and election manipulation. In all of the existing models at least one of these factors is missing.

In our model, unlike in most papers in the literature, voters' election decisions are affected by the government's actions. The policy programs of the second period are influenced by the 'economic inheritance' from the previous period. Voters switch their vote from one party to another when the debt left by the first period government changes. Thus, the first period government may strategically choose tax and public borrowing levels in such a way so as to influence the outcome of the elections. Thus, we have captured an essential hypothesis about the behaviour of politicians in modern democracies, namely that politicians use their political power to make voters vote for them. However, we do not believe that politicians are driven only by the power motive. We assume parties to represent a certain well-defined clientele. The political decision-maker may thus be in conflict of doing the best for his representative voter and staying in power at the same time. Sometimes the policy-maker does not have to compromise because he can pursue the first best policy, which is also best for his constituency, without having to fear a loss in the elections. At other times, pursuing the first best policy will guarantee a sure loss in the elections. Then, the policy-maker has to decide whether it is in the best interest of his voter to deviate from this policy and to stay in power or if this compromise is too costly.

The other novelty of this thesis is the two-dimensionality of the voters' distribution. Consumers vary in two attributes: income and preference over public goods. This captures much better than one-dimensional models the political heterogeneity of a population: for example two voters with the same identical income may nevertheless have opposite ideas concerning the activity of the state. With this we go well beyond the existing literature. An extension like this requires a way of analysis different from the median voter analysis and we consider it one of the major contributions of this thesis that we were able to overcome the median voter analysis. In a two-dimensional distribution there is no single fixed voter who divides the population in half and thus decides on the electoral outcome. In such a set-up the elections outcome is determined by a group of voters. This group is not fixed but changes with the policy programs offered by the parties running in the elections. Another nice and realistic feature introduced in the model is that in contrast to the median voter model the consequences of a change in the fiscal variables are ambiguous. When a government changes its debt policy say, it gains some votes and at the same time loses some. There are very rarely policy measures a whole society approves of (or disapproves of).

Since the model has internal debt, problems of information and beliefs are raised. Consumers need to believe something about the future in order to take their current savings decisions. Part of their beliefs is their expectation about who is going to be in power next period. Knowing these beliefs the government of the first period may choose to behave in such a way that will cause these beliefs to be false. We have pointed out the cases for which a *Rational Expectations* equilibrium exists, i.e. the expectations are self-fulfilling.

The Main Results. Our model shows that the results depend crucially on the voters' distribution and their beliefs. We investigated the optimal fiscal policy of a government in two types of populations, in each we changed the society's political couleur (degree of conservativeness) and traced the changes in the government's optimal decision. We found that only in intermediate societies (societies that are balanced in the sense that they are not skewed in the direction of either the left- or the right-wing party's representative consumer) will a government have to use debt strategically. This result is in contrast to the models by Persson/Svensson [1989] and Alesina/Tabellini [1990a, b]. There, fiscal imbalances are larger the larger the degree of political polarization between the parties, but only if there is a change of government with certainty or high probability. When a government expects with a high probability to stay in power it does not burden itself with a high debt in the future. In that case it exhibits sound fiscal behaviour. From this it becomes obvious that results hinge crucially on the exogeneity of the elections' outcome function. If - as in our model - the incumbent government can exhibit (some) influence on the voting process, then it finds that especially in intermediate (or balanced and thus undecided) societies it is worth fighting. In a very conservative society a right-wing party will win effortlessly whereas in a very liberal society it may decide to give up power. In both cases it will not take extra debt to influence the elections. It is only in intermediate cases that it will attempt to influence the elections and debt will rise. Thus, we can explain debt in situations where a party stays in power: Because reelection is not guaranteed, the government uses its fiscal instruments in order to gain as many votes as necessary to stay in power.

Another fundamental result is that the same party may end up taking opposite measures if the population is different. This is in contrast to most models in which consumers differ in one parameter only and in which the voters' distribution affects only the magnitude but not the direction of fiscal measures taken by a given party. Last but not least, our model can explain how any regime may under certain circumstances take on a high debt.

To sum up, we have shown that the one-dimensionality assumption which is common to all the models in the literature is restricting and limiting. However, one may argue that the introduction of voters with two attributes has made the model vague. The results may go in either direction: A government may wish to increase or decrease its public debt not only as a function of its representative consumer (whether the party represents rich or poor voters), but also as a function of the global configuration of voters in the population. We would like to argue that this property is an advantage rather than a disadvantage of this model; it makes the model not only more interesting but also more realistic. We believe that the aim of research in Political Economy is to investigate what influences the economic policies of governments who may have considerations of power mixed with economic interests. The world in which such arguments are legitimate is unlikely to be so simple that a party will always choose, say, to lower debt just because it represents the rich.

Future Research. Our model has identified a number of parameters that affect fiscal policy, namely the voters' political preferences and their beliefs about the future. Our model has shown that it is possible to (analytically) find out the optimal decision taken by the government. We believe that in order to incorporate politics into theoretical and applied economics, better tools should be developed to measure the political distribution of the voters and their beliefs. Then, it will be possible, analytically or more likely with the help of computers, to simulate fiscal decisions in more realistic situations and test the premises of the models. In order to better approximate the political environment one should develop better models of how the agents (voters and parties) take their decision. It is clear that they are not fully rational in the sense of foreseeing all the consequences of an action they take, they do not consider the distant future nor do they have a clear picture of what that future may look like. However, on the other hand, voters are not totally irrational or 'fiscally illuded'. A model of "boundedly rational" behaviour is needed to understand the effects of the political institutions of the decision-making process in a model with more than two periods or more than two parties where coalitions between parties may form.

In the framework of our model it would be interesting to analyze how the results would be affected if one allowed consumers to vary in their beliefs. For this one needs to know how beliefs are distributed among the income levels. In order to estimate this distribution one would have to integrate political and sociological studies. Interesting questions that arise are for example: Which role does the political future play in the economic decisions of individuals? How do consumers form expectations concerning the future governments? Can these expectations or beliefs be influenced, for example by opinion polls published close to elections' time, and if so, how? Can one develop a good theory for endogenizing beliefs?

Policy Implications. One of the ultimate goals of theoretical economic research is to get a better understanding of the economic processes and to derive the adequate policy recommendations. How then does our model contribute to explaining the real world phenomena as the ones we mentioned in section 2? As our model shows, fiscal imbalances are larger the harder a government has to fight in order to stay in power, which is the case in "intermediate", i.e. more politically balanced, societies. This suggests that the debt has increased in many OECD economies since 1973 (phenomenon 1) because the societies have become more homogeneous. This, one would have to test. Our model provides the analytical tools as well as a suggestion for a measure of the political attitude of a society.

According to our model, the phenomenon that the otherwise similar OECD economies vary in their economic performance can be explained by differences in the populations' distributions and in their political attitude. This implies that a society's specific "character" requires its corresponding politics. We believe that the main contribution of our work to explaining these phenomena is that it provides a basis for a testable framework for analysis and it suggests a measure for determining the "character" (or the political attitude) of a society.

The literature on political economy has shown that debt increases with the degree of political polarization and the less likely it is that a government gets reelected, the less altruism there is (and thus the less the future generation's wishes are taken care of in today's elections), the more decentralized the political decision-making process is and the weaker governments are. Our model has also shown (in agreement with some of the literature, but in greater detail and precision) that debt is influenced by the distribution of the political inclinations of the populations. In particular, we have shown that debt increases when it is more difficult for the ruling party to remain in power, i.e. when the political balance of the population is not decidedly in favour of the ruling party.

These results may be seen to point to an unexpected cost of the democratic process. A sophisticated government, while using fiscal instruments to maximize the long term welfare of its constituents may in the process tilt the elections in its favour. While this is perfectly legal and democratic it may lead to efficiency loss. Under those circumstances it may be better for the population as a whole to have a lower debt.

This raises the question of whether this efficiency loss due to democracy may not be avoided in some way. Such inefficiencies, if they exist, can be remedied by a benevolent planner which replaces the government and the elections. As history has shown, such benevolent planners are hard to come by and once in power are not likely to remain benevolent for long. Any changes and restriction of the democratic process should be carefully and seriously discussed. Could one perhaps go in the direction of a benevolent, independent decision-maker without harming democracy? What one may consider in this case is the possibility of restricting the power of the democratically elected government by introducing a balanced budget rule, a measure widely discussed in the literature[1], or by installing a professional body independent of political pressures which would be in charge of approving any budget before it gets realized[2]. It is telling that the newly elected government in the long established democracy of the UK has gone in this direction. It is particularly interesting that it was the British labour party which is reputed to be less laissez-faire and more in favour of centralized government than the former Tory governments that has taken this crucial step and gave independence to the central bank.

This suggests that some democracies have decided that between the two evils, restricting the government and the cost of not restricting it, the former is the lesser evil. This is, of course, a grave question which should be left for each democracy to answer for itself. Our model cannot give an answer to it. Our model has not even measured the possible inefficiencies from the democratic process. This requires other techniques and should be left for future research. Our model has, however, been able to point out that this phenomenon exists and to describe the machinations that lead to it.

---

[1] See for example Bach [1993] or Palley [1997]

[2] For a discussion see Alesina/Perotti [1995], p.24-26.

A. Appendix

A.1 General Government Net Debt-to-GDP Ratios, 1960-1990

See table A.1.

A.2 From Equation (5.6) to Equation (5.7)

The long run utility of consumer (α, m) is given by equation (5.6):

$$\alpha \log\Big(m-(m-a)\tau_1 - s(m)\Big) + (1-\alpha)\log\Big((K-aN)\tau_1 + S\Big)$$
$$+\delta\Big[\alpha \log\Big(m-(m-a)\tau_2(B) + \rho s(m)\Big)$$
$$+(1-\alpha)\log\Big((K-aN)\tau_2(B) - \rho S\Big)\Big]$$

Multiply the logs in equation (5.6) by 1 (here $(m-a)/(m-a)$ and $(K-aN)/(K-aN)$ respectively) to obtain

$$\alpha \log(m-a)\Big(\frac{m}{m-a} - \tau_1 - \frac{s(m)}{m-a}\Big)$$
$$+(1-\alpha)\log(K-aN)\Big(\tau_1 + \frac{S}{K-aN}\Big)$$
$$+\delta\Big[\alpha\log(m-a)\Big(\frac{m}{m-a} - \tau_2(B) + \frac{\rho s(m)}{m-a}\Big)$$
$$+(1-\alpha)\log(K-aN)\Big(\tau_2(B) - \frac{\rho S}{K-aN}\Big)\Big]$$

Rearranging and using the variables $\tilde{m}, \tilde{s}(m), \tilde{S}$ and $\tilde{K}$ gives

$$\alpha\log(m-a) + \alpha\log\Big(\tilde{m} - \tau_1 - \tilde{s}(m)\Big)$$
$$+(1-\alpha)\log(K-aN) + (1-\alpha)\log(\tau_1 + \tilde{S})$$

Table A.1. General Government Net Debt-to-GDP Ratios, 1960-1996

Year	US	Germany	Italy	Belgium	UK	France
1960	45.0	-13.2	na	82.3	123.2	29.1
1961	44.7	-15.4	na	80.0	120.9	25.8
1962	42.5	-15.5	na	76.8	116.1	22.2
1963	40.4	-13.3	na	74.5	109.2	19.9
1964	38.3	-14.8	23.2	68.9	102.6	18.0
1965	35.3	-12.8	26.2	66.6	96.7	16.1
1966	32.5	-11.9	29.7	65.1	92.5	15.0
1967	32.4	-10.1	29.6	63.3	92.4	14.6
1968	30.7	-8.8	32.0	62.2	86.8	14.8
1969	28.3	-8.9	31.9	59.2	82.1	13.4
1970	27.8	-8.1	34.0	55.5	74.8	11.4
1971	27.9	-7.1	38.1	54.6	70.1	11.1
1972	25.8	-5.7	43.3	52.6	65.3	9.1
1973	23.0	-6.7	45.1	50.9	57.9	8.3
1974	22.2	-4.7	42.7	47.5	54.9	8.7
1975	24.6	1.0	51.9	49.8	57.2	11.1
1976	24.4	4.6	52.7	50.1	56.0	10.9
1977	23.3	7.0	52.7	53.7	55.7	10.2
1978	21.3	9.4	55.3	57.5	53.4	10.2
1979	19.8	11.5	55.3	61.7	48.7	9.7
1980	21.8	11.8	53.0	69.6	36.2	9.1
1981	21.6	15.0	56.4	84.3	37.8	9.9
1982	25.4	17.8	62.6	94.2	37.3	11.3
1983	28.7	19.5	67.4	105.2	37.5	13.4
1984	29.8	20.4	73.0	109.6	30.0[a]	15.2
1985	32.2	20.8	80.0	112.6	30.6	16.8
1986	35.2	21.2	84.3	116.5	31.0	18.2
1987	37.0	22.4	88.5	120.6	29.3	13.0
1988	38.0	23.4	90.9	121.0	23.7	14.2
1989	38.3	22.0	93.9	118.6	19.1	14.8
1990	39.7	20.6	84.4[a]	118.2	18.8	16.3
1991	43.1	22.1	89.4	119.4	19.2	16.5
1992	46.7	26.5	95.7	121.3	26.0	18.6
1993	48.8	35.0	103.7	127.4	35.7	26.9
1994	49.6	39.6	109.1	126.7	35.6	29.3
1995	50.4	44.1	107.5	127.7	42.0	35.3
1996 (est.)	50.0	47.2	108.4	127.2	44.9	38.3

Source: For the period 1960-1979 see Roubini/Sachs [1989b], p.914/915; for the period 1980-1996 see OECD Economic Outlook [1996], p.A38; a) Break in the series starting this year

$$+\delta\alpha\log(m-a)+\delta\alpha\log\left(\tilde{m}-\tau_2(B)+\rho\tilde{s}(m)\right)$$
$$+\delta(1-\alpha)\log(K-aN)+\delta(1-\alpha\log)\left(\tau_2(B)-\rho\tilde{S}\right)$$

Drop all the constants, namely $\log(m-a)$ and $\log(K-aN)$, to obtain equation (5.7)

$$\begin{aligned} U &= \alpha\log\left(\tilde{m}-\tau_1-\tilde{s}(m)\right)+(1-\alpha)\log\left(\tau_1+\tilde{S}\right) \\ &+ \delta\left[\alpha\log\left(\tilde{m}-\tau_2(B)+\rho\tilde{s}(m)\right)+(1-\alpha)\log\left(\tau_2(B)-\rho\tilde{S}\right)\right] \end{aligned}$$

A.3 Total Savings or How to Get Equation(5.9)

The level of total savings in the economy can be obtained by summing (integrating) over all individual savings:

$$S=\int_0^N s(m)f(m)dm$$

Take equation (5.8)

$$\tilde{s}(m)=\frac{1}{\rho(1+\delta)}\left[\tau_2(B)-\delta\rho\tau_1+\tilde{m}(\delta\rho-1)\right]$$

Multiply by $(m-a)$ to get

$$s(m)=\frac{1}{\rho(1+\delta)}\left[\left(\tau_2(B)-\delta\rho\tau_1\right)(m-a)+m(\delta\rho-1)\right]$$

Keeping in mind that we defined by S the sum of all individual savings ($S=\int s(m)f(m)dm$), by K the total income in the economy ($K=\int mf(m)dm$) and by N the number of consumers in the economy, integrating over all consumers gives

$$S=\frac{1}{\rho(1+\delta)}\left[\left(\tau_2(B)-\delta\rho\tau_1\right)(K-aN)+K(\delta\rho-1)\right]$$

($\rho, \delta, \tau_2(B)$ and τ_1 are constants for the saver.)

Dividing by $(K-aN)$ gives equation (5.9).

$$\tilde{S}=\frac{1}{\rho(1+\delta)}\left[\tau_2(B)-\delta\rho\tau_1+\tilde{K}(\delta\rho-1)\right]$$

A.4 Proof: The Left-Wing Party Sets a Higher Tax Rate, $\tau_2(L) > \tau_2(R)$

We want to prove that for the same level of inherited debt the tax rate in the second period set by a left-wing government is higher than the one set by a right-wing government. Recall that the parties vary in two variables, in income m and in preferences for the private relative to public consumption, α. We present the proof in two steps as shown in figure A.1: We first show that for a given preference level α, as m decreases ($\tilde{m}$ increases), τ_2 goes up (arrow 1). Then we show that in income group m_L, as α decreases, τ_2 increases (arrow 2). Hence, $\tau_2(L) > \tau_2(R)$.

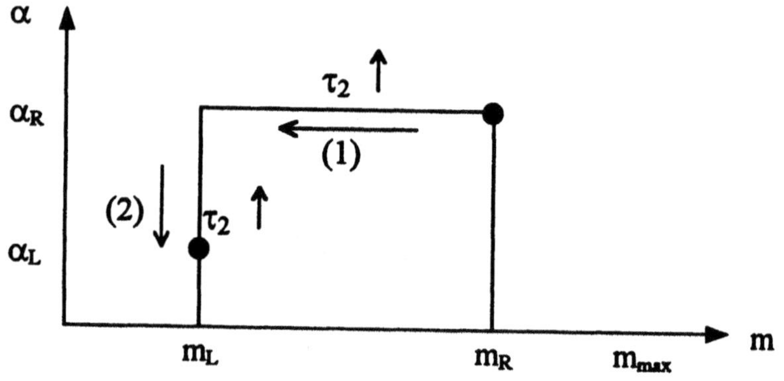

Fig. A.1. The Left-Wing Party Sets a Higher τ_2 than the Right-Wing Party

Let us first analyze how τ_2 (equation 5.12) varies with income holding α fixed.

$$\frac{\partial \tau_2}{\partial \tilde{m}} = (1-\alpha)\left(1+\rho\frac{\partial \tilde{s}(m)}{\partial \tilde{m}}\right)$$

Differentiating equation (5.8) with resepct to $\tilde{m}$ gives

$$\frac{\partial \tilde{s}(m)}{\partial \tilde{m}} = \frac{\delta\rho - 1}{\rho(1+\delta)}$$

Thus,

$$\frac{\partial \tau_2}{\partial \tilde{m}} = (1-\alpha)\left(1+\frac{\delta\rho-1}{1+\delta}\right) > 0$$

Recall that

$$\frac{\partial \tilde{m}}{\partial m} = -\frac{a}{(m-a)^2} < 0$$

That gives

$$\frac{\partial \tau_2}{\partial m} = \frac{\partial \tau_2}{\partial \tilde{m}}\frac{\partial \tilde{m}}{\partial m} = (1-\alpha)\left(1+\frac{\delta\rho - 1}{1+\delta}\right)\frac{-a}{(m-a)^2} < 0$$

As m increases $\tilde{m}$ falls and τ_2 falls, i.e. if the two parties have the same α the richer the voter a party represents the lower the tax rate it will set in the second period.

Let us now analyze how in income group m_L, τ_2 varies with α. Differentiating τ_2 with respect to α gives

$$\frac{\partial \tau_2}{\partial \alpha} = \rho\tilde{S} - \tilde{m} - \rho\tilde{s}(m)$$

From equations (5.8) and (5.9) it follows that

$$\rho\left(\tilde{s}(m) - \tilde{S}\right) = \frac{\delta\rho - 1}{(1+\delta)}(\tilde{m} - \tilde{K})$$

Resubstituting this gives

$$\begin{aligned}\frac{\partial \tau_2}{\partial \alpha} &= -\left[\tilde{m} + \tilde{\rho s}(m) - \rho\tilde{S}\right] = -\left[\tilde{m} + \frac{\delta\rho - 1}{(1+\delta)}(\tilde{m} - \tilde{K})\right] \\ &= -\frac{1}{1+\delta}\left[\tilde{m}\delta(1+\rho) - \tilde{K}(\delta\rho - 1)\right]\end{aligned}$$

We now analyze this expression for $\tilde{m} = \tilde{m}_L$:

$$-\frac{1}{1+\delta}\left[\tilde{m}_L\delta(1+\rho) - \tilde{K}(\delta\rho - 1)\right]$$

Since $\tilde{m}_L > \tilde{K}$[1] and the multiplier of $\tilde{m}_L$ is larger than the multiplier of $\tilde{K}$ ($\delta + \delta\rho > \delta\rho - 1$), the expression in brackets is positive and $\partial\tau_2/\partial\alpha < 0$, q.e.d.

---

[1] Note that for $\tilde{m}$ to be larger than $\tilde{K}$, m has to be smaller than K/N:

$$\begin{aligned}\tilde{m} &> \tilde{K} \\ \frac{m}{m-a} &> \frac{K}{K-aN} \\ mK - maN &> mK - aK \\ m &< \frac{K}{N}\end{aligned}$$

A.5 The Variables Relevant for the Model's Political Dimension

The variables relevant for the voting decision are the levels of private and public consumption, $\tilde{x}_1(m), \tilde{x}_2(m,P), \tilde{y}_1, \tilde{y}_2(P)$ and the interest rate ρ. We now solve the model in these variables. The long run utility function to be maximized given beliefs is

$$\alpha \log\left(\tilde{m} - \tau_1 - \tilde{s}(m)\right) + (1-\alpha)\log\left(\tau_1 + \tilde{S}\right) +$$
$$\delta\left[\alpha \log\left(\tilde{m} - \tau_2(B) + \rho\tilde{s}(m)\right) + (1-\alpha)\log\left(\tau_2(B) - \rho\tilde{S}\right)\right]$$

A.5.1 Optimal Individual Savings

The individual (α, m) chooses $\tilde{s}(m)$ in order to maximize the above utility function. The first order condition is given by

$$\frac{-\alpha}{\tilde{m} - \tau_1 - \tilde{s}(m)} + \frac{\delta\rho\alpha}{\tilde{m} - \tau_2(B) + \rho\tilde{s}(m)} = 0$$

The consumer chooses his optimal savings level by equating the marginal utilities of an extra unit of private income in the two periods. Rearranging gives

$$\tilde{m} - \tau_2(B) + \rho\tilde{s}(m) = \delta\rho\left(\tilde{m} - \tau_1 - \tilde{s}(m)\right) \tag{A.1}$$

Rewriting this in the above variables we get

$$\tilde{x}_2(m,B) = \delta\rho\tilde{x}_1(m)$$

A.5.2 Total Savings

The level of total savings can be derived from integrating over individual savings, given in equation (A.1). Summing gives

$$\begin{aligned} \tilde{K} - \tau_2(B) + \rho\tilde{S} &= \delta\rho(\tilde{K} - \tau_1 - \tilde{S}) \\ \text{or } \delta\rho(\tilde{S} + \tau_1) &= \tau_2(B) - \rho\tilde{S} + \tilde{K}(\delta\rho - 1) \end{aligned}$$

Rewriting this in the above variables gives

$$\delta\rho\tilde{y}_1 = \tilde{y}_2(B) + \tilde{K}(\delta\rho - 1)$$

A.5.3 The Optimal Tax Decision in the Second Period

A party P chooses $\tau_2(P)$ so as to maximize the second period utility of its representative voter (α_P, m_P):

$$V = \alpha_P \log\left(\tilde{m}_P - \tau_2(P) + \rho\tilde{s}(m_P)\right) + (1-\alpha_P)\log\left(\tau_2(P) - \rho\tilde{S}\right)$$

The first order condition is given by

$$\frac{-\alpha_P}{\tilde{m}_P - \tau_2(P) + \rho\tilde{s}(m_P)} + \frac{1-\alpha_P}{\tau_2(P) - \rho\tilde{S}} = 0$$

or

$$\alpha_P\left(\tau_2(P) - \rho\tilde{S}\right) = (1-\alpha_P)\left(\tilde{m}_P - \tau_2(P) + \rho\tilde{s}(m_P)\right)$$

Rewriting this in the above variables gives

$$\alpha_P\tilde{y}_2(P) = (1-\alpha_P)\tilde{x}_2(m_P, P)$$

A.5.4 An Additional Equation: The Consumers' Budget Constraint

The consumers' net income (after taxes) has to be sufficient to pay for private goods: From the point of view of the second period this requirement is given by

$$(1+\rho)\tilde{m} - \rho\tau_1 - \tau_2 = \rho\tilde{x}_1 + \tilde{x}_2$$

Adding 0, $(\rho\tilde{S} - \rho\tilde{S})$ and rearranging gives

$$\begin{aligned}(1+\rho)\tilde{m} &= \rho\tilde{x}_1 + \tilde{x}_2 + \rho\tau_1 + \tau_2 + \rho\tilde{S} - \rho\tilde{S}\\ &= \rho\tilde{x}_1 + \tilde{x}_2 + \rho(\tau_1 + \tilde{S}) + (\tau_2 - \rho\tilde{S})\end{aligned}$$

Rewriting this in the above variables gives

$$(1+\rho)\tilde{m} = \rho\tilde{x}_1 + \tilde{x}_2 + \tilde{y}_1 + \tilde{y}_2$$

We have thus identified four equations for the above five variables, which leaves us with one degree of freedom.

A.6 The Relationship Between $\tilde{y}_1$ and ρ

Taking the derivative of $\tilde{y}_1$ in equation (5.13) with respect to ρ gives

$$\frac{\partial\tilde{y}_1}{\partial\rho} = -\frac{(1-\alpha_B)\tilde{m}_B - \frac{\alpha_B+\delta}{\delta}\tilde{K}}{(1+\delta)\rho^2}$$

This is positive if

$$\frac{\alpha_B + \delta}{\delta}\tilde{K} > (1 - \alpha_B)\tilde{m}_B$$

$$\text{When } \alpha_B = 0 \qquad \tilde{K} > \tilde{m}_B$$

$$\text{When } \alpha_B = 1 \qquad \frac{1+\delta}{\delta}\tilde{K} > 0$$

Continuity ensures that as long as α_B is not too close to 0

$$\frac{\partial \tilde{y}_1}{\partial \rho} > 0$$

A.7 How to Get from Equation (5.14) to Equation (5.15)

Isolating all terms influenced by α in equation (5.14) on the LHS, denoting α by $\alpha^{ind}(m)$ and rearranging give

$$\alpha^{ind}(m)\Big[\log\left(\tilde{m} + \rho\tilde{s}(m) - \tau_2(L)\right) - \log\left(\tilde{m} + \rho\tilde{s}(m) - \tau_2(R)\right)$$

$$+\log\left(\tau_2(R) - \rho\tilde{S}\right) - \log\left(\tau_2(L) - \rho\tilde{S}\right)\Big]$$

$$= \log\left(\tau_2(R) - \rho\tilde{S}\right) - \log\left(\tau_2(L) - \rho\tilde{S}\right)$$

Using the fact that $\log a - \log b = \log(a/b)$ we obtain

$$\alpha^{ind}(m)\left[\log\frac{\tilde{m} + \rho\tilde{s}(m) - \tau_2(L)}{\tilde{m} + \rho\tilde{s}(m) - \tau_2(R)} + \log\frac{\tau_2(R) - \rho\tilde{S}}{\tau_2(L) - \rho\tilde{S}}\right] = \log\frac{\tau_2(R) - \rho\tilde{S}}{\tau_2(L) - \rho\tilde{S}}$$

Dividing by the multiplier of $\alpha^{ind}(m)$ gives equation (5.15)

$$\alpha^{ind}(m) = \frac{\log\frac{\tau_2(L)-\rho\tilde{S}}{\tau_2(R)-\rho\tilde{S}}}{\log\frac{\tau_2(L)-\rho\tilde{S}}{\tau_2(R)-\rho\tilde{S}} + \log\frac{\tilde{m}+\rho\tilde{s}(m)-\tau_2(R)}{\tilde{m}+\rho\tilde{s}(m)-\tau_2(L)}}$$

A.8 Proof: The Curve of Indifferent Consumers is Decreasing in m or How to Get Equation (5.16)

When differentiating $\alpha^{ind}(m)$ (equation (5.15)) with respect to m we notice that the logarithm in the numerator and the first logarithm in the denominator are both independent of m. Hence, it suffices to analyze the second logarithm in the denominator. It is obvious that

$$\frac{\tilde{m}+\rho\tilde{s}(m)-\tau_2(R)}{\tilde{m}+\rho\tilde{s}(m)-\tau_2(L)} > 1 \quad \text{since } \tau_2(R) < \tau_2(L)$$

Adding $(-\tau_2(L)+\tau_2(L)=0)$ to the numerator gives

$$\frac{\tilde{m}+\rho\tilde{s}(m)-\tau_2(L)+\tau_2(L)-\tau_2(R)}{\tilde{m}+\rho\tilde{s}(m)-\tau_2(L)} = 1+\frac{\tau_2(L)-\tau_2(R)}{\tilde{m}+\rho\tilde{s}(m)-\tau_2(L)}$$

Let us look at the fraction on the RHS of that equation. As m goes up, $\tilde{m}$ and hence $\tilde{s}(m)$ decrease, i.e. the whole fraction increases. Hence, the logarithm of that expression increases and the whole RHS of equation (5.15) becomes smaller. In order for (5.15) to be still fulfilled $\alpha^{ind}(m)$ has to decrease: As m increases the indifferent preference level decreases:

$$\frac{\partial\alpha^{ind}(m)}{\partial m} < 0$$

A.9 Proof: The Indifferent Consumers' Curve's Reaction to Changes in ρ

Expressions for later use

We first define some useful variables:

$$\begin{aligned}
A &= \frac{\tau_2(L)-\rho\tilde{S}}{\tau_2(R)-\rho\tilde{S}}\\
B &= \frac{\tilde{m}+\rho\tilde{s}(m)-\tau_2(R)}{\tilde{m}+\rho\tilde{s}(m)-\tau_2(L)}\\
C &= \tilde{m}+\rho\tilde{s}(m)-\tau_2(R)\\
D &= \tilde{m}+\rho\tilde{s}(m)-\tau_2(L)\\
E &= \tau_2(L)-\rho\tilde{S}\\
F &= \tau_2(R)-\rho\tilde{S}
\end{aligned}$$

Recall the following expressions:

$$\begin{aligned}
\tau_2(P) &= \alpha_P\rho\tilde{S}+(1-\alpha_P)\Big(\tilde{m}_P+\rho\tilde{s}(m_P)\Big)\\
\rho\tilde{s}(m)(1+\delta) &= \tau_2-\delta\rho\tau_1+\tilde{m}(\delta\rho-1)\\
\rho\tilde{S}(1+\delta) &= \tau_2-\delta\rho\tau_1+\tilde{K}(\delta\rho-1)\\
\rho\tilde{s}(m)-\rho\tilde{S} &= (\tilde{m}-\tilde{K})\frac{\delta\rho-1}{1+\delta}
\end{aligned}$$

Derivation of an expression for $(1-\alpha_P)/\big(\tau_2(P)-\rho\tilde{S}\big)$

$$\begin{aligned}\tau_2(P) - \rho\tilde{S} &= (1-\alpha_P)(\tilde{m}_P + \rho\tilde{s}(m_P) - \rho\tilde{S}) \\ &= (1-\alpha_P)\left(\tilde{m}_P + (\tilde{m}_P - \tilde{K})\frac{\delta\rho - 1}{1+\delta}\right)\end{aligned}$$

Rearranging then gives

$$\frac{1-\alpha_P}{\tau_2(P) - \rho\tilde{S}} = \frac{1+\delta}{\tilde{m}_P\delta(1+\rho) - \tilde{K}(\delta\rho - 1)} \tag{A.2}$$

Derivation of an expression for $E + D = C + F$

$$\begin{aligned}E + D &= \tau_2(L) - \rho\tilde{S} + \tilde{m} + \rho\tilde{s}(m) - \tau_2(L) \\ &= \tilde{m} + \rho\tilde{s}(m) - \rho\tilde{S} = C + F\end{aligned}$$

$$\tilde{m} + \rho\tilde{s}(m) - \rho\tilde{S} = \frac{1}{1+\delta}\left(\tilde{m}\delta(1+\rho) - \tilde{K}(\delta\rho - 1)\right) \tag{A.3}$$

Proof

In order to ease calculations we first rewrite equation (5.15) using the definitions from above

$$\alpha^{ind}(m) = \frac{\log\frac{\tau_2(L)-\rho\tilde{S}}{\tau_2(R)-\rho\tilde{S}}}{\log\frac{\tau_2(L)-\rho\tilde{S}}{\tau_2(R)-\rho\tilde{S}} + \log\frac{\tilde{m}+\rho\tilde{s}(m)-\tau_2(R)}{\tilde{m}+\rho\tilde{s}(m)-\tau_2(L)}} = \frac{\log A}{\log A + \log B}$$

Rearranging gives

$$\begin{aligned}\log A + \log B &= \frac{\log A}{\alpha^{ind}(m)} \\ 1 + \frac{\log B}{\log A} &= \frac{1}{\alpha^{ind}(m)} \\ \frac{\log B}{\log A} &= \frac{1}{\alpha^{ind}(m)} - 1\end{aligned}$$

Resubstituting the values for A and B gives equation (A.4)

$$\frac{1}{\alpha^{ind}(m)} - 1 = \frac{\log\frac{\tilde{m}+\tilde{s}(m)\rho-\tau_2(R)}{\tilde{m}+\tilde{s}(m)\rho-\tau_2(L)}}{\log\frac{\tau_2(L)-\tilde{S}\rho}{\tau_2(R)-\tilde{S}\rho}} = \frac{\log\frac{C}{D}}{\log\frac{E}{F}} \tag{A.4}$$

We now differentiate the indifferent consumer in income group m, $\alpha_{ind}(m)$, as in equation (A.4) with respect to ρ in order to show that the curve of indifferent voters increases on the left side and decreases on the right side when ρ increases (see figure 4.5). Differentiating the right hand side of (A.4) with respect to ρ, one finds that the derivative has the same sign as the numerator of the derivative (the denominator is positive in any case)

$$\log\frac{E}{F}\Big[\frac{\tilde{m}-\tilde{K}-(1-\alpha_R)(\tilde{m}_R-\tilde{K})}{C}-\frac{\tilde{m}-\tilde{K}-(1-\alpha_L)(\tilde{m}_L-\tilde{K})}{D}\Big]$$
$$-\log\frac{C}{D}\Big[\frac{(1-\alpha_L)(\tilde{m}_L-\tilde{K})}{E}-\frac{(1-\alpha_R)(\tilde{m}_R-\tilde{K})}{F}\Big] \quad (A.5)$$

So if (A.5) is positive, the derivative of the left hand side of equation (A.4) with respect to ρ is positive, i.e. $\alpha^{ind}(m)$ decreases with ρ, $\partial\alpha^{ind}(m)/\partial\rho < 0$. If (A.5) is negative, the reverse holds, $\partial\alpha^{ind}(m)/\partial\rho > 0$.

We now show that expression (A.5) is negative for m in the neighbourhood of m_L and positive for m in the neighbourhood of m_R. In fact we show more: (A.5) is negative for all $m \le m_L$ and positive for all $m \ge m_R$: In the left end the curve of indifferent consumers increases with ρ and in the right end it decreases with ρ (see figure 4.5).

Expression (A.5) is negative iff

$$\frac{\frac{\tilde{m}-\tilde{K}-(1-\alpha_R)(\tilde{m}_R-\tilde{K})}{C}-\frac{\tilde{m}-\tilde{K}-(1-\alpha_L)(\tilde{m}_L-\tilde{K})}{D}}{\frac{(1-\alpha_L)(\tilde{m}_L-\tilde{K})}{E}-\frac{(1-\alpha_R)(\tilde{m}_R-\tilde{K})}{F}} < \frac{\log\frac{C}{D}}{\log\frac{E}{F}} \quad (A.6)$$

The outline of the proof is simple: we estimate the right hand side (RHS) of equation (A.6) from above (by some smaller value) and show that this is still larger than the left hand side (LHS) of equation (A.6):

$$\text{LHS of (A.6)} \le \text{estimate of RHS of (A.6)} < \text{RHS of (A.6)}$$

From that it follows that (A.6) holds.

For the estimation we use the inequalities

$$x-1 > \log x > 1-\frac{1}{x} \quad (A.7)$$

In order to estimate the RHS of (A.6) from below we substitute the numerator of (A.6) by something smaller $(1-1/x)$ and the denominator by something larger $(x-1)$. The estimate (est) is

$$\text{est} = \frac{1-\frac{1}{x}}{x-1} = \frac{\frac{C-D}{C}}{\frac{E-F}{F}} = \frac{F}{C}$$

(Note that $C-D = E-F = \tau_2(L)-\tau_2(R)$.)

We now show that

$$\text{LHS of (A.6)} = \frac{\frac{\tilde{m}-\tilde{K}-(1-\alpha_R)(\tilde{m}_R-\tilde{K})}{C}-\frac{\tilde{m}-\tilde{K}-(1-\alpha_L)(\tilde{m}_L-\tilde{K})}{D}}{\frac{(1-\alpha_L)(\tilde{m}_L-\tilde{K})}{E}-\frac{(1-\alpha_R)(\tilde{m}_R-\tilde{K})}{F}} \le \frac{F}{C} = \text{est}$$

Multiplying by C/F gives

$$\frac{\tilde{m}-\tilde{K}-(1-\alpha_R)(\tilde{m}_R-\tilde{K})-\frac{C}{D}\left(\tilde{m}-\tilde{K}-(1-\alpha_L)(\tilde{m}_L-\tilde{K})\right)}{\frac{F}{E}(1-\alpha_L)(\tilde{m}_L-\tilde{K})-(1-\alpha_R)(\tilde{m}_R-\tilde{K})} \leq 1 \quad \text{(A.8)}$$

Since $\tilde{m}_L > \tilde{K} > \tilde{m}_R$, the denominator of this expression is positive. In order for (A.8) to hold, the numerator has to be less or equal to the denominator:

$$(1-\alpha_L)(\tilde{m}_L-\tilde{K})\left(\frac{C}{D}-\frac{F}{E}\right) \leq (\tilde{m}-\tilde{K})\left(\frac{C}{D}-1\right)$$

$$(1-\alpha_L)(\tilde{m}_L-\tilde{K})\left(\frac{C}{D}-\frac{D}{D}+\frac{E}{E}-\frac{F}{E}\right) \leq (\tilde{m}-\tilde{K})\frac{C-D}{D}$$

$$(1-\alpha_L)(\tilde{m}_L-\tilde{K})\left(\frac{C-D}{D}+\frac{E-F}{E}\right) \leq (\tilde{m}-\tilde{K})\frac{C-D}{D}$$

Multiplying by $D/(C-D)$ then gives

$$(1-\alpha_L)(\tilde{m}_L-\tilde{K})\left(1+\frac{D}{E}\right) \leq \tilde{m}-\tilde{K}$$

Dividing both sides by $E+D$ and rearranging gives

$$\frac{1-\alpha_L}{E}(\tilde{m}_L-\tilde{K}) \leq \frac{\tilde{m}-\tilde{K}}{E+D}$$

Substituting (A.2) for $(1-\alpha_L)/E$ on the LHS and (A.3) for $E+D$ on the RHS we get

$$\frac{\tilde{m}_L-\tilde{K}}{\tilde{m}_L\delta(1+\rho)-\tilde{K}(\delta\rho-1)} \leq \frac{\tilde{m}-\tilde{K}}{\tilde{m}\delta(1+\rho)-\tilde{K}(\delta\rho-1)} \quad \text{(A.9)}$$

At $\tilde{m}=\tilde{m}_L$ (A.9) holds in equality. As $\tilde{m}$ increases, i.e. m decreases, the RHS of (A.9) increases:

$$\frac{\partial \text{RHS of } (A.9)}{\partial \tilde{m}} = \frac{\tilde{m}\delta(1+\rho)-\tilde{K}(\delta\rho-1)-(\tilde{m}-\tilde{K})\delta(1+\rho)}{\left(\tilde{m}\delta(1+\rho)-\tilde{K}(\delta\rho-1)\right)^2} > 0 \quad \text{(A.10)}$$

So $\forall \tilde{m} > \tilde{m}_L$, or equivalently $\forall m < m_L$[2], expression (A.9) holds in inequality. We have thus shown, that

for all $m < m_L$	estimate of RHS of (A.6) > LHS of (A.6)
at $m = m_L$	estimate of RHS of (A.6) = LHS of (A.6)

[2] Recall that

$$\frac{\partial \tilde{m}}{\partial m} = -\frac{a}{(m-a)^2} < 0$$

Hence the LHS is strictly smaller than the RHS of (A.6) for all $m \leq m_L$. Continuity of all the functions in inequality (A.6) ensures that (A.6) holds as a strict inequality also for some interval to the right of m_L. This result is demonstrated in figure 4.5: As ρ increases the curve of indifferent consumers goes up in the low income group.

Along the same line of argument we now show that the curve of indifferent consumers goes down in the higher income group as ρ increases (see figure 4.5). If we can show that the derivative of (A.4) with respect to ρ is positive, i.e.

$$\frac{\partial\left(\frac{1}{\alpha^{ind}(m)} - 1\right)}{\partial \rho} > 0$$

we have proved that, in some income group m, as ρ increases the indifferent preference level $\alpha^{ind}(m)$ goes down. As we have shown above, the derivative of (A.4) with respect to ρ has the same sign as expression (A.5). So if (A.5) is positive, $\partial\alpha^{ind}(m)/\partial\rho < 0$, i.e. the curve of indifferent consumers shifts down in its right end.

Expression (A.5) is positive iff

$$\frac{\frac{\tilde{m}-\tilde{K}-(1-\alpha_R)(\tilde{m}_R-\tilde{K})}{C} - \frac{\tilde{m}-\tilde{K}-(1-\alpha_L)(\tilde{m}_L-\tilde{K})}{D}}{\frac{(1-\alpha_L)(\tilde{m}_L-\tilde{K})}{E} - \frac{(1-\alpha_R)(\tilde{m}_R-\tilde{K})}{F}} > \frac{\log\frac{C}{D}}{\log\frac{E}{F}} \tag{A.11}$$

In order to get rid of the logs, we now estimate the RHS of (A.11) from above and show that this estimate is still less or equal to the LHS of (A.11):

$$\text{LHS of (A.11)} \geq \text{estimate of RHS of (A.11)} > \text{RHS of (A.11)} \tag{A.12}$$

Again using (A.7), the estimate is given by

$$\frac{x-1}{1-\frac{1}{x}} = \frac{\frac{C}{D}-1}{1-\frac{F}{E}} = \frac{C-D}{D}\frac{E}{E-F} = \frac{E}{D}$$

We now show that this estimate is less or equal to the LHS of (A.11).

$$\frac{\frac{\tilde{m}-\tilde{K}-(1-\alpha_R)(\tilde{m}_R-\tilde{K})}{C} - \frac{\tilde{m}-\tilde{K}-(1-\alpha_L)(\tilde{m}_L-\tilde{K})}{D}}{\frac{(1-\alpha_L)(\tilde{m}_L-\tilde{K})}{E} - \frac{(1-\alpha_R)(\tilde{m}_R-\tilde{K})}{F}} \geq \frac{E}{D}$$

Multiplying by D/E and rearranging gives

$$(1-\alpha_R)(\tilde{m}_R-\tilde{K})(\frac{E}{F}-\frac{F}{F}+\frac{C}{C}-\frac{D}{C}) \geq (\tilde{m}-\tilde{K})(1-\frac{D}{C})$$

$$(1-\alpha_R)(\tilde{m}_R-\tilde{K})(\frac{E-F}{F}+\frac{C-D}{C}) \geq (\tilde{m}-\tilde{K})(\frac{C-D}{C})$$

Multiplying by $C/(C-D)$ gives

$$(1-\alpha_R)(\tilde{m}_R - \tilde{K})\frac{C+F}{F} \geq \tilde{m} - \tilde{K}$$

$$\frac{1-\alpha_R}{F}(\tilde{m}_R - \tilde{K}) \geq \frac{\tilde{m} - \tilde{K}}{C+F}$$

Substituting (A.2) for $(1-\alpha_R)/F$ on the LHS and (A.3) for $C+F$ on the RHS we get

$$\frac{\tilde{m}_R - \tilde{K}}{\tilde{m}_R\delta(1+\rho) - \tilde{K}(\delta\rho - 1)} \geq \frac{\tilde{m} - \tilde{K}}{\tilde{m}\delta(1+\rho) - \tilde{K}(\delta\rho - 1)} \tag{A.13}$$

At $\tilde{m} = \tilde{m}_R$ expression (A.13) holds in equality, $\forall \tilde{m} < \tilde{m}_R$, (or $\forall m > m_R$), (A.13) holds in inequality as the RHS of (A.13) decreases (same argument as above, see equation (A.10). So,

for all $m > m_R$ estimate of RHS of (A.11) < LHS of (A.11)
at $m = m_R$ estimate of RHS of (A.11) = LHS of (A.11)

Hence the LHS is strictly greater than the RHS of (A.11) for all $m \geq m_R$, the curve of indifferent consumers shifts down in its right end as ρ increases. Continuity of all the functions in inequality (A.11) ensures that (A.11) holds as a strict inequality also for some interval to the left of m_R as in figure 4.5.

Moreover, a stronger result can be shown: Any two curves of indifferent consumers have a single intersection as shown in figure 4.5, i.e. as a reaction to a change in ρ the curve shifts up for all m less than a certain income and it shifts down for all m larger than that income. (Note that this crucial income changes with ρ.) We omit the proof of this stronger result since the weaker property as shown above is sufficient for our purposes.

A.10 Proof: Parties' Reactions when the Debt to Repay Increases

We now show how ρ influences the optimal tax and public goods decisions of the two parties in the second period. We first show that as ρ increases, both parties set a higher $\tau_2(\cdot)$, but the left-wing party increases τ_2 by more than the right-wing party:

$$\frac{\partial\tau_2(L)}{\partial\rho} > \frac{\partial\tau_2(R)}{\partial\rho}$$

We then show that as a reaction to a higher ρ, the left-wing party increases the level of public goods in the second period, $\partial y_2(L)/\partial\rho > 0$, whereas the right-wing party provides less public goods, $\partial y_2(R)/\partial\rho < 0$.

A.10.1 $\tau_2(\cdot)$ as a Function of ρ

The derivative of τ_2, equation 5.12, with respect to ρ is given by

$$\frac{\partial \tau_2}{\partial \rho} = \alpha \tilde{S} + (1-\alpha)\tilde{s} = \tilde{s} + \alpha(\tilde{S} - \tilde{s})$$

From equations 5.8 and 5.9 we see that $\tilde{s}$ and $\tilde{S}$ also depend on ρ. The derivative then becomes

$$\begin{aligned}\frac{\partial \tau_2}{\partial \rho} &= \frac{1}{\rho(1+\delta)}\Big[\tau_2(B) - \delta\rho\tau_1 + \tilde{m}(\delta\rho - 1)\Big] + \alpha\frac{\delta\rho - 1}{\rho(1+\delta)}(\tilde{K} - \tilde{m}) \\ &= \frac{1}{\rho(1+\delta)}\Big[\tau_2(B) - \delta\rho\tau_1\Big] + \alpha\frac{\delta\rho - 1}{\rho(1+\delta)}\tilde{K} + \tilde{m}\frac{\delta\rho - 1}{\rho(1+\delta)}(1-\alpha)\end{aligned}$$

We now show that this expression increases as m goes down, i.e. for a given α a "poorer" party increases τ_2 as a function of ρ by more than a "richer" party (arrow 1 in figure A.2). We then show that in income group $\tilde{m}_L$, $\partial\tau_2/\partial\rho$ goes

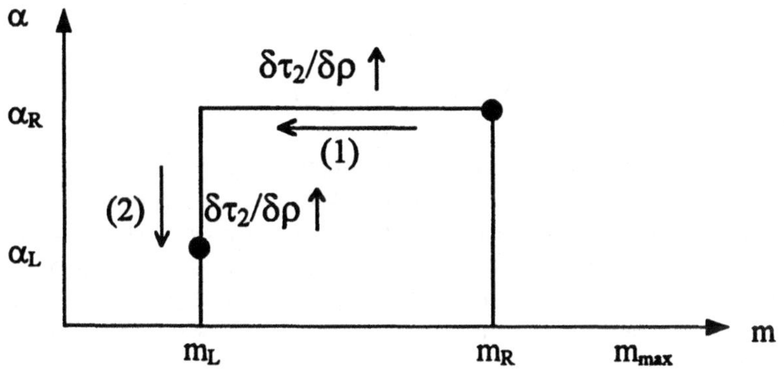

Fig. A.2. Parties' Tax Reactions in the Second Period to an Increase in ρ

up as α goes down (arrow 2 in figure A.2). Hence, at (α_L, m_L), $\partial\tau_2/\partial\rho$ is larger than at (α_R, m_R).

Arrow 1 in figure A.2.

$$\frac{\partial}{\partial \tilde{m}}\frac{\partial \tau_2}{\partial \rho} = \frac{\delta\rho - 1}{\rho(1+\delta)}(1-\alpha) > 0$$

$$\text{i.e. } \frac{\partial}{\partial m}\frac{\partial \tau_2}{\partial \rho} < 0$$

Arrow 2 in figure A.2.

$$\frac{\partial}{\partial \alpha}\frac{\partial \tau_2}{\partial \rho} = \frac{\delta\rho - 1}{\rho(1+\delta)}\tilde{K} - \frac{\delta\rho - 1}{\rho(1+\delta)}\tilde{m}_L$$

At $\tilde{m} = \tilde{m}_L$ this expression is negative since $\tilde{m}_L > \tilde{K}$, see footnote 1.

A.10.2 $y_2(\cdot)$ as a Function of ρ

Recall the expression for y_2

$$y_2 = \frac{1}{1+\delta}(1-\alpha)\left[(1+\rho)\delta\tilde{m} - (\delta\rho - 1)\tilde{K}\right]$$

The derivative of this expression with respect to ρ is given by

$$\frac{\partial y_2}{\partial \rho} = \frac{1}{1+\delta}(1-\alpha)(\delta\tilde{m} - \delta\tilde{K})$$

This is negative for $\tilde{m} = \tilde{m}_R$, ($\tilde{m}_R < \tilde{K}$) and positive for $\tilde{m} = \tilde{m}_L$ independent of α: The right-wing party lowers the levels of public goods as ρ increases, whereas the left-wing party increases it.

A.11 The Problem of Intersecting μ-Curves

The reason for keeping the average income fixed when we compare different societies follows from similar arguments as the ones we proposed when we introduced the special types of distributions we are now working with. We have difficulties in deriving clear-cut results when curves of indifferent consumers intersect in the area where consumers are distributed. This was the reason why we introduced the two types of societies in section 5.3.2. In these distributions, the curves of indifferent consumers are ordered as a function of the first government politics and the following holds: Increasing the level of public goods makes a government more likely to win (lose) the elections.

Some pairs of societies cannot be compared as the example of figure A.3(a) shows. According to our definition society G is more conservative for all $m < m_{intersect}$ and society F is more conservative for all $m > m_{intersect}$. But the population is distributed on both sides of $m_{intersect}$ and we are hence incapable of determining which society is overall more conservative. So we can only compare societies whose sets μ-curves do not intersect as in figure A.3(b). The condition that enables us to compare different societies is that these societies have the same average income K/N (mean preserving change). As we now show, societies with the same K/N have the same $\tilde{K}$. Hence, they have the same $\tau_2(\cdot)$, equation (5.12), $\tilde{S}$, equation(5.9), and the same sets of indifferent consumers' curves $\alpha_{ind}(m)$, equation (5.15). Note

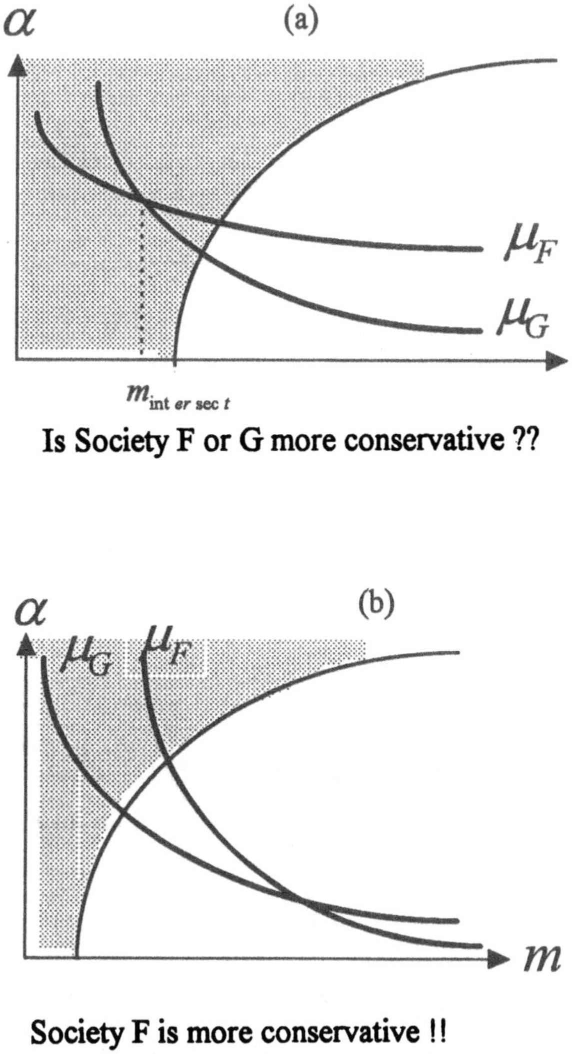

Fig. A.3. The Problem of Intersecting μ-Curves

that societies can have the same average income even if they are of different size (N) or vary in their total income(K). Let us verify this by adding to a society a group of n consumers with total income k such that this group has the same average income as the society:

$$\frac{k}{n} = \frac{K}{N}$$

In order for this new larger society to have the same $\tilde{K}$ as the old one the following has to hold:

$$\tilde{K} = \frac{K}{K - aN} = \frac{K + k}{K + k - a(N + n)} \tag{A.14}$$

Note that from $k/n = K/N$ it follows that $k = (n/N)K$. We can then rewrite the right hand side of equation (A.14) as

$$\frac{K(1 + \frac{n}{N})}{K(1+)\frac{n}{N} - aN(1 + \frac{n}{N})} = \frac{K}{K - aN} \qquad \text{q.e.d.}$$

A.12 The Optimal Levels of Private and Public Goods, $\tilde{x}_1, \tilde{x}_2, \tilde{y}_1$ and $\tilde{y}_2$

The levels of $\tilde{x}_1, \tilde{y}_1, \tilde{x}_2$ and $\tilde{y}_2$ in general form are given by

$$\begin{aligned} \tilde{x}_1 &= \tilde{m}_P - \tau_1 - \tilde{s}(m_P) \qquad & \tilde{y}_1 = \tau_1 + \tilde{S} \\ \tilde{x}_2 &= \tilde{m}_P - \tau_2 + \rho\tilde{s}(m_P) \qquad & \tilde{y}_2 = \tau_2 - \rho\tilde{S} \end{aligned}$$

We now substitute for $\tilde{s}(m_P), \tilde{S}$ and $\tau_2(P)$ the expressions for their optimal levels as given by equations (5.8), (5.9) and (5.12):

$$\begin{aligned} \tilde{s}(m_P) &= \frac{1}{\rho(1+\delta)}\left[\tau_2(B) - \delta\rho\tau_1 + \tilde{m}_P(\delta\rho - 1)\right] \\ \tilde{S} &= \frac{1}{\rho(1+\delta)}\left[\tau_2(B) - \delta\rho\tau_1 + \tilde{K}(\delta\rho - 1)\right] \\ \tau_2(T) &= \alpha_T\rho\tilde{S} + (1 - \alpha_T)(\tilde{m}_T + \rho\tilde{s}(m_T)) \end{aligned}$$

(where P denotes the party in power in the first period and T the party that actually wins the elections and governs in the second period.)

The variables of the first period ($\tilde{s}(m), \tilde{S}$) are based on beliefs about the future. These beliefs enter in the levels of individual and total savings through $\tau_2(B)$, $B = L, R$. The variable of the second period (τ_2) on the other hand, is influenced by the party that actually won the elections, T. Thus, the τ_2 that enters in the variables of the second period is different from the $\tau_2(B)$ that determines the first period variables.

We first derive expressions for $\tau_2(B)$, the tax rate that - in the first period - people believe will be set in the second period and for $\tau_2(T, B)$, the tax rate that will actually be set in the second period by the reigning T-party, given the beliefs B people had.

The tax rate set by the party people believe will win the elections is given by

$$\tau_2(B) = \alpha_B \rho \tilde{S} + (1 - \alpha_B)\big(\tilde{m}_B + \rho \tilde{s}(m_B)\big)$$

Substituting for $\tilde{S}$ and $\tilde{s}(m_B)$ gives

$$\begin{aligned} \tau_2(B) &= \alpha_B \frac{1}{1+\delta}\Big[\tau_2(B) - \delta\rho\tau_1 + \tilde{K}(\delta\rho - 1)\Big] \\ &+ (1 - \alpha_B)\left[\tilde{m}_B + \frac{1}{1+\delta}\Big(\tau_2(B) - \delta\rho\tau_1 + \tilde{m}_B(\delta\rho - 1)\Big)\right] \end{aligned}$$

After simplifying and rearranging we get

$$\tau_2(B) = (1+\rho)(1-\alpha_B)\tilde{m}_B + \frac{\delta\rho - 1}{\delta}\alpha_B \tilde{K} - \rho\tau_1 \tag{A.15}$$

The tax rate set by the party that will actually be in power in the second period, given beliefs, is

$$\tau_2(T, B) = \alpha_T \rho \tilde{S} + (1 - \alpha_T)\big(\tilde{m}_T + \rho \tilde{s}(m_T)\big)$$

Substituting for $\tilde{S}$ and $\tilde{s}(m_T)$ gives

$$\begin{aligned} \tau_2(T, B) &= \alpha_T \frac{1}{1+\delta}\Big[\tau_2(B) - \delta\rho\tau_1 + \tilde{K}(\delta\rho - 1)\Big] \\ &+ (1 - \alpha_T)\left[\tilde{m}_T + \frac{1}{1+\delta}\big(\tau_2(B) - \delta\rho\tau_1 + \tilde{m}_T(\delta\rho - 1)\big)\right] \\ &= \frac{1}{1+\delta}\tau_2(B) - \frac{\delta\rho}{1+\delta}\tau_1 + \alpha_T \frac{\delta\rho - 1}{1+\delta}\tilde{K} + (1-\alpha_T)\tilde{m}_T \frac{\delta(1+\rho)}{1+\delta} \end{aligned}$$

Multiply both sides by $(1+\delta)$ and subtracting $\tau_2(T, B)$ gives

$$\delta\tau_2(T, B) = \tau_2(B) - \tau_2(T, B) - \delta\rho\tau_1 + \alpha_T(\delta\rho - 1)\tilde{K} + (1-\alpha_T)\tilde{m}_T\delta(1+\rho)$$

We now derive an expression for $\tau_2(B) - \tau_2(T, B)$:

$$\begin{aligned} \tau_2(B) - \tau_2(T, B) &= \alpha_B\Big(\rho\tilde{S} - \rho\tilde{s}(m_B)\Big) - \alpha_T\Big(\rho\tilde{S} - \rho\tilde{s}(m_T)\Big) \\ &+ (1-\alpha_B)\tilde{m}_B - (1-\alpha_T)\tilde{m}_T + \rho\tilde{s}(m_B) - \rho\tilde{s}(m_T) \end{aligned}$$

Substituting for $\tilde{S}$ and $\tilde{s}(\cdot)$ gives

$$\begin{aligned}\tau_2(B) - \tau_2(T,B) &= \alpha_B \frac{1}{1+\delta}(\tilde{K} - \tilde{m}_B)(\delta\rho - 1) - \alpha_T \frac{1}{1+\delta}(\tilde{K} - \tilde{m}_T)(\delta\rho - 1) \\ &+ (1-\alpha_B)\tilde{m}_B - (1-\alpha_T)\tilde{m}_T + \frac{1}{1+\delta}(\tilde{m}_B - \tilde{m}_T)(\delta\rho - 1) \\ &= (1-\alpha_B)\tilde{m}_B \frac{\delta(1+\rho)}{1+\delta} - (1-\alpha_T)\tilde{m}_T \frac{\delta(1+\rho)}{1+\delta} \\ &+ \frac{\delta\rho - 1}{1+\delta}(\alpha_B - \alpha_T)\tilde{K}\end{aligned}$$

Substituting this back in the equation for $\tau_2(T,B)$ and dividing by δ gives

$$\begin{aligned}\tau_2(T,B) = \frac{1+\rho}{1+\delta}(1-\alpha_B)\tilde{m}_B + \frac{(1+\rho)\delta}{1+\delta}(1-\alpha_T)\tilde{m}_T \\ + \frac{\delta\rho - 1}{(1+\delta)\delta}\alpha_B \tilde{K} + \frac{\delta\rho - 1}{1+\delta}\alpha_T \tilde{K} - \rho\tau_1\end{aligned} \tag{A.16}$$

Note that when the government in the second period coincides with peoples' beliefs (rational expectations) the tax rate is given by

$$\tau_2(T,T) = (1+\rho)(1-\alpha_T)\tilde{m}_T + \frac{\delta\rho - 1}{\delta}\alpha_T \tilde{K} - \rho\tau_1 \tag{A.17}$$

(Note that this is the same as $\tau_2(B)$ in equation (A.15). Of course, in the first period people believe that there beliefs are correct.)

We can now finally derive expressions for $\tilde{x}_1, \tilde{y}_1, \tilde{x}_2$ and $\tilde{y}_2$ using $\tau_2(B)$ as in equation (A.15) for the variables of the first period and $\tau_2(T,B)$ from equation (A.16) for the variables of the second period.

$$\begin{aligned}\tilde{x}_1 &= \tilde{m}_P - \tau_1 - \tilde{s}(m_P) \\ &= \left(1 - \frac{\delta\rho - 1}{\rho(1+\delta)}\right)\tilde{m}_P - \left(1 - \frac{\delta}{1+\delta}\right)\tau_1 - \frac{1+\rho}{\rho(1+\delta)}(1-\alpha_B)\tilde{m}_B \\ &- \frac{\delta\rho - 1}{\delta\rho(1+\delta)}\alpha_B \tilde{K} + \frac{1}{1+\delta}\tau_1 \\ &= \frac{1+\rho}{\rho(1+\delta)}\tilde{m}_P - \frac{1+\rho}{\rho(1+\delta)}(1-\alpha_B)\tilde{m}_B - \frac{\delta\rho - 1}{\delta\rho(1+\delta)}\alpha_B \tilde{K}\end{aligned}$$

$$\begin{aligned}\tilde{y}_1 &= \tau_1 + \tilde{S} \\ &= \tau_1 + \frac{1}{\rho(1+\delta)}\left[\tau_2(B) - \delta\rho\tau_1 + (\delta\rho - 1)\tilde{K}\right] \\ &= \frac{1+\rho}{\rho(1+\delta)}(1-\alpha_B)\tilde{m}_B + \frac{\delta\rho - 1}{\delta\rho(1+\delta)}(\alpha_B + \delta)\tilde{K}\end{aligned}$$

and

$$\begin{aligned}
\tilde{x}_2 &= \tilde{m}_P - \tau_2(T,B) + \rho\tilde{s}(m_P) \\
&= \tilde{m}_P - \frac{(1+\rho)\delta}{1+\delta}(1-\alpha_T)\tilde{m}_T - \frac{1+\rho}{1+\delta}(1-\alpha_B)\tilde{m}_B \\
&- \frac{\delta\rho-1}{(1+\delta)\delta}\alpha_B\tilde{K} - \frac{\delta\rho-1}{1+\delta}\alpha_T\tilde{K} + \rho\tau_1 \\
&+ \frac{1}{1+\delta}\Big[\tau_2(B) - \delta\rho\tau_1 + \tilde{m}_P(\delta\rho-1)\Big] \\
&= \frac{\delta(1+\rho)}{1+\delta}\tilde{m}_P - \frac{\delta(1+\rho)}{1+\delta}(1-\alpha_T)\tilde{m}_T - \frac{\delta\rho-1}{1+\delta}\alpha_T\tilde{K}
\end{aligned}$$

$$\begin{aligned}
\tilde{y}_2 &= \tau_2(T,B) - \rho\tilde{S} \\
&= \frac{1+\rho}{1+\delta}(1-\alpha_B)\tilde{m}_B + \frac{(1+\rho)\delta}{1+\delta}(1-\alpha_T)\tilde{m}_T + \frac{\delta\rho-1}{(1+\delta)\delta}\alpha_B\tilde{K} \\
&+ \frac{\delta\rho-1}{1+\delta}\alpha_T\tilde{K} - \rho\tau_1 - \frac{1}{1+\delta}\Big[(1+\rho)(1-\alpha_B)\tilde{m}_B + \frac{\delta\rho-1}{\delta}\alpha_B\tilde{K} \\
&- \rho\tau_1 - \delta\rho\tau_1 + (\delta\rho-1)\tilde{K}\Big] \\
&= \frac{1}{1+\delta}(1-\alpha_T)\Big((1+\rho)\delta\tilde{m}_T - (\delta\rho-1)\tilde{K}\Big)
\end{aligned}$$

Note that the variables of the second period, as they enter in the long run utility function to be maximized by the P-party in the first period, are independent of the beliefs.

A.13 The Long Run Utility Function to Be Maximized in Reduced Form

The long run utility function to be maximized is given by

$$\begin{aligned}
U_P &= \alpha_P\left(\frac{1+\rho}{\rho(1+\delta)}\tilde{m}_P - \frac{1+\rho}{\rho(1+\delta)}(1-\alpha_B)\tilde{m}_B - \frac{\delta\rho-1}{\delta\rho(1+\delta)}\alpha_B\tilde{K}\right) \\
&+ (1-\alpha_P)\left(\frac{1+\rho}{\rho(1+\delta)}(1-\alpha_B)\tilde{m}_B + \frac{\delta\rho-1}{\delta\rho(1+\delta)}(\alpha_B+\delta)\tilde{K}\right) \\
&+ \delta\left[\alpha_P\left(\frac{\delta(1+\rho)}{1+\delta}\tilde{m}_P - \frac{\delta(1+\rho)}{1+\delta}(1-\alpha_T)\tilde{m}_T - \frac{\delta\rho-1}{1+\delta}\alpha_T\tilde{K}\right)\right. \\
&+ \left.(1-\alpha_P)\left(\frac{1}{1+\delta}(1-\alpha_T)\Big((1+\rho)\delta\tilde{m}_T - (\delta\rho-1)\tilde{K}\Big)\right)\right]
\end{aligned}$$

Subtracting or adding constants changes the overall utility level but leaves the maximum points the same.

$$
\begin{aligned}
U_P &= \alpha_P \left[\log \left((1+\rho)\tilde{m}_P - (1+\rho)(1-\alpha_B)\tilde{m}_B - \frac{\delta\rho - 1}{\delta}\alpha_B \tilde{K} \right) - \log \rho \right] \\
&- \alpha_P \log(1+\delta) \\
&+ (1-\alpha_P) \left[\log \left((1+\rho)(1-\alpha_B)\tilde{m}_B + \frac{\delta\rho - 1}{\delta}(\alpha_B + \delta)\tilde{K} \right) - \log \rho \right] \\
&- (1-\alpha_P)\log(1+\delta) \\
&+ \delta \Bigg[\alpha_P \log \left(\delta(1+\rho)\tilde{m}_P - \delta(1+\rho)(1-\alpha_T)\tilde{m}_T - (\delta\rho - 1)\alpha_T \tilde{K} \right) \\
&+ (1-\alpha_P)\log \left((1+\rho)\delta\tilde{m}_T - (\delta\rho - 1)\tilde{K} \right) \Bigg] \\
&- \delta \left(\alpha_P \log(1+\delta) + (1-\alpha_P)\log(1+\delta) \right)
\end{aligned}
$$

Neglecting the constant $(1+\delta)\log(1+\delta)$ gives equation (6.5)

$$
\begin{aligned}
&= \alpha_P \left[\log \left((1+\rho)\tilde{m}_P - (1+\rho)(1-\alpha_B)\tilde{m}_B - \frac{\delta\rho - 1}{\delta}\alpha_B \tilde{K} \right) - \log \rho \right] \\
&+ (1-\alpha_P) \left[\log \left((1+\rho)(1-\alpha_B)\tilde{m}_B + \frac{\delta\rho - 1}{\delta}(\alpha_B + \delta)\tilde{K} \right) - \log \rho \right] \\
&+ \delta \Bigg[\alpha_P \log \left(\delta(1+\rho)\tilde{m}_P - \delta(1+\rho)(1-\alpha_T)\tilde{m}_T - (\delta\rho - 1)\alpha_T \tilde{K} \right) \\
&+ (1-\alpha_P)\log \left((1+\rho)\delta\tilde{m}_T - (\delta\rho - 1)\tilde{K} \right) \Bigg]
\end{aligned}
$$

A.14 The Derivative of U_P With Respect to ρ

In order to find the maximum of the long run utility function in equation (6.5) we take its derivative with respect to ρ:

$$
\begin{aligned}
\frac{\partial U_P}{\partial \rho} &= \alpha_P \left[\frac{\tilde{m}_P - (1-\alpha_B)\tilde{m}_B - \alpha_B \tilde{K}}{(1+\rho)\tilde{m}_P - (1+\rho)(1-\alpha_B)\tilde{m}_B - \frac{\delta\rho-1}{\delta}\alpha_B \tilde{K}} - \frac{1}{\rho} \right] \\
&+ (1-\alpha_P) \left[\frac{(\alpha_B + \delta)\tilde{K} + (1-\alpha_B)\tilde{m}_B}{(1+\rho)(1-\alpha_B)\tilde{m}_B + \frac{\delta\rho-1}{\delta}(\alpha_B + \delta)\tilde{K}} - \frac{1}{\rho} \right] \\
&+ \delta \Bigg[\alpha_P \frac{\tilde{m}_P - \delta(1-\alpha_T)\tilde{m}_T - \delta\alpha_T \tilde{K}}{\delta(1+\rho)\tilde{m}_P - \delta(1+\rho)(1-\alpha_T)\tilde{m}_T - (\delta\rho - 1)\alpha_T \tilde{K}}
\end{aligned}
$$

$$+ \quad (1-\alpha_P)\frac{\delta\tilde{m}_T - \delta\tilde{K}}{(1+\rho)\delta\tilde{m}_T - (\delta\rho - 1)\tilde{K}}\Bigg]$$

$$= \quad \alpha_P \frac{-\tilde{m}_P + (1-\alpha_B)\tilde{m}_B - \frac{\alpha_B}{\delta}\tilde{K}}{\rho\Big[(1+\rho)\tilde{m}_P - (1+\rho)(1-\alpha_B)\tilde{m}_B - \frac{\delta\rho-1}{\delta}\alpha_B\tilde{K}\Big]}$$

$$+ \quad (1-\alpha_P)\frac{\frac{\alpha_B+\delta}{\delta}\tilde{K} - (1-\alpha_B)\tilde{m}_B}{\rho\Big[(1+\rho)(1-\alpha_B)\tilde{m}_B + \frac{\delta\rho-1}{\delta}(\alpha_B+\delta)\tilde{K}\Big]}$$

$$+ \quad \delta^2\Bigg[\alpha_P\frac{\tilde{m}_P - (1-\alpha_T)\tilde{m}_T - \alpha_T\tilde{K}}{\delta(1+\rho)\tilde{m}_P - \delta(1+\rho)(1-\alpha_T)\tilde{m}_T - (\delta\rho-1)\alpha_T\tilde{K}}$$

$$+ \quad (1-\alpha_P)\frac{\tilde{m}_T - \tilde{K}}{(1+\rho)\delta\tilde{m}_T - (\delta\rho-1)\tilde{K}}\Bigg]$$

Note that the denominators are equivalent to $\tilde{x}_1, \tilde{y}_1, \tilde{x}_2$ and $\tilde{y}_2$. Hence, all denominators are positive.

A.15 The Long Run Utility Functions for the Special Cases of Our Model

We now show that - in the relevant range $1/\delta \leq \rho \leq \Big(\tau_2(K - aN)\Big)/S$ - and given the assumptions $\tilde{m}_L \sim \tilde{K} \sim \tilde{m}_R$ and $\alpha_R \to 1$, the long run utility functions of an L- as well as of an R-party in power in the first period are decreasing functions of ρ. We calculate the long run utility functions for eight different cases, namely for a given incumbent party in the first period P, given beliefs B and the "true" party governing in the second period T. The cases are summarized in table A.2. We will see that given our assumptions the

Table A.2. Overview Over the Possible Political Constellations

Case	P	B	T	Comments
1	R	R	L	
2	R	R	R	Dictatorship, Rational Expectations Equilibrium
3	R	L	L	Rational Expectations Equilibrium
4	R	L	R	Dictatorship
5	L	R	L	Dictatorship
6	L	R	R	Rational Expectations Equilibrium
7	L	L	L	Dictatorship, Rational Expectations Equilibrium
8	L	L	R	

beliefs do not matter for the relationship between an incumbent's long run utility function and ρ, so that we get the same values for the derivatives of the long run utility functions with respect to ρ, equation (6.6), i.e. for cases 1 and 3, cases 2 and 4, cases 5 and 7 and cases 6 and 8.

Recall that for $B = P$ the first two terms of equation (6.6) reduce to

$$\alpha_P \frac{-\tilde{m}_P - \frac{1}{\delta}\tilde{K}}{\rho\left[(1+\rho)\tilde{m}_P - \frac{\delta\rho-1}{\delta}\tilde{K}\right]}$$
$$+(1-\alpha_P)\frac{\frac{\alpha_P+\delta}{\delta}\tilde{K} - (1-\alpha_P)\tilde{m}_P}{\rho\left[(1+\rho)(1-\alpha_P)\tilde{m}_P + \frac{\delta\rho-1}{\delta}(\alpha_P+\delta)\tilde{K}\right]}$$

and that for $T = P$ the last two terms reduce to

$$\delta^2 \frac{\tilde{m}_P - \tilde{K}}{(1+\rho)\delta\tilde{m}_P - (\delta\rho-1)\tilde{K}}$$

Case 1: P=R, B=R, T=L

$$\begin{aligned}
\frac{\partial U_{R\to L,B=R}}{\partial\rho} &= \alpha_R \frac{-\tilde{m}_R + (1-\alpha_R)\tilde{m}_R - \frac{\alpha_R}{\delta}\tilde{K}}{\rho\left[(1+\rho)\tilde{m}_R - \frac{\delta\rho-1}{\delta}\tilde{K}\right]} \\
&+ (1-\alpha_R)\frac{\frac{\alpha_R+\delta}{\delta}\tilde{K} - (1-\alpha_R)\tilde{m}_R}{\rho\left[(1+\rho)(1-\alpha_R)\tilde{m}_R + \frac{\delta\rho-1}{\delta}(\alpha_R+\delta)\tilde{K}\right]} \\
&+ \delta^2\left[\alpha_R \frac{\tilde{m}_R - (1-\alpha_L)\tilde{m}_L - \alpha_L\tilde{K}}{\delta(1+\rho)\tilde{m}_R - \delta(1+\rho)(1-\alpha_L)\tilde{m}_L - (\delta\rho-1)\alpha_L\tilde{K}}\right. \\
&+ \left.(1-\alpha_R)\frac{\tilde{m}_L - \tilde{K}}{(1+\rho)\delta\tilde{m}_L - (\delta\rho-1)\tilde{K}}\right]
\end{aligned}$$

Given our assumptions the second and fourth term become insignificant and the first and third term are both negative. Recall that all the denominators in equation (6.6) are positive. Hence, it suffices to check the signs of the numerators. It is obvious to see that the numerator of the first term is negative ($\alpha_R = 1$). In the numerator of the third term a convex-combination of $\tilde{m}_L$ and $\tilde{K}$ is subtracted from $\tilde{m}_R$. Since both $\tilde{m}_L$ and $\tilde{K}$ are larger than $\tilde{m}_R$, the numerator is negative. Hence,

$$\frac{\partial U_{R\to L,B=R}}{\partial\rho} < 0$$

Case 2: P=R, B=R, T=R

$$\begin{aligned}\frac{\partial U_{R\to R,B=R}}{\partial\rho} &= \alpha_R\frac{-\tilde{m}_R-\frac{1}{\delta}\tilde{K}}{\rho\left[(1+\rho)\tilde{m}_R-\frac{\delta\rho-1}{\delta}\tilde{K}\right]}\\ &+ (1-\alpha_R)\frac{\frac{\alpha_R+\delta}{\delta}\tilde{K}-(1-\alpha_R)\tilde{m}_R}{\rho\left[(1+\rho)(1-\alpha_R)\tilde{m}_R+\frac{\delta\rho-1}{\delta}(\alpha_R+\delta)\tilde{K}\right]}\\ &+ \delta^2\frac{\tilde{m}_R-\tilde{K}}{(1+\rho)\delta\tilde{m}_R-(\delta\rho-1)\tilde{K}}\end{aligned}$$

Since the first term is negative and all others become insignificant,

$$\frac{\partial U_{R\to R,B=R}}{\partial\rho}<0$$

Case 3: P=R, B=L, T=L

$$\begin{aligned}\frac{\partial U_{R\to L,B=L}}{\partial\rho} &= \alpha_R\frac{-\tilde{m}_R+(1-\alpha_L)\tilde{m}_L-\frac{\alpha_L}{\delta}\tilde{K}}{\rho\left[(1+\rho)\tilde{m}_R-(1+\rho)(1-\alpha_L)\tilde{m}_L-\frac{\delta\rho-1}{\delta}\alpha_L\tilde{K}\right]}\\ &+ (1-\alpha_R)\frac{\frac{\alpha_L+\delta}{\delta}\tilde{K}-(1-\alpha_L)\tilde{m}_L}{\rho\left[(1+\rho)(1-\alpha_L)\tilde{m}_L+\frac{\delta\rho-1}{\delta}(\alpha_L+\delta)\tilde{K}\right]}\\ &+ \delta^2\left[\alpha_R\frac{\tilde{m}_R-(1-\alpha_L)\tilde{m}_L-\alpha_L\tilde{K}}{\delta(1+\rho)\tilde{m}_R-\delta(1+\rho)(1-\alpha_L)\tilde{m}_L-(\delta\rho-1)\alpha_L\tilde{K}}\right.\\ &+ \left.(1-\alpha_R)\frac{\tilde{m}_L-\tilde{K}}{(1+\rho)\delta\tilde{m}_L-(\delta\rho-1)\tilde{K}}\right]\end{aligned}$$

Given our assumptions, the second and fourth terms become insignificant, the third term is negative (same argument as in case 1). With our assumptions the first term reduces to

$$\frac{-\tilde{m}_R+(1-\alpha_L)\tilde{m}_R-\frac{\alpha_L}{\delta}\tilde{m}_R}{\rho\left[(1+\rho)\tilde{m}_R-(1+\rho)(1-\alpha_L)\tilde{m}_R-\frac{\delta\rho-1}{\delta}\alpha_L\tilde{m}_R\right]}=$$

$$\frac{-\alpha_L\tilde{m}_R(1+\frac{1}{\delta})}{\rho\alpha_L\tilde{m}_R(1+\rho-\frac{\delta\rho-1}{\delta})}=-\frac{1}{\rho}<0$$

Hence,

$$\frac{\partial U_{R\to L,B=L}}{\partial \rho} < 0$$

Case 4: P=R, B=L, T=R

$$\begin{aligned}\frac{\partial U_{R\to R,B=L}}{\partial \rho} &= \alpha_R \frac{-\tilde{m}_R + (1-\alpha_L)\tilde{m}_L - \frac{\alpha_L}{\delta}\tilde{K}}{\rho\left[(1+\rho)\tilde{m}_R - (1+\rho)(1-\alpha_L)\tilde{m}_L - \frac{\delta\rho-1}{\delta}\alpha_L\tilde{K}\right]}\\ &+ (1-\alpha_R)\frac{\frac{\alpha_L+\delta}{\delta}\tilde{K} - (1-\alpha_L)\tilde{m}_L}{\rho\left[(1+\rho)(1-\alpha_L)\tilde{m}_L + \frac{\delta\rho-1}{\delta}(\alpha_L+\delta)\tilde{K}\right]}\\ &+ \delta^2\frac{\tilde{m}_R - \tilde{K}}{(1+\rho)\delta\tilde{m}_R - (\delta\rho-1)\tilde{K}}\end{aligned}$$

The first term is negative (see case 3), all others become insignificant. Hence,

$$\frac{\partial U_{R\to R,B=L}}{\partial \rho} < 0$$

Case 5: P=L, B=R, T=L

$$\begin{aligned}\frac{\partial U_{L\to L,B=R}}{\partial \rho} &= \alpha_L \frac{-\tilde{m}_L + (1-\alpha_R)\tilde{m}_R - \frac{\alpha_R}{\delta}\tilde{K}}{\rho\left[(1+\rho)\tilde{m}_L - (1+\rho)(1-\alpha_R)\tilde{m}_R - \frac{\delta\rho-1}{\delta}\alpha_R\tilde{K}\right]}\\ &+ (1-\alpha_L)\frac{\frac{\alpha_R+\delta}{\delta}\tilde{K} - (1-\alpha_R)\tilde{m}_R}{\rho\left[(1+\rho)(1-\alpha_R)\tilde{m}_R + \frac{\delta\rho-1}{\delta}(\alpha_R+\delta)\tilde{K}\right]}\\ &+ \delta^2\alpha_L\frac{\tilde{m}_L - \tilde{K}}{\delta(1+\rho)\tilde{m}_L - (\delta\rho-1)\tilde{K}}\end{aligned}$$

The third term is insignificant. With our assumptions, the first two terms reduce to

$$\alpha_L\frac{-\tilde{m}_L(1+\frac{1}{\delta})}{\rho\tilde{m}_L(1+\rho-\frac{\delta\rho-1}{\delta})} + (1-\alpha_L)\frac{\tilde{m}_L\frac{1+\delta}{\delta}}{\rho\tilde{m}_L\frac{1+\delta}{\delta}(\delta\rho-1)} = -\frac{\alpha_L}{\rho} + \frac{1-\alpha_L}{\rho(\delta\rho-1)}$$

This is negative, if

$$\begin{aligned}1-\alpha_L-\alpha_L(\delta\rho-1) &< 0\\ \text{or}\quad 1-\alpha_L\delta\rho &< 0\end{aligned}$$

Hence, if α_L is not too close to 0

$$\frac{\partial U_{L\to L,B=R}}{\partial \rho} < 0$$

Case 6: P=L, B=R, T=R

$$\begin{aligned}\frac{\partial U_{L\to R,B=R}}{\partial\rho} &= \alpha_L\frac{-\tilde{m}_L+(1-\alpha_R)\tilde{m}_R-\frac{\alpha_R}{\delta}\tilde{K}}{\rho\Big[(1+\rho)\tilde{m}_L-(1+\rho)(1-\alpha_R)\tilde{m}_R-\frac{\delta\rho-1}{\delta}\alpha_R\tilde{K}\Big]}\\ &+ (1-\alpha_L)\frac{\frac{\alpha_R+\delta}{\delta}\tilde{K}-(1-\alpha_R)\tilde{m}_R}{\rho\Big[(1+\rho)(1-\alpha_R)\tilde{m}_R+\frac{\delta\rho-1}{\delta}(\alpha_R+\delta)\tilde{K}\Big]}\\ &+ \delta^2\Bigg[\alpha_L\frac{\tilde{m}_L-(1-\alpha_R)\tilde{m}_R-\alpha_R\tilde{K}}{\delta(1+\rho)\tilde{m}_L-\delta(1+\rho)(1-\alpha_R)\tilde{m}_R-(\delta\rho-1)\alpha_R\tilde{K}}\\ &+ (1-\alpha_L)\frac{\tilde{m}_R-\tilde{K}}{(1+\rho)\delta\tilde{m}_R-(\delta\rho-1)\tilde{K}}\Bigg]\end{aligned}$$

The third and fourth terms are insignificant, the first two terms are negative if α_L is not too close to 0, see case 5. Hence,

$$\frac{\partial U_{L\to R,B=R}}{\partial\rho}<0$$

Case 7: P=L, B=L, T=L

$$\begin{aligned}\frac{\partial U_{L\to L,B=L}}{\partial\rho} &= \alpha_L\frac{-\tilde{m}_L-\frac{1}{\delta}\tilde{K}}{\rho\Big[(1+\rho)\tilde{m}_L-\frac{\delta\rho-1}{\delta}\tilde{K}\Big]}\\ &+ (1-\alpha_L)\frac{\frac{\alpha_L+\delta}{\delta}\tilde{K}-(1-\alpha_L)\tilde{m}_L}{\rho\Big[(1+\rho)(1-\alpha_L)\tilde{m}_L+\frac{\delta\rho-1}{\delta}(\alpha_L+\delta)\tilde{K}\Big]}\\ &+ \delta^2\frac{\tilde{m}_L-\tilde{K}}{\delta(1+\rho)\tilde{m}_L-(\delta\rho-1)\tilde{K}}\end{aligned}$$

The last term is insignificant, the first two terms can be reduced to

$$\alpha_L\frac{-\tilde{m}_L(\frac{1+\delta}{\delta})}{\rho\tilde{m}_L(1+\rho-\frac{\delta\rho-1}{\delta})}+(1-\alpha_L)\frac{\alpha_L\tilde{m}_L\frac{1+\delta}{\delta}}{\rho\tilde{m}_L\frac{(1+\delta)(\delta\rho-\alpha_L)}{\delta}}=$$

$$-\frac{\alpha_L}{\rho}+(1-\alpha_L)\frac{\alpha_L}{\rho(\delta\rho-\alpha_L)}=\frac{(1-\delta\rho)}{\delta\rho-\alpha_L}<0$$

Since $\delta\rho>1>\alpha_L$ this expression is negative and

$$\frac{\partial U_{L\to L,B=L}}{\partial\rho}<0$$

Case 8: P=L, B=L, T=R

$$\begin{aligned}
\frac{\partial U_{L\to L,B=L}}{\partial \rho} &= \alpha_L \frac{-\tilde{m}_L - \frac{1}{\delta}\tilde{K}}{\rho\left[(1+\rho)\tilde{m}_L - \frac{\delta\rho-1}{\delta}\tilde{K}\right]} \\
&+ (1-\alpha_L)\frac{\frac{\alpha_L+\delta}{\delta}\tilde{K} - (1-\alpha_L)\tilde{m}_L}{\rho\left[(1+\rho)(1-\alpha_L)\tilde{m}_L + \frac{\delta\rho-1}{\delta}(\alpha_L+\delta)\tilde{K}\right]} \\
&+ \delta^2\left[\alpha_L \frac{\tilde{m}_L - (1-\alpha_R)\tilde{m}_R - \alpha_R\tilde{K}}{\delta(1+\rho)\tilde{m}_L - \delta(1+\rho)(1-\alpha_R)\tilde{m}_R - (\delta\rho-1)\alpha_R\tilde{K}}\right. \\
&+ \left.(1-\alpha_L)\frac{\tilde{m}_R - \tilde{K}}{(1+\rho)\delta\tilde{m}_R - (\delta\rho-1)\tilde{K}}\right]
\end{aligned}$$

This whole expression is negative, the third and fourth terms are insignificant, for the argument concerning the first and second term see case 7. Hence

$$\frac{\partial U_{L\to R,B=L}}{\partial \rho} < 0$$

A.16 The Influence of the Beliefs on the Optimal Policy Choice $\tilde{y}_1^*$

We now show that the $\tilde{y}_1$ the first period government has to set in order to achieve a certain ρ is higher when $B = L$ than when $B = R$. Let us write the expression for the level of public goods in the first period as a function of ρ and the party people believe to be in power in the second period (α_B, m_B): $y_1(\rho, \alpha_B, m_B)$. We now show that

$$\tilde{y}_1(\rho, \alpha_R, m_R) < \tilde{y}_1(\rho, \alpha_L, m_L) \tag{A.18}$$

Recall the expression for $\tilde{y}_1$

$$\tilde{y}_1 = \frac{1+\rho}{\rho(1+\delta)}(1-\alpha_B)\tilde{m}_B + \frac{\delta\rho-1}{\delta\rho(1+\delta)}(\alpha_B+\delta)\tilde{K}$$

It is immediate to see that

$$\frac{\partial \tilde{y}_1}{\partial \tilde{m}_B} > 0$$

For a given α, the higher $\tilde{m}_B$, i.e. the "poorer" the party people believe will be in power in the second period is, the higher the corresponding $\tilde{y}_1$. We thus know that

$$\tilde{y}_1(\rho, \alpha_R, m_R) < \tilde{y}_1(\rho, \alpha_R, m_L)$$

Let us now check whether for a given income, in particular income $\tilde{m}_L$, $\tilde{y}_1$ is a negative function of α_B. Then inequality A.18 holds.

$$\begin{aligned}
\frac{\partial \tilde{y}_1}{\partial \alpha_B} &= -\frac{1+\rho}{\rho(1+\delta)}\tilde{m}_B + \frac{\delta\rho - 1}{\delta\rho(1+\delta)}\tilde{K} \\
&= \frac{-(\delta+\delta\rho)\tilde{m}_B + (\delta\rho - 1)\tilde{K}}{\delta\rho(1+\delta)} \\
&= \frac{-\delta\tilde{m}_B - \tilde{K} - \delta\rho(\tilde{m}_B - \tilde{K})}{\delta\rho(1+\delta)}
\end{aligned}$$

For $\tilde{m}_B = \tilde{m}_L$, this expression is negative: in income group $\tilde{m}_L$ as α_B decreases, $\tilde{y}_1$ increases and hence

$$\tilde{y}_1(\rho, \alpha_R, m_R) < \tilde{y}_1(\rho, \alpha_R, m_L) < \tilde{y}_1(\rho, \alpha_L, m_L)$$

References

1. Aghion, P./ Bolton, P. (1990) Government Domestic Debt and the Risk of Default: A Political-Economic Model of the Strategic Role of Debt. In: Public Debt Management: Theory and Practice, ed. by R.Dornbusch and M.Draghi, Cambridge, pp. 315-345
2. Alesina, A. (1988) Credibility and Policy Convergence in a Two-Party System with Rational Voters. American Economic Review 78, No.4, September, pp. 796-805
3. Alesina, A. (1989) Politics and Business Cycles in Industrialized Democracies. Economic Policy, Vol. 8, pp. 55-98
4. Alesina, A./ Drazen, A. (1991) Why are Stabilizations Delayed? American Economic Review 82, No.5, December, pp. 1170-1188
5. Alesina, A./ Perotti, R. (1995) The Political Economy of Budget Deficits. IMF Staff Papers, Vol. 42, No.1, March, pp. 1-31
6. Alesina, A./ Prati, A./ Tabellini, G. (1990) Public Confidence and Debt Management: A Model and a Case Study of Italy. In: Public Debt Management: Theory and Practice, ed. by R.Dornbusch and M.Draghi, Cambridge, pp. 94-118
7. Alesina, A./ Tabellini, G. (1988) Credibility and Politics. European Economic Review 32, pp. 542-550
8. Alesina, A./ Tabellini, G. (1990a) A Positive Theory of Fiscal Deficits and Government Debt. Review of Economic Studies 57, pp. 403-414
9. Alesina, A./ Tabellini, G. (1990b) Voting on the Budget Deficit. American Economic Review 80, No.1, March, pp. 37-49
10. Alesina, A./ Tabellini, G. (1992) Positive and Normative Theories of Public Debt in Historical Perspective. European Economic Review 36, pp. 337-344
11. Aschauer, D.A. (1988) The Equilibrium Approach to Fiscal Policy. Journal of Money, Credit and Banking 20, No.1, pp. 41-62
12. Atkinson, A.B./ Stiglitz, J.E. (1980) Lectures on Public Economics. New York, McGraw-Hill
13. Bach, S. (1993) Institutionelle Beschränkungen der Staatsverschuldung vor dem Hintergrund der Auseinandersetzungen um das "Balanced Budget Amendment" in den USA, der Maastrichter Verträge und der Rechtssprechung des Bundesverfassungsgerichts. Konjunkturpolitik 39, H.1/2, pp. 1-27
14. Backus, D./ Driffill, J. (1985a) Rational Expectations and Policy Credibility after a Change of Regime. Review of Economic Studies 52, pp. 211-222
15. Backus, D./ Driffill, J. (1985b) Inflation and Reputation. American Economic Review 75, No. 3, June, pp. 530-538
16. Baron, D.P./ Frerejohn, J.A. (1989) Bargaining in Legislatures. American Political Science Review 83, No.4, pp. 1181-1206
17. Barro, R.J. (1974) Are Government Bonds Net Worth? Journal of Political Economy, Vol.82, pp. 1095-1117

18. Barro, R.J. (1979) On the Determination of the Public Debt. Journal of Political Economy, Vol.87, pp. 940-971
19. Barro, R.J./ Grilli, V. (1994) European Macroeconomics. London, Macmillan
20. Belke, A. (1993) Theorien des Politischen Konjunkturzyklus. WISU 11, pp. 919-922
21. Bernheim, B.D./ Shleifer, A./ Summers, L.H. (1985) The Strategic Bequest Motive. Journal of Political Economy, Vol.93, pp. 1045-1076
22. Berthold, N./ Fehn, R. (1994) Verursachen Wahlen einen Politischen Konjunkturzyklus? WiSt Heft 4, pp. 166-174
23. Bingham Powell, A. (1982) Contemporary Democracies - Participation, Stability and Violence. Cambridge, Harvard University Press
24. Blanchard, O.J./ Chouraqui, J.C./ Hagemann, R.P./ Sartor, N. (1990) The Sustainability of Fiscal Policy: New Answers to an Old Question. OECD Economic Studies No.15, pp. 7-36
25. Blanchard, O.J./ Fischer, S. (1989) Lectures on Macroeconomics. Cambridge, MIT University Press
26. Blankart, C.B. (1991) Öffentliche Finanzen in der Demokratie: Eine Einführung in die Finanzwissenschaft. München, Vahlen
27. Bliss, C./ Nalebuff, B. (1984) Dragon-Slaying and Ballroom Dancing: The Private Supply of a Public Good. Journal of Public Economics 25, pp. 1-12
28. Bombach, G. (1989) Von der nationalen zur internationalen Verschuldungsproblematik. Schriftenreihe des wirtschaftswissenschaftlichen Seminars Ottobeuren, Band 18. Tübingen, J.C.B. Mohr, pp. 3-39
29. Bruno, M. (1990) Economic Analysis and the Political Economy of Policy Formation. European Economic Review 34, pp. 273-301
30. Buchanan, J.M. (1960) La Scienza Delle Finanze: The Italian Tradition in Public Finance. In his: Fiscal Theory and Political Economy. Chapel Hill, Chapel Hill University Press, pp. 145-173
31. Buchanan, J.M. (1987) Public Debt. In: The New Palgrave Dictionary of Economics, Vol. 3, pp. 1045-47
32. Buiter, W.H./ Kletzer, K. (1992) Fiscal Policy Coordination as Fiscal Federalism: Economic Integration, Public Goods and Efficiency in Growing Economies. European Economic Review 36, pp. 647-653
33. Buiter, W.H./ Tobin, J. (1989) Debt Neutrality: A Brief Review of Doctrine and Evidence. In: Social Security versus Private Savings. ed. by G.M. von Fürstenberg, Cambridge
34. Calvo, G. (1978) On the Time Consistency of Optimal Policy in a Monetary Economy. Econometrica 46, pp. 1411-1428
35. Casella, A./ Frey, B. (1992) Federalism and Clubs: Towards an Economic Theory of Overlapping Jurisdictions. European Economic Review 36, pp. 639-646
36. Chiang, A.C. (1984) Fundamental Methods of Mathematical Economics. New York, Mc Graw-Hill
37. Cukierman, A. (1992) Central Bank Strategy, Credibility and Independence: Theory and Evidence. Cambridge
38. Cukierman, A./ Edwards, S./ Tabellini, G. (1992) Seignorage and Political Instability. American Economic Review 82, No.3, June, pp. 537-556
39. Cukierman, A./ Meltzer, A. (1989) A Positive Theory of Government Debt and Deficits in a Neo-Ricardian Framework. American Economic Review 79, No.4, September, pp. 713-732
40. Domar, E.D. (1944) The "Burden of the Debt" and the National Income. American Economic Review 34, pp. 798-827
41. Downs, A. (1957) An Economic Theory of Democracy. New York, Harper & Row

42. Drazen, A./ Grilli, V. (1993) Benefits of Crises for Economic Reform. American Economic Review 83, No. 3, June, pp. 598-607
43. The Economist (1995) Buying Votes. November 25th, 1995, pp. 41-42
44. The Economist (1996) The Burdensome National Debt. February 10th, 1996, pp. 70-71
45. Eisner, R. (1986) How Real is the Federal Deficit? New York, Macmillan
46. Eisner, R. (1987) Burden of the Debt. In: The New Palgrave Dictionary of Economics, Vol.1, pp. 294-296
47. Eisner, R. (1992) Deficits: Which, How Much and So What? American Economic Review 82, No.2, May, pp. 295-298
48. Ekelund, R.B./ Hebert, R.F. (1990) A History of Economic Theory and Method. Third ed. New York, McGraw-Hill
49. Emerson, M. (1988) What Model for Europe? Cambridge, Massachusetts
50. Fiorina, M. (1978) Legislative Facilitation of Government Growth: Universalism and Reciprocity Practices in Majority Rule Institutions. Paper presented at the Conference on the Causes and Consequences of Public Sector Growth, Puerto Rico
51. Fiorina, M./ Noll, R.G. (1978) Voters, Bureaucrats and Legislators: A Rational Choice Perspective on the Growth of Bureaucracy. Journal of Public Economics 9, pp. 239-254
52. Frerejohn, J.A. (1974) Pork Barrel Politics: Rivers and Harbours Legislation 1947-68. Stanford, Stanford University Press
53. Galbraith, J.K./Darity, W. Jr. (1995) A Guide to the Deficit. Challenge, July-August, pp. 5-12
54. Gandenberger, O. (1988) Was kann die Staatsverschuldung in Zukunkt leisten? In: Zimmermann, H. (ed.): Die Zukunft der Staatsfinanzierung. Stuttgart: Wissenschaftliche Verlagsgesellschaft, pp. 173-183
55. Giavazzi, F./ Pagano, M. (1990) Confidence Crises and Public Debt Management. In: Public Debt Management: Theory and Practice, ed. by R.Dornbusch and M.Draghi, Cambridge, pp. 125-143
56. Gilboa, I./ Schmeidler, D. (1994) Case-Based Decision Theory. Quarterly Journal of Economics, pp. 635-639
57. Gordon, G. (1987) National Debt. In: The New Palgrave Dictionary of Economics, Vol. 3, pp. 588-590
58. Grilli, V./ Masciandaro, D./ Tabellini, G. (1991) Institutions and Policies: Political and Monetary Institutions and Public Financial Policies in the Industrial Countries. Economic Policy, Vol.13, pp. 341-392
59. Hansard, T.C. (1819) Parliamentary Debates. Vol.40, London
60. Hibbs, D.A. (1977) Political Parties and Macroeconomic Policy. American Political Science Review 71, pp. 1467-1487
61. Hotelling, H. (1929) Stability in Competition. Economic Journal 39, March, pp. 41-57
62. Hughes, G./ Smith, S. (1991) Economic Aspects of Decentralized Government: Structure, Functions and Finance. Economic Policy 13, October, pp. 425-459
63. Hurd, M.D. (1989) Mortality Risk and Bequests. Econometrica 57, pp. 779-813
64. Inman, R.P. (1990) Public Debts and Fiscal Politics: How to Decide. American Economic Review 80, No.2, May, pp. 81-85
65. Inman, R.P./ Rubinfeld, D. (1992) Fiscal Federalism in Europe: Lessons from the United States Experience. European Economic Review 36, pp. 654-660
66. Kalecki, M. (1943) Political Aspects of Full Employment. Political Quarterly 7, pp. 322-331
67. Kennan, J./ Wilson, R. (1988) Strategic Bargaining Methods and Interpretation of Strike Data. Unpublished manuscript, New York University

68. Kromphardt, J. (1987) Arbeitslosigkeit und Inflation. Göttingen, Vandenhoeck & Ruprecht
69. Kydland, F.E./ Prescott, E.C. (1977) Rules Rather than Discretion: The Inconsistency of Optimal Plans. Journal of Political Economy 85, pp. 473-491
70. Lucas, R./ Stokey, N. (1983) Optimal Fiscal and Monetary Policy in an Economy without Capital. Journal of Monetary Economics 12, pp. 55-94
71. Maier, C. (1975) Recasting Bourgeois Europe: Stabilization in France, Germany and Italy in the Decade after World War II. Princeton, Princeton University Press
72. Malinvaud, E. (1991) Discussion of Grilli et al. [58], therein, pp. 376-79
73. Maré, M./ Sarcinelli, M. (1994) The European Union: How to Assign the Functions of Government. Banca Nazionale del Lavorno Quarterly Review, No.191, pp. 341-377
74. McRae, D.(1977) A Political Model of the Business Cycle. Journal of Political Economy 85, pp. 239-264
75. Milesi-Ferretti, G.M. (1995a) Do Good or Do Well? Public Debt Management in a Two-Party Economy. Economics and Politics 7, No.1, pp. 59-78
76. Milesi-Ferretti, G.M. (1995b) The Disadvantage of Tying Their Hands: On the Political Economy of Policy Commitments. The Economic Journal 105 (November), pp. 1381-1402
77. Milesi-Ferretti, G.M./ Spolaore, E. (1994) How Cynical can an Incumbent be? Strategic Policy in a Model of Government Spending. Journal of Public Economics 55, pp. 121-140
78. Musgrave, R.A. (1958) Theorie der öffentlichen Schuld. In: Gerloff, W./Neumark, F., Handbuch der Finanzwissenschaften, Band 3. Tübingen, pp. 68-137
79. Musgrave, R.A./ Musgrave, P.B. (1989) Public Finance in Theory and Practice. 5th edn, New York, McGraw-Hill
80. Myles, G.D. (1995) Public Economics. Cambridge, Cambridge University Press
81. Neumann, F. (1995) Bundestagswahlen. In: Gesellschaft und Staat. Lexikon der Politik. 9th edition, ed. by Drechsler, H./ Hilligen, W./ Neumann, F., pp. 129-132
82. Nicholson, W. (1985) Microeconomic Theory: Basic Principles and Extensions. Third edition. New York, The Dryden Press
83. Nordhaus, W.D. (1975) The Political Business Cycle. Review of Economic Studies 42, pp. 169-190
84. O'Driscoll, G.P. (1977) The Ricardian Non-Equivalence Theorem. Journal of Political Economy, Vol. 85, pp. 207-210
85. OECD (Organization for Economic Cooperation and Development) (1995) Wirtschaftsausblick (Economic Outlook) 57. June. Paris
86. OECD (Organization for Economic Cooperation and Development) (1996) Wirtschaftsausblick (Economic Outlook) 60. December. Paris
87. Pagano, M. (1991) Discussion of Grilli et al. [58], therein, pp. 379-381
88. Palley, T. (1997) State of the Union: The Sorry Politics of the Balanced Budget. Challenge, May-June, pp. 5-13
89. Persson, T. (1988) Credibility of Macroeconomic Policy: An Introduction and a Broad Survey. European Economic Review 32, pp. 519-532
90. Persson, M./ Persson, T./ Svensson, L. (1988) Time Consistency of Fiscal and Monetary Policy. Econometrica 55, pp. 1419-1432
91. Persson, T./ Svensson, L.E. (1989) Why a Stubborn Conservative would run a Deficit: Policy with Time-Inconsistent Preferences. Quarterly Journal of Economics, May, pp. 325-345

92. Persson, T./ Tabellini, G. (1990) Macroeconomic Policy, Credibility and Politics. Chur, Harwood Academic Publishers
93. Persson, T./ Tabellini, G. (1994a) Monetary and Fiscal Policy. Vol. 1: Credibility. Cambridge, MIT Press
94. Persson, T./ Tabellini, G. (1994b) Monetary and Fiscal Policy. Vol. 2: Politics. Cambridge, MIT Press
95. Rae, D. (1967) The Political Consequences of Electoral Laws. New Haven, Yale University Press
96. Ramsey, F.P.(1927) A Contribution to the Theory of Taxation. Economic Journal 37, pp. 47-61
97. Richter, W.F./ Wiegard, W. (1993) Zwanzig Jahre 'Neue Finanzwissenschaft'. Zeitschrift für Wirtschafts- und Sozialwissenschaften 102, pp. 169-224 and 337-400
98. Riley, J. (1980) Strong Evolutionary Equilibrium and the War of Attrition. Journal of Theoretical Biology 82, pp. 383-400
99. Rogoff, K. (1990) Equilibrium Political Business Cycles. American Economic Review 80, No.1, March, pp. 21-36
100. Roubini, N./ Sachs, J. (1989a) Fiscal Policy: Government Spending and Budget Deficits in the Industrial Countries. Economic Policy 8, pp. 99-132
101. Roubini, N./ Sachs, J. (1989b) Political and Economic Determinants of Budget Deficits in the Industrialized Economies. European Economic Review 33, pp. 903-938
102. Rubinstein, A. (1995) Lectures on Modeling Bounded Rationaility. CORE Foundation. Louvain-La-Neuve
103. Sachs, J.D./ Larrain, F. (1993) Macroeconomics in the Global Economy. Englewood Cliffs, Prentice-Hall
104. Sanguinetti, P.J. (1993) The Politics of Intergovernmental Transfers and Local Government Deficits: Theory and Evidence. Estudios Economicos 8, pp. 87-109
105. Sargent, T.J./ Wallace, N. (1981) Some Unpleasant Monetarist Arithmetic. Federal Reserve Bank of Minneapolis Quarterly Review, January, pp. 1-17
106. Shepsle, K. A./ Weingast, B. (1981) Institutional Arrangements and Equilibrium in Multidimensional Voting Models. American Journal of Political Science 25, pp. 96-111
107. Smith, A. (1776) An Inquiry into the Nature and Causes of the Wealth of Nations. Ed. by E. Cannan (1937) New York: Random House
108. Spolaore, E. (1993) Policy Making and Economic Efficiency: Coalition Governments versus Majority Governments. Unpublished manuscript, ECARE, Université Libre Bruxelles
109. Steunenberg, B. (1994) Decision Making under Different Institutional Arrangements: Legislation by the European Community. Journal of Institutional and Theoretical Economics 150/4, pp. 642-669
110. Stockmann, D. (1975) The Social Pork Barrel. Public Interest 39, pp. 3-30
111. Tabellini, G. (1986) Money, Debt and Deficits in a Dynamic Game. Journal of Economic Dynamics and Control 8, pp. 427-442
112. Tabellini, G. (1988) Centralized Wage Setting and Monetary Policy in a Reputational Equilibrium. Journal of Money, Credit and Banking 20, pp. 102-118
113. Tabellini, G. (1991) The Politics of Intergenerational Redistribution. Journal of Political Economy, Vol.99, pp. 335-357
114. Wagner, H. (1990) Demokratie und Inflation - Eine "rationale" wahlpolitische Theorie eines Inflationsbias. In: Jahrbücher für Nationalökonomie und Statistik, Vol. 207, pp. 356-373

115. Weingast, B./ Marshall, W. (1988) The Industrial Organization of Congress or Why Legislatures, like Firms, are not Organized as Markets. Journal of Political Economy 96, February, pp. 132-163
116. Weingast, B.R./ Shepsle, K.A./ Johnsen, C. (1981) The Political Economy of Benefits and Costs: A Neoclassical Approach to Distributive Politics. Journal of Political Economy, Vol. 89, pp. 642-664
117. von Weizsäcker, R.K. (1992) Staatsverschuldung und Demokratie. KYKLOS 45, pp. 51-67
118. Wittmann, D. (1977) Candidates with Policy Preferences: A Dynamic Model. Journal of Economic Theory, February, pp. 180-189
119. Wittmann, D. (1983) Candidate Motivation: A Synthesis of Alternative Theories. American Political Science Review 77, pp. 142-157

Contributions to Economics

Hagen Bobzin
Indivisibilities
1998. ISBN 3-7908-1123-8

Helmut Wagner (Ed.)
Current Issues in Monetary Economics
1998. ISBN 3-7908-1127-0

Peter Michaelis/Frank Stähler (Eds.)
Recent Policy Issues in Environmental and Resource Economics
1998. ISBN 3-7908-1137-8